Rawlyk

C12

D0205492

Two Worlds

McGILL-QUEEN'S STUDIES IN THE
HISTORY OF RELIGION

George A. Rawlyk, Editor

Volumes in this series are being supported by the
Jackman Foundation of Toronto.

Two Worlds

The Protestant Culture of Nineteenth-Century Ontario

WILLIAM WESTFALL

McGill-Queen's University Press
Kingston and Montreal

© McGill-Queen's University Press 1989
ISBN 0-7735-0669-1

Legal deposit 1st quarter 1989
Bibliothèque nationale du Québec

Printed in Canada on acid-free paper

This book has been published with the help of a grant
from the Canadian Federation for the Humanities,
using funds provided by the Social Sciences and
Humanities Research Council of Canada.

Canadian Cataloguing in Publication Data

Westfall, William, 1945–
    Two worlds: the Protestant culture of nineteenth-
century Ontario
    (McGill-Queen's studies in the history of religion; 2)
    Includes bibliographical references and an index.
    ISBN 0-7735-0669-1
    1. Protestantism – Ontario – History – 19th century.
    2. Ontario – History – 19th century. I. Title.
    II. Series.
    BR575.05W48 1989   280'.4'09713   C88-090342-2

To the memory of my father,
Russell Edward Westfall

And the earth was without form, and void; and
darkness was upon the face of the deep. And the
Spirit of God moved upon the face of the waters.

Genesis 1:2

everything divides by two or is uneven
poetry consists in the doubling of words
doubled words are poetic words
this is the true meaning of poetry
each poem speaks to another poem
the language of poetry is a secret language
these are true doubles.

Eli Mandel, "The Double,"
Out of Place

Contents

Acknowledgments

This book must begin by thanking those people who have helped me along the way. While the text and especially the notes acknowledge the debts I owe to the insights of many scholars, I would like to take this opportunity to give special thanks to friends and colleagues who have played a special part in the history of this work.

Four distinguished professors at the University of Toronto watched over the genesis of the study. Carl Berger introduced me to the study of ideas, Maurice Careless helped to turn my attention to the study of religion in Ontario, Donald Creighton sustained my course and by his living example helped me to grasp the relationship between art and history, and Michael Cross (now at Dalhousie University) shepherded me with great care and encouragement through my doctoral studies, continually sharpening my understanding of society and class.

My scholarly interest in religious and social history was broadened into the study of culture largely through the pleasure of working at York University in the interdisciplinary program in Canadian Studies; to my colleagues in the Division of Humanities and the Division of Social Science – John Warkentin, Eli Mandel, Ron Bloore, Michael Quealey, Ted Rathé, Tom Traves, and Paul Craven – I offer a special vote of thanks.

The Social Sciences and Humanities Research Council of Canada provided a grant that allowed me to spend part of a sabbatical in Britain working in the rich and underused resources of a number of archives. York University helped me in several ways. Atkinson College awarded me a leave fellowship to complete the manuscript, and Secretarial Services in the Faculty of Arts made me compatible with WordPerfect. Pat Humenyk, a true friend, deserves special thanks.

The manuscript has benefited enormously from the careful reading of Keith Walden and John Webster Grant, and the two anonymous readers from the Social Science Federation of Canada did their critical duty with force and insight (may the offer of a bottle of claret allow me to thank them personally). Douglas Richardson and Malcolm Thurlby made many helpful suggestions on matters architectural, while Cathy Mastin worked with dispatch to help prepare the illustrative materials.

The task of advancing from manuscript to book was far more complex and time-consuming than I had ever imagined. To my great good fortune McGill-Queen's has been the very model of a scholarly press. The original work was guided through the tortuous channels of evaluation by Donald Akenson and then revised and edited under the watchful eye of Joan McGilvray and the sharp but authoritative pencil of Freya Godard.

Finally, I would like to acknowledge a special debt to three friends: Donald Swainson, who once offered to introduce dynamite to the study of Gothic architecture, taught me the value of the straight line; Eli Mandel, poet and teller of stories, explained to me the trickery of doubles; and Brian McKillop, who has walked the same path, set three goals that this book has journeyed to reach – to affirm the inherent value of ideas, to discern patterns of structure, and to search for coherence.

Two Worlds

CHAPTER ONE

The Dominion of the Lord: Protestant Ontario and the Study of Religion and Culture

He shall have dominion also from sea to sea, and from the river unto the ends of the earth.

Psalm 72:8

The vision of a new dominion "from sea to sea" captured the imagination of the Fathers of Confederation and sustained an ambitious program of nation building. Taking up the powers that the British North America Act placed in their hands, these men set out to fulfil a dream of empire and power, hoping that westward expansion, railways, immigration, and protective tariffs would transform a disparate collection of superfluous British colonies into a prosperous, integrated, and modern society. Economic development would carry Canada to its appointed destiny.

The apparent fulfilment of this dream has imparted to the stages of its progress an aura of myth and legend. From generation to generation historians have told a tale of daring and drama in which the seemingly mundane considerations of party advantage and commercial profit have taken on a heroic stature. Politicians and businessmen have become statesmen and nation builders, while their economic policies provide the themes of the great Canadian epic. The myth of our creation is a decidedly materialistic one, with the days of Canada's genesis reckoned in lines of boxcars and acres of wheat. The words of the Seventy-second Psalm seem to capture this ethos and provide a fitting motto for the new dominion: *A mari usque ad mare*, a nation from sea to sea.[1]

At the same time, however, these words express another vision that challenges the unbridled materialism of Canada's national development, for in the biblical passage from which Tilley drew the phrase, the word "dominion" has a spiritual meaning.[2] Here the geographical extent of the new land amplifies the social and moral qualities that will grace this future state. The Psalmist lifts up his voice in praise of a time when the true justice of God's commandments will triumph over the selfishness and wickedness of men. It is the *just* King who "shall have dominion also from sea to sea, and from the river unto the ends of the earth." The psalm is a commentary on power in society, but instead of dwelling on the means of gaining power, it describes the moral and social goals that power should pursue. The verses themselves anticipate the Beatitudes:

Yea, all kings shall fall down before him: all nations shall serve him.
For he shall deliver the needy when he crieth; the poor also, and him that hath no helper.
He shall spare the poor and needy, and shall save the souls of the needy.
He shall redeem their soul from deceit and violence: and precious shall their blood be in his sight.[3]

The Lord will save the impoverished and the downtrodden; times of suffering and violence will end; a new world will replace the old. In the ninth chapter of Zechariah, where the same phrase appears, another prophecy enriches the contrast between the old world and the one that has not yet come to pass: "Rejoice greatly, O daughter of Zion; shout, O daughter of Jerusalem: behold, thy King cometh unto thee: he is just, and having salvation; lowly, and riding upon an ass. ... He shall speak peace unto the heathen: and his dominion shall be from sea even to sea, and from the river even to the ends of the earth."[4] Here the vision of a dominion that will extend "from sea even to sea" heralds the ultimate dispensation – the coming of the Messiah and the millennial triumph of Christ.

In effect, the motto of the Canadian nation brings together a material vision and a spiritual vision that point in two very different directions. On the surface the words speak to the physical growth of Canada itself, to the well-known historical narrative of politics, railways, and tariffs, but buried beneath this materialistic ethos rests a deeply spiritual vision. The biblical passages foretell a new type of society on the earth when the wilderness of sin and injustice will become the dominion of the Lord.

I

In joining the materialism of their own age with a religious understanding of life, the Fathers of Confederation were participating in an ageless tradition. Throughout history individuals, societies, and nations have tried to impart meaning to their lives by relating their experiences and beliefs to an overarching explanation of existence. Since religions explain the meaning of place and time, humanity has continually turned to religion to reconcile its own world with a world that transcends the limits of its own consciousness.

Canadians have participated fully in this most human of endeavours. In nineteenth-century Quebec, for example, a particular strain of ultramontanism infused the life and thought of French Canadian society with a strong messianic quality. Contemporary events were interpreted according to a distinctive mission given by God to this most Catholic of nations.[5] English Canadian Protestants were drawn just as deeply into the same attempt to link history and experience to religious goals. In the early decades of the nineteenth century a rather obscure and ambitious clergyman in Upper Canada set out to explain to his British audience the singularly important place that the affairs of this distant colony could have in God's grand design for the world. If the mother country supported the established church in the colony and endowed a church university, Upper Canada would enjoy an unrivalled state of happiness and prosperity and in time become a shining light to a world darkened by chaos and rebellion. First the British Empire and then the whole world would follow the colony's example: "For as the influence of Christian principles extend ... murmurs will give way to blessings and praise; and one-fourth of the human race being thus reclaimed, the remainder will gradually follow, and thus the whole earth become the garden of the Lord."[6] From the very beginning many English Canadians believed they had a special role to play in converting the world.

Similar religious associations appear in the mythology that grew up around the United Empire Loyalists. These immigrants received a special place in Canadian history because society interpreted their reasons for coming and their long-term significance through a well-known religious narrative. Like the Jews of old, this exiled remnant held fast to its faith while suffering in the wilderness and in time became a new nation in a promised land.[7] In fact, prophecy and promised lands are central to the interpretation of Canadian history. The popular predictions that the Canadian west would become a new garden and that the twentieth century would belong to Canada also testify to the strength of the bonds that link history and religion.[8]

But the interweaving of the material and the spiritual went far beyond these interpretations of Canadian history, the same pattern reappearing in a wide variety of institutional and cultural settings. In mid-nineteenth-century Ontario, for example, religious institutions waged an unceasing struggle to create a spiritual refuge within a secular society undergoing rapid social and economic change. The great crusades for temperance and Sabbath observance were part of this larger struggle to provide Victorians with a moral pathway through the hazards of a materialistic world.[9] That this endeavour was not in vain is suggested by the province's notorious ability to combine business acumen with a narrow Protestant morality.[10]

Education provides another interesting example of the integration of religious and secular goals. In the first decades of the Victoria era, the established church lost its favoured position at almost all levels of education as the state took control of the instruction of the youth of the colony. This process of "secularization," however, reorganized rather than rejected the close relationship between religion and education. The "reform" of the provincial university removed the church from King's College, but it also accelerated the proliferation of denominational colleges in the province.[11] Queen's, Victoria, and Trinity all tried to integrate religion and education, although the form of this integration varied from one institution to another.[12] Nor was the new provincial university at Toronto as godless an institution as certain Anglican critics asserted, for in fact religion appeared at many points in the curriculum and the texts approved by the government for religious instruction were the same ones that the Protestant denominations used in their own colleges.[13]

Even at the elementary levels of education, where the new state reigned supreme, the advance of secularism was met by a stern defence of the importance of instilling an unshakeable religious code in the minds of youth. Egerton Ryerson, to whom is ascribed such praise for creating the system of public education, never questioned the necessity of religious instruction in his schools. Indeed, he hoped that the creation of a system of public education would expand the place of religion in the classroom by removing special privileges and creating "a common patriotic ground of comprehensiveness and avowed Christian principles."[14] Public education would place religious instruction on a firmer and less contentious foundation. To that end he introduced a set of textbooks that imparted a strong moral tone to the classroom and tied the study of practical subjects to the study of the Bible. He even introduced a special course that embraced "the entire History of the Bible, its instructions, cardinal doctrines and morals, together with the evidences of its authenticity." The textbook for this course, *First Lessons in Christian Morals*,[15] Ryerson wrote himself.

The Protestant account of history and salvation also provided the new school system with an intellectual structure capable of integrating diverse and seemingly contradictory secular and religious goals. As many historians of education have noted, the school reformers expressed a number of conflicting attitudes and beliefs. Although they were confident that schools would improve society, they also betrayed a deep concern for the social problems created by a large class of non-institutionalized youth. Schools, they asserted, provided a way to meet this social crisis by taking children off the streets and teaching them to respect the existing structure of society.[16] What was once regarded as a movement for social reform is now seen as an attempt to control social change. But the conflict between social reform and social control, between optimistic and pessimistic attitudes towards childhood, tends to disappear as both sets of goals find a comfortable place within a single system of religious thought. School promoters could preach control *and* reform because they justified public education by appealing to a secularized version of the basic story of Christian redemption. Since all people bore the weight of original sin, society must sustain public order by supporting schools, prisons, courts, and churches, which moderated the anti-social repercussions of human nature. But in precisely the same way that religion could redeem individuals from the fall and win for them the joys and happiness of salvation, so too could public education redeem the youth of the province and raise society to a higher level of existence. Schools, in effect, were religious surrogates, able to control and redeem at the same time. Perhaps it was the ability of education to justify itself in this religious language that explains why society so readily accepted the relatively new doctrine that the state should provide a system of public education.

The same pattern is evident in the way the Victorians interpreted many aspects of their lives. The nature of the family, for example, was often explained in relation to two distinct categories of reality that were then drawn together through a religious account of time and place. The well-documented practice of dividing human nature into masculine and feminine spheres relied once again on the basic categories of the religious and the secular. Sex and religion were closely joined: man was material and practical, while woman was moral and spiritual; man had power, woman had taste; man was active, woman reflective; man was rational, woman intuitive. In the words of a popular moral guide to almost every conceivable aspect of Victorian life, man was "the creature of interest and ambition ... But a woman's whole life is the history of the affections. The heart is her world."[17] The union of these secular and sacred elements in wedlock sanctified the family and transformed the home into a "sacred asylum" to which the "care-worn heart retreats to find rest from the toils and inquietudes of life." Home, in effect, was presented as a heaven on earth clearly set apart from the "harassings of business." Indeed the movement from an external material environment to an internal spiritual one was seen as an everyday enactment of the future journey from life on this earth to "heaven itself, ... the home for whose acquisition we are to strive the most strongly."[18]

The rhetoric of nationalism, the pronouncements on education, and the language of family life all rely on an interpretation of place and time that divided everything into two elements. For the Canadian nation, material success was combined with moral fulfilment. In education, a knowledge of practical and useful subjects was tied to a knowledge of religious truth. In work, six days of labour were weighed against one day of rigidly enforced non-labour. In society, the public world of masculine competition was yoked to the domestic world of feminine virtue. The Victorian cosmology was made up of two worlds: the material and the moral, the human and the divine, or, to use the language of the age, the secular and the sacred.

The secular world of nineteenth-century Canada does not require an elaborate introduction because it figures so prominently in the great nineteenth-century odes to economic expansion, machine technology, and material progress.[19] In fact, some of the most important watchwords of the age were discipline, efficiency, and development. But many Victorians argued that secular and material forces could not adequately explain the character and meaning of reality and that society and history were also shaped by other powers, quite different from those associated with materialism. As might be expected, religious leaders testified fervently to the reality of the other side of the dichotomy. The Rev. Alexander Sutherland, an important figure in the unification of Methodism, and an uncompromising crusader for prohibition, began his popular history of Methodism with an unequivocal affirmation of the power and reality of the sacred in human history: "For be it understood that what I have to relate is not the method whereby men of mingled passions like ourselves planned and reared a Babel-Tower to their own ambition, but it is the process of a divine evolution whereby God made them to be a people

... and raised up the weak things of the world to confound the mighty."[20] Another Methodist historian also emphasized the presence of the hand of God in human affairs. When Egerton Ryerson explained the extraordinary growth of Methodism he began by asking two rhetorical questions: "Is such a development natural or supernatural? Is it the growth of nature or the work of grace?" The expansion of Methodism, he answered, must be ascribed to "that which is above the powers or laws of nature ... that which is produced by a Divine agency – the immediate power of God."[21] When these men looked at the world they both saw two different and at times competing forces; in their worlds they found abundant evidence of the power and presence of both the secular and the sacred.

Although many Victorians believed that the two worlds were quite different, they refused to separate the secular and the sacred into two rigid and static categories. On the one hand they divided human nature, institutions, and social structures into two parts; on the other they tried to bind the two parts together. In the rhetoric of national fulfilment, for example, moral goals were dependent on economic expansion; in education, secular ambitions must be harnessed by a strong moral code before society could advance materially and spiritually; in the language of everyday life, the masculine had to be united with the feminine – the secular sphere with the sacred – for the family to attain its exalted character.

In one sense the world was divided into distinct categories; in another the two categories were joined closely together. This concurrent division and integration created enormous cultural tensions, for Victorian culture seemed intent on pulling apart what it believed to be inseparable while fusing into one entity two elements that, it argued, were of different natures. But such tensions also imparted a strength to the age that can fascinate those who look back upon it.

II

In the period between 1820 and 1870, a distinctive Protestant culture took root in Ontario and came to have a profound influence on the life of the province. What are the origins of this culture, what was its character, and how did it influence Ontario society? The origins must be approached by looking first inside the culture, and then examining the external forces that shaped the process of cultural development. The internal approach focuses upon the way new cultures build upon the remnants of older ones. In this instance the Protestant culture of Ontario cobbled together ideas, beliefs, and symbols left behind by cultures that could no longer explain the world. As old concepts broke down, their shards provided the materials for building something new. The second approach relates cultural creation to social, economic, and political change. The way a society sees the world is tied closely to the world which that culture tries to explain, and in the middle of the nineteenth century the world of Ontario was changing very rapidly. Protestant culture grew up at precisely the time that capitalism was reshaping almost every aspect of Ontario life. Older patterns of culture lost their authority because capitalism was destroying the worlds they had once explained and creating many problems that the new culture had to address.

The impressive statistical foundations of the new Protestant culture that emerged from the old demonstrate the extent to which the religious structure of the province was assuming a new form.[22] At the start of the Victorian period the province contained a large number of relatively small Protestant groups, and almost a quarter of the population did not reveal their religious affiliation or said they were not attached to any particular religious group. By 1881 the picture had changed dramatically. Only 6 per cent of the population belonged to the smaller Protestant bodies, and quite remarkably, less than 1 per cent claimed to enjoy no religious affiliation whatsoever. And by that date four Protestant bodies had come to dominate the religious structure of the province. Between 1842 and 1881 the growth in the number of the Methodists, Presbyterians, Baptists, and Anglicans was staggering. The Methodist groups, who were at this time undergoing the often difficult process of church union, increased their combined membership more than sevenfold, from 82,923 to 591,503. Over the same period the Presbyterians, who achieved church union in 1875, grew by a factor of 5.5 and the Baptists grew at only a slightly lower rate. The Anglicans, whose size was most likely inflated by the census of 1842, nonetheless grew by a factor of 3.4.

When these statistics are examined in relation to the increase in the provincial population, the growth of these four groups becomes even more dramatic. Between 1842 and 1881 the population of the region almost quadrupled, from 487,053 to 1,923,228. Such rapid growth, many sociologists have argued, often occasions severe social dislocation that provides a fertile ground for the proliferation of new sects.[23] In this instance, however, these major Protestant bodies not only coped well (at least in a statistical sense) with the possibility of disruption, but in fact strengthened their position within the religious structure of the province. Except for the Anglicans, each of these groups easily outpaced the rate of population growth for the province, and even the Anglicans added over a quarter of a million new adherents, which left them only slightly behind the general rate of population increase. By 1881 these four Protestant denominations had become almost synonymous with religion in Ontario. After subtracting the Catholic population (which between 1851 and 1881 remained at about 17 per cent),[24] these four groups constituted close to 98 per cent of the population of Ontario.

During the same period these groups also came to share a common outlook on a number of essential religious and social questions. By mid-century the animosity and bitterness that had divided the Anglicans and the Methodists had begun to disappear, and the way was open for the development of an informal Protestant alliance on a large number of moral issues.[25] This growing religious consensus provided the institutional and intellectual foundations for a Protestant culture. Through educational institutions, moral crusades, and a distinct style of worship, Ontario Protestantism proclaimed a body of ideas and attitudes that shaped the way the society interpreted the world. Protestant Ontario created a Protestant culture.

Two distinctive features of this new Protestant culture were the way it organized place and the way it organized time. All cultures must define a sense of place and time, for without these definitions culture could not explain reality. But whereas the need to explain place and time is universal, each culture answers these questions differently. In the Protestant culture of Ontario these concepts were defined in a particular way, which in turn shaped the systems of explanation that the culture provided. The necessity of explaining place and time provides a way of approaching a culture, and the particular response to this necessity leads us to the very heart of the Protestant culture of Ontario.

The growth of this powerful and distinctive culture raises some important sociological questions. How did the culture as a whole influence the social system? How did the relationship that the culture defined between the secular and the sacred help maintain social stability during a period of intense social change? How did this Protestant culture affect the process of secularization? How did religion penetrate, at least in a cultural sense, the fabric of Canadian life? And finally, what were the forces that undermined these important cultural relationships and in time destroyed the very understanding of place and time that Protestant culture had worked so hard to define?

III

"Protestant culture" is a complex term and can lead to confusion if its specific meaning and theoretical implications are not defined clearly. Since questions of method, theory, and the art of history are central to this analysis, it is important to explain briefly how the study uses this term and how this usage helps to establish the intellectual framework of the study as a whole.

The word "Protestant" is used in three different ways. It can refer to a series of historical events that divided Western Christianity into two opposing camps – Protestants and Catholics. To a remarkable degree the history of the Protestant Reformation formed an important part of the collective memory of Ontario. Events that happened in the sixteenth and seventeenth centuries were as fresh in people's minds as if they had taken place only a few years before. People observed the rituals of the Reformation with devotion, and the division between Protestant and Catholic remained one of the primary facts of the religious and social life of the province well beyond the nineteenth century.[26] Protestant is also used to describe a number of religious groups that traced their ancestry more or less directly to the original separation from Rome. The institutional history of these "denominations" (as they came to be called), especially the relationship between them, forms another major theme in the study. Third and perhaps most important, the word refers to a rather amorphous body of religious, moral and social attitudes that provided a series of reference points for approaching a wide range of questions and issues – from wearing fashionable styles of dress and enjoying certain amusements to the role of the clergy in helping the individual achieve salvation and the place of God in contemporary events.

The term "culture" is also complex and has both a historical and methodological meaning. In the period that this study examines, it often referred to a state of achievement or level of social development that an individual or group could attain after passing through a number of preliminary (and by implication "uncultured") stages. A society became "cultured" when people learned to live and act in a certain way and produced certain "cultural" achievements – such as great works of architecture, painting, literature, or history. This historical use of the term is closely related to what is now termed "high culture" and implies moral refinement and social respectability. The study uses "culture" in this sense when it is describing a particular set of historical assumptions about moral character, society, and art. The popular Victorian phrase "moral and cultural progress" is one example of this historical and descriptive usage.[27]

The second meaning of culture is more important. Here the term means a set of ideas, beliefs, and attitudes through which an individual, society, or group interprets existence. Culture, in this sense, is a pattern of interpretation for organizing the unstructured data of life. Every individual seeks understanding and adopts a complex language of words and symbols to order the world; every social system contains such patterns of interpretation.[28]

This conception of culture as a pattern of interpretation introduces the importance of religion, especially the Protestant religion, in this study. Religions provide the ideas and concepts that make up a culture, or to state the relationship in a slightly different way, religions are systems of belief that answer the questions that cultures ask. Religions have creeds that set out doctrines, and stories that attempt to explain the deepest mysteries of life. For this reason the way religions – in this case the Protestant religion – answer questions of meaning defines to a considerable degree the character of the cultural system. Protestantism not only shaped how people saw God, it also shaped the culture through which that society interpreted the world.

But why should systems of religious belief be given such special stature in a culture? They may answer questions of meaning, but do not other systems of ideas also answer these same questions? Are not religions only one system of explanation among many? On a continent that sanctifies free will and individual liberty, are we not all free to create our own explanations of existence? Why then should culture be tied so closely to religion?

The tension between competing systems of explanations is very important. In Victorian Ontario, for example, the Protestant culture was continually threatened on a number of fronts. The statistics that reveal such a remarkable degree of religious affiliation did not give Protestantism an absolutely secure place in the culture of this period. Protestantism allows enormous scope to individual convictions, which can easily change, and religious leaders were very aware of the threats posed by competing systems of belief to the hegemony of the Protestant religion. The influence of Darwinian science reveals at least in one sense the vulnerability of religious accounts of life and history.[29]

At the same time religion in general and Ontario Protestantism in particular enjoyed a very special authority. Religions seek to understand the sacred and to tie life to an understanding of the divine, and for this reason attain an authority that other accounts of time and place cannot realize. Christianity does not say "I believe"; it says "I believe in God." All religions take part in an age-old quest to express a relationship to the transcendent.[30] It is this bonding of belief to the sacred that elevates the stature of religious systems of explanation.[31]

Nevertheless, religions still had to compete with other systems of belief – the ability to seek the transcendent also allows one to ignore it. Every individual could continue to create a distinctive interpretation of the world, but without the sacred these interpretations had to rely for their authority upon the notoriously unstable compound of individual self-interest and mere personal opinion, which often led their adherents to alienation rather than understanding. The sacred, in short, helped religion to solve the problem caused by the inherent instability of individual belief by giving religion an authority that society considered unassailable. In this way the culture of Protestant Ontario seemed able to rise above the powers of the world that had helped to shape it.

The power of the sacred also drew other systems of belief into the orbit of religion. Our own age has perhaps lost sight of the extraordinary force that a conception of the sacred can exert upon social thought. If today we acknowledge religion at all, we tend to limit its authority severely. Since science and psychology can answer most questions, we only need religion to deal with those issues that science has not (or not yet) explained. But in societies that are less modern than our own, the power of the sacred broke down any barriers that attempted to limit its sovereignty. The sacred forced other systems of belief to reach an accommodation with the dominant set of religious beliefs. In the Protestant worlds of early nineteenth-century Canada, it was the sacred that gave Protestant culture the ability to penetrate the entire social system, to shape the very consciousness of society. If our age reduces all things to material and psychological causes, ages past tied all things to God. The sacred sphere tried to encompass everything and obliterate in cultural terms the distinction between the secular and the sacred.

At this point we can begin to identify the place of religion and culture in the social system. At the centre of the social system is a cultural pattern through which society organizes and understands the world. This culture is tied to a set of religious beliefs that enhance the authority of the culture and allow it to oversee other systems of explanation. The important position of culture in the social system allows it to serve a number of crucial functions. Culture helps to hold society together by providing ways of ordering and explaining the phenomena of existence; it answers questions of meaning and reduces the disruptive power of events that can threaten the social system itself. In this way religion and culture impart to society a stability and coherence that delight the many sociologists who have studied the role of religion in society.

This general interpretation raises one of the most important issues in the study of society and religion. Sociologists such as Max Weber, Vilfredo Pareto, Emile Durkheim, and Karl Marx have been preoccupied with the relationship between religion, authority, and social stability, especially when it appeared that religion was losing both its authority and the ability to stabilize the social system.[32] More recently the long and often unintelligible work of the American sociologist Talcott Parsons has taken up the same issue and has concluded that religion holds society together by sustaining a system of common values.[33] He in fact carries this tradition of sociological analysis to the point that religion makes the social system so stable that disruption and social change become almost unthinkable.[34] Only in America could one create a voluntary theocracy.

Although this tradition of sociological analysis offers many insights into the relationship between religion and social order, it has largely ignored the question of religious and cultural change. It assumes that change is an aberration rather than the norm. Yet the history of nineteenth-century Ontario is to a large extent the history of change, for both the social system and the culture of the province changed dramatically during this period. Protestant culture was itself born of the process of change, and it is somewhat ironic that at the very point it attained the height of its power, it was undermined by the continuing process of social development. Change after all is inherent in the very concept of stability, and this study attempts to understand not only how religion contributes to social order, but also how religion relates to the process of social and cultural change.

But how does a culture change? How can one understand the changes that take place in the way a society sees itself? To a considerable degree the nature of culture itself answers these important questions. Since culture is a pattern through which a society explains the world, the relationship between categories of cultural explanation and the phenomena that they are trying to explain can help us understand cultural change. The systems that attempt to explain the world do not necessarily perform this task effectively, or if they can explain the world at one moment in time they may not maintain that ability over a longer period. In effect, it is the tension between what explains and what needs to be explained that shapes the process of cultural transformation.

When cultures change, they change in relation to *both* the forces that shape this conflict. When the categories of culture lose their meaning, the culture must search for new ways of explaining the world; but the materials for explaining the world exist only in the culture itself. One must guard against the methodological heresy of assuming that the phenomena of existence define the categories that explain those phenomena;[35] the categories of culture make up a world of their own and a culture must search within itself to find the concepts that will explain the world. To do this the new culture can take parts of the old culture and put them together in different ways. Parts that used to play only minor roles can move to the centre of the cultural stage and acquire new significance. In addition every category of explanation defines an alternative category of explanation. In proper ontological fashion, the meaning of "good" defines the meaning of "evil", or the character of the hero defines the character of the villain. As a category becomes a prominent feature of a culture, it casts a shadow that becomes an alternative category for cultural explanation. Once again the character of a culture provides the materials for building a new cultural form out of the old.

Although a culture must look inside itself to explain the world, the world itself exerts continual pressure on a culture. It is not enough to explain the world at one moment in time, because the world must be ordered and explained over and over again, for every person at every moment. In Ontario during the nineteenth century, social change challenged the patterns of cultural explanation on countless occasions. The province was undergoing a process of capitalistic economic development that changed and reorganized almost every aspect of society and undermined the cultures that attempted to explain the character and meaning of Ontario life. The world seemed to be out of step with the course that culture had defined for the future.

Tensions of this type forced the culture to search within itself for new ways of explaining a new world. Out of this complex process would in time emerge a new culture. Once this new culture was able to explain the world, religion could perform its appointed tasks within the social system. The new culture could influence the pace and character of social change itself and shape the very reality it set out to explain. So the circle of cultural history runs its necessary course.

History and historians occupy a special place in a culture. The myths of history that historians use to organize the past restate and reinforce the myths that are at the centre of religion and culture. This close relationship also means that the process of religious and cultural change deeply influences the way a society interprets its past; the forces that transform a pattern of culture also transform the way a society interpets these same forces. For this reason the writing of history is always a commentary on history itself.

Social and cultural change has had an especially important influence on the study of the history of religion in English-speaking Canada. A century ago religion was at the centre of academic life in Canada. Almost every college and university, whether Protestant or Catholic, built its curriculum around the study of religion. Courses in natural history and moral philosophy attempted to integrate and synthesize academic life by defining the relationship between the great doctrines of religious belief and life in contemporary society.[36] In the same way that Protestant culture tried to join the secular and the sacred world, the study of religion tried to bridge the gap between the material and the moral universe.

In our own age, however, religion has fallen from this noble position. Social and cultural change has reduced the strength of institutionalized religion and broken the bonds that once held religion and knowledge together. Education has been fragmented into a number of discrete and narrow disciplines, and academic life in general has become aggressively secularist in the way it interprets space and time. The land and staple products have replaced moral character and romantic visions as the dominant themes of historical explanation.

In this new process the study of religion did not disappear completely but rather retreated from the centre of academic life into a narrow and restricted sphere. The study of religion became yet another type of specialized knowledge that might be of use as preparation for a particular type of career. To enjoy the blessings of academic respectability, it had to accept the terms set by the new concepts of knowledge.[37] In the study of Canadian history, for example, religion became merely another factor that could help to round out the picture defined by political and economic forces. Religion became a dependent variable and was relegated to the second rank of historical explanation. When religion entered the house of man it did so as a servant that must see to the needs of the master. In the light of this process of social and religious change, this study makes one important assertion: the sacred must be returned to the history of religion in Canada, for it is the sacred that makes religion a meaningful category of historical analysis. Only when this fact has been recognized can the importance of religion in the history of Canada be appreciated.

The process of secularization has also limited the appreciation of culture and cultural history. The growing preoccupation with material forces in history has reinforced a long-standing positivism in the Canadian historical profession that treats the past as a variety of discrete materials that can be weighed and measured according to the standards of value-free research. Historians see themselves as masons whose studies are bricks for reconstructing the many mansions of the past.

This study proceeds from a different set of assumptions about the nature of history and culture. Although it draws upon a large body of historical materials, it tries to look beyond this material to the structures of thought and perception that give meaning to these phenomena. In essence the study is a search for form rather than content. In a broader sense the writing of history is also a search for form. All history attempts to give order and meaning to the past, and for this reason historians act out, either consciously or unconsciously, the central act in the art of life. There is no real boundary between the historian and history. At one level this study describes a people in the mid-nineteenth century that was searching for a form that would give order and meaning to its collective existence. At another level it marks the historian's search for a form that will give order and meaning to this historical quest. In both cases the form itself tells the real story.

CHAPTER TWO

Order and Experience: The Religious and Cultural Roots of Protestant Ontario

Erroneous tests of godliness have been instituted among them, whereby feelings instead of an enlightened judgment and a life-reforming faith, have been set forth as the criteria of true religion.

The Rev. Charles Forest to the Lord Bishop of Montreal, 1 July 1848

On 3 July 1825 John Strachan, the rector of York in the seemingly insignificant colony of Upper Canada, preached a sermon on the life and character of Bishop Jacob Mountain. At the time of his death Mountain had been the Anglican Bishop of Quebec for over thirty years, and Strachan was determined to interpret for his parishioners the historical significance of the Bishop's long career in Canada. The task of glorifying Mountain, however, was not easy, even for someone like Strachan who took considerable pride in his literary skill. The progress of the church, at least in Strachan's eyes, had not been especially rapid during Mountain's episcopate; indeed in 1825 the church was still in a very precarious position. For this reason Strachan feared that some "future historian" might be "inclined to find fault in the little that [had] been done by the first Protestant Bishop of Quebec."[1]

Strachan tried to anticipate this possibility by setting out his own interpretation of the history of the last forty years. In effect, he became one of the first historians of early nineteenth-century English Canada, and like the historians who followed him, he reconstructed the past by giving prominence to certain themes and events while ignoring others. In due course Mountain's life began to appear in a more favourable light.

Strachan asked his congregation "to pause before pronouncing judgment in order to examine the many obstacles in his Lordship's way during the whole of his Episcopacy." When Mountain arrived in Quebec "the colony was a greater spiritual than a natural wilderness." There were few congregations and almost no clergy. To serve the needs of his wilderness charge, the Bishop set out to create a proper parish system of churches and schools, but his hard work was met with hostility and indifference. The Papists, of course, opposed him, and worse still, the small Protestant population showed a singular want of enthusiasm for Mountain's attempt to bestow the uncountable benefits of an Anglican establishment on the colony. Nevertheless, Mountain had managed to advance the cause of the church by slow degrees. If he had not left the church in a position of prosperity, he had nonetheless constructed "a fair foundation ... for the diffusion of Christianity throughout the Diocese." Strachan's rhetorical strategy was simple. By dwelling on the adversities of history and circumstance, he hoped to elevate the Bishop's rather meagre accomplishments to the point where his episcopate might be seen as an important preliminary stage in what would surely be the eventual triumph of the Church of God in the Canadas. Evidently pleased with his handiwork, Strachan had the sermon published and sent copies of it to England, where it might help the friends of the colonial church in that most important arena of politics, wealth, and power.

In retrospect, Strachan's defence of Mountain appears artificial and unconvincing. By dwelling upon the glory of Bishop Mountain's intentions and the difficulties he faced rather than the goals he actually reached, Strachan almost inevitably turned the Bishop into a minor historical figure. Even if one were content with sure foundations rather than the monuments that such foundations were meant to support, little historical immortality could be claimed for the recently departed ecclesiastic.[2] In this light Strachan's sermon might well have contributed to the problem that it was supposed to forestall. Certainly a "future historian" would have to challenge many of Strachan's judgments in order to reach a more balanced and judicious assessment of the life and character of Jacob Mountain.[3]

This short sermon nonetheless remains one of the most important documents in the religious and cultural history of early nineteenth-century Canada. Although the sermon did not achieve what it set out to do, its historical significance lies in the assumptions Strachan brought to his text and in the structure of his argument rather than in the elaborate apologia for the life of the Bishop. To defend Mountain, Strachan wrote a brief history of his own times that imposed a sense of order on the chaos of religion and politics flourishing at that time. This history rested on a number of beliefs and assumptions which reveal a good deal about the way Strachan and many others understood their own world, especially the crucial relationship between God and creation. As Strachan well understood, however, any one way of seeing the world defines an antithetical mode of perception. He was so determined to praise Mountain because he feared that someone who saw the world differently might examine his life from a different point of view and reach a very different conclusion. And in fact his fears were justified, although he did not anticipate the fury and the impact of the challenge to his argument. Certain passages in his sermon provoked an immediate – and what became a famous – attack on his representation of the character of God and creation, and when the attack came it was John Strachan, rather than Jacob Mountain, who had to bear the force of the assault.

I

Strachan began his interpretation of the past by dividing the population of Upper Canada into three religious groups, each of which he placed at a particular point on a religious spectrum that he constructed according to his own appreciation of the proper forms of ecclesiastical polity and religious practice. At one end he placed the Roman Catholics; at the other, a rather loosely defined group of "Protestant dissenters," and between these "extravagant and dangerous extremes,"[4] his own church – the United Church of England and Ireland – and the Church of Scotland. According to Strachan the centre always had to fight against the extremes: from one end of the spectrum the church had to confront the new-world embodiment of the age-old powers of Popery; from the other it had to meet the challenge of the Methodists and a host of other sects.

Typically, Strachan's representation of the religious world of Upper Canada contains a rich mixture of Anglican self-interest and historical accuracy. Strachan was constantly pleading for money, and this particular analysis certainly tried to further that goal. By putting his church in the centre, he was repeating one of the basic arguments for a well-endowed religious establishment. Since certain religious groups had spawned and sustained revolution and rebellion, the state had to protect itself from both the heirs of the Catholic counter-reformation and the descendants of the Puritan commonwealth. Since public order demanded a degree of conformity not only to the legal statutes but also to the religious canons of the nation, the state must provide the revenue to create an Anglican establishment in Upper Canada.[5] Strachan needed enemies in order to promote his own goals.

At the same time, this representation of the religious structure of the colony captured a number of very important social, political, and ideological truths. The clear line that Strachan drew between Roman Catholics and his church, for example, was not merely a financial notation, for it marked a set of attitudes that the Protestant population of the colony accepted as a matter of course. Strachan was a Protestant who saw the world in Protestant terms, and even though he later developed a strong doctrine of the church and protected certain higher churchmen from the attacks of their more evangelical brethren,[6] he nonetheless regarded Roman Catholicism as a jumble of irrational superstitions and a system of religious idolatry and temporal slavery.[7] Although in Upper Canada Catholics were not subject to the same legal restrictions as they were elsewhere and Protestants usually directed their attacks at Catholics as a group, rather than as individuals, Catholics must have suffered personally from the intense prejudices that ran through Upper Canadian society. Indeed anti-Catholicism forms a persistent theme in the religious history of the nineteenth century in Canada.

At the other end of the religious spectrum were the "Protestant dissenters," a term that seemed to encompass the "old dissenters," (such as the Congregationalists, Baptists, and dissenting Presbyterians) and especially the new enthusiasms of Methodism and many other recent sectarian creations. Here the accuracy of Strachan's representation of this part of the religious world of Upper Canada can be measured in two ways. First, his assumptions about the Christian religion (and above all the relationship between church and state) clearly separated him and his church from the dissenting extreme. Secondly, the rage his words provoked in these dissenters confirmed the accuracy of Strachan's analysis of Upper Canadian religion.

Above all John Strachan was a clergyman and a teacher, and at the conclusion of this sermon he revealed his basic religious beliefs: "the doctrine of the atonement – the satisfaction made for sinners by the blood of Christ – the corruption of human nature – the insufficiency of man, unassisted by divine grace – the efficacy of the prayer of faith, and the purifying, directing, sustaining, and sanctifying influence of the Holy Spirit."[8] In short, Christianity was a religion of salvation, offering the means to redeem people from sin, to reconcile God and humanity, and to draw heaven and earth together.

To be saved a person had to proceed along a specific path. Strachan began with the fall when God punished Adam and Eve for their disobedience and expelled them from a state of harmony and innocence. All their descendants continued to suffer under the weight of their original sin. The world had fallen from grace;

people had become the creatures of their instincts and passions. The first step towards redemption, therefore, was to restrain the "selfish passions and appetites" and learn to abide by the rules that God had given to humanity. Both the character of the world and divine revelation taught people that they could only attain true happiness by recognizing their own sinfulness, having faith in God, and living a life of virtue and good works. Then as time moved forward, as more and more people came to understand the eternal benefits that such obedience would bring, society itself would slowly change and humanity would return to God. Then everyone would enjoy the freedom and order that had been lost when our ancestors' apostasy led them out of Eden. Strachan concluded his sermon with a truly breathtaking vision of a future earthly millennium: "For as the influence of Christian principles extend ... murmurs will give way to blessings and praise; and one fourth of the human race being thus reclaimed, the remainder will gradually follow and thus the whole earth become the garden of the Lord."[9]

This way of interpreting redemption helps to explain why Strachan so strongly advocated the need for a religious establishment. Since redemption was a slow and gradual process, people had to be taught continually how to control their passions and lead a life of virtue and moderation. Therefore they needed a well-educated and resident clergyman to "bring [them] daily into the presence of God and [their] Saviour,"[10] churches to house the faithful, and schools and teachers to educate the youth of the province. People were needed who could devote their entire lives to this important task. Only the financial resources of the state could sustain such a system, without which society could not be saved.

The state also helped the church in a less direct way. Since redemption began with order and restraint, the restraint that the state and the law placed upon the passions of the people served a positive religious good. A loyal and ordered population was the basis for a Christian society, and thus the institutions of the state were, in effect, ancillary religious bodies. At the same time the church returned the favour by helping the state achieve its objectives. Christianity taught people to live virtuous lives, and virtue made people into useful and productive subjects. Faith manifests itself in good works - Christians (to quote one of Strachan's more memorable phrases), "pant after the felicity of doing good."[11] A religious population would be a loyal population. In brief, the alliance of church and state rested upon a reciprocity of interests. Strachan summarized his defence of an Anglican establishment in a single phrase: "A Christian nation without a religious establishment is a contradiction."[12] His "garden of the Lord" would be a pious, rational, and ordered place, founded upon strong religious and social institutions and filled with reasonable, virtuous, and happy people.

It is against this background of restraint, order, and establishmentarianism that one can begin to see the wide gulf that separated the church and the dissenting end of the religious spectrum in early nineteenth-century Upper Canada. The way Strachan described the latter group is revealing. Towards the conclusion of his sermon he referred to "other denominations connected by no bond of union, no common principles of order."[13] He compared the settled, well-educated, and sober-minded clergy of his own church and the Church of Scotland with the emotional, poorly trained Methodist preachers who wandered through the colony, disrupting in the name of salvation the slow and careful work of redemption that his church was trying so hard to carry out. He further suggested that the American origins of some of these preachers raised serious doubts about the social and political implications of their religious teachings. His specific charges form but a small part of his general discourse, and they flow logically from his overall argument: they were sound, reasonable, and perfectly consistent. But others saw them very differently, and removed his phrases from their theological context, giving them a prominence they still enjoy. These Methodists were "uneducated itinerant preachers, who leaving their steady employment, betake themselves to preaching the Gospel from idleness, or a zeal without knowledge, by which they are induced without any preparation, to teach what they do not know, and which from pride, they disdain to learn."[14]

These were the words that provoked such outrage. In what later generations interpreted as an instance of divine intervention, one of the "uneducated," the young Egerton Ryerson, came forth from obscurity to do battle with the Anglican Goliath. In a long, vituperative, and rather meandering letter, the Methodist preacher set out to discredit Strachan and to challenge his assertions. Although he tried to convey an air of moderation, even praising some Anglicans and certain aspects of the Anglican Church, he proceeded to charge the Hon. and Rev. John Strachan D.D. with slander, bigotry, ignorance and even pettifoggery – of action that "better comports with the character of a passionate lawyer" than a dignified ecclesiastic. Ryerson's letter caused a sensation; it was reprinted quickly in pamphlet form and spread like wildfire throughout the colony. The Methodist cause in Upper Canada had gained a new champion.[15]

Egerton Ryerson's place in the hagiography of Canadian history is still reasonably secure. Although some historians have tried to argue that his underlying intentions were quite conservative, he is still numbered among the saints of progress and liberalism[16] – certainly his response to Strachan has been seen as a ringing defence of religious and political freedom. But if one reads his actual words with care, it becomes clear that the standard categories in which historians have analysed this debate – the tory Strachan *versus* the liberal Ryerson – are not especially useful. For the issue here was primarily religious, and the two men's many political disagreements grew out of the fact that they saw the world in different religious terms. The debate reveals two distinct interpretations of the character of God and the world, and in a somewhat ironic manner confirms the accuracy of the way Strachan divided the religious structure of the colony.

Ryerson's response accepted implicitly the same three-part division. Like Strachan, he quickly segregated the Catholic population of the colony; as a good God-fearing Protestant he had a general antipathy towards all things Roman. In his letter, for example, Ryerson quoted with approval a passage from the Anglican book of homilies that branded Rome as the "harlot, the most filthy of all harlots, the greatest that has ever been."[17] He also attempted to discredit Strachan and the Anglican Church by associating them with the Church of Rome, arguing that all establishments were essentially Romish. "When did popish and corrupt doctrines receive countenance and support in the church? When religious establishments commenced their existence. When did papal domination, which has crimsoned the Christian world from age to age, commence her infernal sway? When religious establishments got the vogue."[18] Ryerson attacked the very idea of religious establishments: "Our saviour never intimated the union of his church with the civil polity of any country."[19] Furthermore, in Upper Canada there was neither the need nor the legal basis for such an establishment, and if there was no establishment there could be no dissenters. Consequently, Strachan and his church were trying to corrupt both the religious and political life of the colony by imposing what neither God nor nature had intended.

This attack on establishments confirms the other main division in Strachan's religious structure. Though Ryerson argued, in effect, that the Anglicans should be treated like any other Protestant group – indeed he tried to present himself as the loyal son of many Anglican traditions, praising the liturgy and ordinances of the church – once he tried to divide the church from the state, he undercut his own argument. He was trying to divide the indivisible and to put assunder something that history had joined together for several centuries in a long and tolerably happy union. For the early nineteenth century the separation of church and state was a radical idea that could not be supported on historical grounds. To pull the church and establishment apart and treat the Anglicans like just another denomination was like telling the Methodists that their religion would be quite acceptable if they gave up revivalism and itinerancy. Acceptable it might be, but it would no longer be Methodism.

Ryerson's response also illustrates the gap that separated dissenters and churchmen, for his letter expresses a body of beliefs about the relationship between God and the world that stands in marked contrast to the ordered, rational, and institutional doctrines of Strachan's religious world. Strachan, for example, argued that the Anglican liturgy "presents with great force, simplicity, and beauty, the ways, means, and appointments of God, to restore our fallen nature to purity and everlasting life."[20] Ryerson labelled this "all pompous panegyric," rejecting the liturgy as a means of conversion and proclaiming with as much force as he could muster the absolute necessity of "preaching the gospel." This phrase did not mean "reading of one or two dry discourses every Sabbath."[21] He quoted St Paul's second letter to Timothy: "preach the word; be instant in season and out of season; reprove, rebuke, exhort with all long suffering and doctrine."[22] Preaching should not instruct and enlighten but admonish and convert. Conversion was not slow and gradual: it was sudden and immediate, the dramatic experience of being overwhelmed by the redeeming spirit of God. Once again the passages of scripture that sustained his counter-attack illustrate these attitudes. Casting Strachan in the role of Nicodemus, he alluded to the third chapter of St John: "except a man be born of water and the Spirit he cannot enter into the Kingdom of God." In a similar way, he referred to the conversion of Saul and the words of Ananias, "Brother Saul, the Lord, even Jesus, that appeared unto thee in the way as thou comest, hath sent me, that thou mightest receive thy sight, and be filled with the Holy Ghost."[23]

The same preoccupation with conversion and the immediate experience of the spirit of God shaped the way Ryerson replied to the charge that Methodists were "uneducated." Instead of describing the training that an itinerant received and the close supervision that the senior members of the Methodist Church exercised over their prospective preachers, he chose instead to argue that education was not necessary. While formal learning might be useful and pleasing, it could never replace the necessity of experiencing the transforming power of the spirit. A preacher must be redeemed; education was a secondary consideration. He turned Strachan's words on their head: knowledge without zeal was a positive evil.

Ryerson's concluding vision of the future of the world once again points out the same basic contrast. Strachan expressed the hope that careful instruction and good example could gradually convert the people to Christianity and transform the whole earth into "the garden of the Lord." Ryerson also dreamed of a glorious future, but his millennial vision turned upon a series of immediate and powerful juxtapositions. He described the drama of sudden conversion, using images of violence and war: "The day is not very far distant 'when the banners of the Lamb will wave triumphant over the blood-stained car of the Juggernaut; when the Shaster and Koran shall be exchanged for the oracles of truth'; when the plundering Arab, the degraded Huttentot, and the inflexible Chinese, with the polished European, and the uncultivated American, will sit down under the tree of life, and all acknowledge 'one Spirit, one Lord, one Faith, one Baptism, and one God.'"[24]

II

The dispute between Strachan and Ryerson reveals several important aspects of religion and culture in Upper Canada in the early nineteenth century. On the one hand Strachan and Ryerson shared a good deal – they both considered themselves to be servants of the same God; they both proclaimed their allegiance to the Protestant Reformation; and they both read the same Bible and drew many of the same conclusions from it. But on the other hand they disagreed strongly about a number of crucial religious questions: What is the nature of salvation? What is the character of God? What is the proper relationship between God and humanity? These differences sustained some of the basic religious divisions in Upper Canada and shaped a number of elements in the culture of the colony.

To a certain extent the differences between Strachan and Ryerson can be attributed to differences in their character, background, and personality; one was from Scotland, the other from Upper

Canada; one had a university education, the other did not. As with any two human beings, such differences helped to shape different attitudes and beliefs. At the same time these differences had a larger significance, for the two men were representative figures whose ideas and beliefs were part of two general intellectual and cultural patterns. The expressions that Strachan had used in his sermon were not original and can be found in any number of sermons and discourses that he and others had delivered over the course of the previous twenty years.[25] Indeed it is their very generality (and Strachan's ability to promulgate them through the state, the church, and the schools) that gives them a powerful resonance. Similarly, Ryerson's words could have been spoken by many others. His preoccupation with the immediate experience of the spirit of God and the rhetoric in which he clothed his conviction were part of Methodist thought and practice at that time; indeed, they reached far beyond the institutional limits of Methodism. Ryerson was also able to carry these ideas to a large audience, both through his work as a minister and through his distinguished career in education.

In sum, the contest between Strachan and Ryerson over these "uneducated itinerant preachers" is not only a debate between two important historical figures but also an extraordinarily valuable commentary on religion and culture in the early nineteenth century. The points of agreement and disagreement in the debate highlight the general nature of Protestant thought as well as the divisions in the Protestant world of Upper Canada. A study of the debate also introduces the links between religious thought and culture. As both Strachan and Ryerson show so clearly, religion is not restricted to what goes on in a church: the way these men (and so many others) saw God also shaped the way they saw the world.

To move from the specific debate to these more general issues of religion and culture, it is best to begin at the point where most Protestants began their own interpretation of God and the world. At the centre of Protestant Christianity was the Bible, which embodied the very word of God; it was the cornerstone of the faith, the text that held the keys to the nature and purpose of life. Since the Bible was an unassailable authority and the court of final judgment for all disputes and controversies,[26] it is important to understand how Protestants interpreted this unique text.

In the early nineteenth century most Protestants agreed that the Bible was essentially a sacred book of history telling a story with a single theme that began at the beginning of time and concluded at the end of the world. All the passages of scripture quoted so epigrammatically by so many preachers in the nineteenth century were joined together by this basic narrative. The Bible was not only a history text; it was the only history text.

The specific history that was drawn from the Bible was built around a single grand theme: the separation and reconciliation of God and humanity. In the beginning God created the heavens and the earth. The first man and woman lived in harmony with their creator, in a state of innocence and peace. It was Adam's apostasy that shattered this unity, drove Adam and Eve from Eden, and separated humanity from God. The Lord, however, did not abandon the inhabitants of the world completely. During the era described in the Old Testament, God made a number of promises to the people, telling them that if they obeyed certain conditions they could enjoy at least a portion of divine favour. God entered, for example, into a series of covenants to protect and reward a chosen people and in the same era provided a glimpse of the next stage in the progress of reconciliation. The Bible foretold, primarily through the prophets, the approach of a new era and a new relationship between God and the world. In the fullness of time this era came to pass in the series of historical events that form the central episode in the Protestant interpretation of the Bible – the life, death, and resurrection of Christ. By his death Christ atoned for the sins of the world and offered a fallen humanity a way of escaping from the horrific consequences of Adam's original sin. The Gospel held out the hope of salvation, the promise of a future reconciliation between God and creation – a new heaven and a new earth.[27]

Protestant Christianity, then, was a religion of salvation rooted in a distinctive representation of the whole of human history. The past, present, and future were drawn together through a series of strong teleological assumptions. When people read the Bible they assumed that the past foretold the present and that the future would fulfil the prophecies of the past. The eternal present was placed in turn at a critical juncture in this structure of time, standing on the precipice between separation and reconciliation. Although people were still sinners, suffering under the enormous weight of their ancestors' transgressions, they could be saved and the world made into something new. When the Bible was read in this way, it gave time and place a distinct form and meaning.[28]

Although this general interpretation of the nature of the Bible was accepted by most Protestants as a matter of course, it nonetheless remained at a certain distance from the people and the society of the day. It provided, as it were, a broad representation of the nature of time and place, but it did not address directly the specific events of everyday existence, in this case the world of Upper Canada. In order to reach this more immediate and practical level, the Bible had to be interpreted through metaphors and images that integrated this sacred text and the living world that it had to explain.

It was precisely at this point that the general Protestant consensus began to break down. When Protestants tried to fit their own lives and society into the general Biblical representation of the tragedy and triumph of human history, sharp divisions on a number of critical issues quickly arose. In the early nineteenth century there were in general two contrasting patterns of interpretation through which different groups of Protestants attempted to reconcile the Bible and their own existence. From this perspective the battle between Strachan and Ryerson was a battle over which pattern should dominate the way Upper Canada interpreted God and the world.

Both patterns divided reality into two general categories, relying heavily upon a series of paired concepts such as heaven and earth, good and evil, salvation and sin. The two differed, however, when they tried to reconcile these dualities, and this difference sustained two quite distinct representations of the very nature of God and the world. The first pattern of interpretation was based on a distinctive interpretation of "nature."[29] Its representation of religion was highly rational and systematic and appealed to the values of order and reason. The second pattern turned over the cultural coin and appealed to the other side of early nineteenth-century psychology – the feelings[30] – by reworking the Bible into a religion of intense personal experience. From the story of the resurrection it drew the paramount doctrine that to be saved one must directly experience the saving grace of God.

The first interpretation looked back to the foundation of the Christian universe, to the first verse of the first chapter of Genesis. Since God had created heaven and earth, the character of creation revealed the nature of God and the meaning of existence. The argument proceeded, as a general rule, through an extended and well-known analogy.[31] By observing nature one readily learns that order is the primary attribute of the universe. As in a well-made watch, every element in creation fits together within a grand system and suits perfectly the task it performs. And just as the existence of a watch demonstrates the existence of a watchmaker, so too does the perfect order of nature prove beyond doubt the existence of a higher rational intelligence who has imparted such order to the universe. "The works of creation [present] the demonstrative proof to every reasonable mind of the being, nature, and attributes of God."[32] As Strachan explained to his students at Cornwall in 1807 (and repeated on many occasions throughout his life), "the Sun, the Moon, and the Stars, the inhabitants of the land and water so wonderfully suited to their different stations, and habits of life, loudly proclaim a first cause of infinite power and wisdom."[33]

The structure of the world also revealed the purpose of creation and, by implication, the role that each of the inhabitants of creation should play. God made the world with a particular end in view: he ordered creation in a rational and integrated manner so that the system would not only function but function for the benefit of all. If God was a God of love, would he have created the world to produce misery rather than happiness? Seeds are nurtured by soil and rain to produce food; people are given arms to gather and teeth to eat. Each part fulfils its function, and together all parts promote the happiness of the whole.

This image of God and life made duty and self-interest into thoroughly compatible virtues. To follow God's will one must accept the order of nature and society; everything had a place in this grand design. But at the same time one should pursue happiness and contentment. All was order, all was rational, all was happy: "all things work together for good."[34] Strachan argued that "the purpose of creation" was to "confer happiness upon a greater number of rational beings."[35] If people accepted the order of creation and pursued their true self-interest rationally and reasonably, they would realize the happiness that God had provided for the inhabitants of creation to enjoy.

But as it now stood, this way of understanding God and the world could easily drift away from its Christian moorings, for it wavered on the very edge of deism, that heresy that proved so attractive to the apostles of reason and order.[36] If it could be demonstrated that the physical universe was perfectly rational and that rational thought and action were the keys to human happiness, a person might worship reason and order as if they were gods in themselves. The Bible or revelation or even Christ might not be necessary when the world and reason explained the nature and meaning of life quite satisfactorily. This interpretation seemed to lead to a decidedly worldly attitude.

The doctrine of "happiness" created a similar problem. If the term was not defined precisely, the pursuit of happiness could lead to chaos rather than order. If individuals were allowed to define happiness for themselves, they could easily delude themselves into believing that selfishness made them happy and that general selfishness would promote the happiness of all. In this way the interpretation that emphasized the importance of order opened the door to a host of disruptive activities. Society became the battleground of thousands of people trying to satisfy their insatiable passion for worldly pleasure. When carried to its logical conclusion, happiness might prove to be the antithesis of order rather than its concomitant.

To address these problems this interpretation tempered its preoccupation with reason and happiness by stressing the necessity of prophecy and revelation.[37] These provided a strong future orientation that lessened the disruptive potential of the expediency that went hand in hand with the doctrine of rational self-interest and also tied the interpretation more closely to the basic doctrines of Christianity. The argument proceeded this way. The structure of creation, if *rightly* understood, proclaimed the existence of God and strengthened the sacred injunction to lead a rational, ordered, and happy life; but unfortunately the fall had obscured these important lessons. Adam's apostasy had made the people of the world creatures of instinct and passion who were now too ignorant to understand the true meaning of the world. "If it be admitted on all hands that God could have no other end in view in creating the world but the diffusion of happiness, it may be allowed that this end had failed, for mankind were ignorant of the things most essential to their happiness."[38] The structure of creation was not enough; people needed to be instructed more directly. Prophecy and revelation performed this vital task by presenting a series of precise moral instructions and explaining that human happiness included the pleasures not only of this world but also of the world to come. Christian revelation, declared Strachan, "raises our thoughts above the frivolous joys of this life, and presents us with the most glorious prospects beyond the grave."[39]

The study of nature could offer abundant examples of the virtues of order, reason, and piety, but it could not supply an eschatological framework to link individual and social action to goals that transcended the limitations of worldly time and place. In effect, the well-crafted watch of nature could not tell time. The prophecies about the future (which of course were always completely fulfilled) and the specific glimpses of the future provided by revelation set the values of order and reason securely within the biblical account of redemption and the life of the world to come. Rational action must consider two goals: happiness in the present and happiness in the future. In this way prophecy and revelation gave expediency a decidedly Christian dimension. It was not enough to pursue a life of earthly pleasures and immediate gratification; the long-term goal of everlasting happiness in the kingdom of heaven must also be considered. "The primary end of our existence is to promote and secure our spiritual happiness for God delights in the happiness of all his creatures."[40]

Revelation and prophecy can be explosive material; indeed the history of Christianity is filled with groups and individuals who have attempted to use their own interpretations of prophecy and revelation to transform their own lives and societies. In this case, however, revelation and prophecy sustained the values of order and stability running through this interpretation. While the insights of revelation exceeded the scope of reason by answering questions the human mind could not fathom on its own, the answers they gave in fact secured order and happiness. Nothing in revelation undermined these social values or even led anyone to question them. Did not the fact that all prophecies were fulfilled confirm that God and the design of history were perfectly rational? Were not the teachings of Christ – his admonishments to sinners to lead a virtuous life – fully compatible with reason? Did not the beneficial social results of a faith in the world to come demonstrate the reasonableness and utility of the Christian religion?

Order was the virtue that informed this pattern of interpretation. God was a God of order, nature revealed the workings of an ordered and rational intelligence, and reason, sustained by revelation, explained the nature of God and the pathway to salvation. Order was also evident in the way the system as a whole was built on a set of fixed principles such as rational self-interest and the pursuit of happiness. There was nothing extraordinary or unpredictable here: all the pieces came together, and everything worked in an orderly and integrated way. If people led virtuous lives (and after all it was in their own self-interest to do so), they would achieve everlasting happiness, humanity would regain the order and perfection that it had lost at the fall, and the earth would become the garden of the Lord. It was, in effect, a highly ordered pattern that proclaimed above all the value of order itself.

This interpretation of the Bible and the world answered a number of basic theological questions by explaining the relationship between the secular and the sacred: a person who had faith in God, led a virtuous life, and performed a number of good works would enjoy the benefits of life everlasting. The very fact, however, that this was a theological system gave it a significance that went far beyond theological issues. Because this interpretation explained the meaning of life, it tried to encompass all aspects of existence. Thus the way it explained creation also explained the immediate environment, the way it saw God was also the way people should see themselves, and the way it approached the knowledge of God also defined how all knowledge should be approached. A religious pattern was also a social pattern, and order was not only a religious but also a social virtue.

Strachan's statements concerning the relationship between church and state illustrate how religious beliefs become cultural assumptions. In his eyes there was an exact parallel between religious and social obligations. A love of order not only led to salvation but it also helped to create the proper type of society, which in turn helped the church perform its mission. A religious population was also a loyal population, since people imbued with religion led reasonable and circumspect lives. Christianity, therefore, was the cornerstone of social order. This simple syllogism also demonstrated the necessity of a close relationship between the church and the state: both promoted a common set of goals, and both sustained order and happiness.

The same pattern of ideas and values recurs throughout this period. The ordered and hierarchical character of the natural world, for example, not only explained the character of God, but also justified the hierarchy of wealth and power in society at large. Like nature, society was an integrated system, and just as the various parts of nature could exist only as elements in an ordered and integrated system, so could individuals only exist as part of a social system. Order was the very basis of society; without it there could be no liberty or happiness. The principle of social rank followed from the same logic. In the same way that each rank in nature had to accept its place for the system to work, so too each person had to accept their station within the social hierarchy for society to promote the general happiness and prosperity of all.[41]

It should come as no surprise that those groups which were in positions of power and authority in this hierarchy continually called upon religion to justify their exalted stature. To lead a virtuous life and do good works became central parts of a code of aristocratic gentility that bound together the small elites that dominated provincial affairs. Canadian historians have commented upon how the image these elites had of themselves as a refined, public-spirited, and useful group sustained a common social and political ideology, and when the leaders of this group declaimed on the character of their society, they returned time and again to the link between religion, their own virtue, and social stability. John Beverley Robinson, to cite one important example, captured perfectly the close association between religious and social values within this culture of order: "There is a meaning in the moral world no less visible than in the great works of Nature – order, stability, peace, security the great blessings of social existence ... can be reaped only as the rewards of a religious adherency to what is right and true ... The foundations of a people's welfare must be laid in public virtue." According to Robinson (and many others) the fact that he and his associates were virtuous men justified their social authority and the way they exercised that authority.[42]

In a more general way, the culture of order defined a particular approach to knowledge and truth. One began with certain general principles from which one drew certain arguments or theories that could be applied to a number of specific issues. The original premise could then be evaluated in the light of this examination. Knowledge, then, was acquired as one moved from the general to the specific and then from the specific to the general. Once again religion sustained culture: the method for ascertaining the evidence of Christianity was the method of Baconian experimentation – natural theology was perfectly compatible with the world of Isaac Newton. Indeed, in this era there was no clear division between religion and science; religion actively encouraged the study of natural phenomena, and as Professor McKillop has shown so clearly, in the period before the writings of the younger Darwin, science sustained and enhanced the authority of religion.[43]

This culture also encouraged a certain intellectual style. To be accepted as truth, an argument, discourse, or sermon had to be presented in a certain manner. After a brief exordium that introduced the general issue, the topic was divided into three parts: the primary principles that define the question were set out, then these principles were applied to the specific topic, and finally the whole piece was drawn together in a pleasing and systematic way. Everything should be rational and coherent: each point should stand on the conclusions of the previous one. All should be sober, careful, and consistent. A later (and more romantic) generation would find this style dry and lifeless, a seemingly endless series of pious axioms and deductions; but given the pattern of truth that sustained it, the style at least for this era was lucid, forceful, and effective.[44]

This overriding concern with order points out the extraordinary conservatism of the culture. The highly mechanistic representation of the universe was one that discounted even the possibility of sudden and radical change. God did not intervene in the world to change the principles of order, and heaven remained at a reasonably safe distance. The hierarchical social system and institutions of this culture again suggest that conservatism was the political and social ideology that inevitably accompanied the culture of order.

The belief that order was a religious and social necessity was undoubtedly the cornerstone of tory ideology in Upper Canada, but the culture of order also contained elements that could weaken the very values and institutions that Upper Canadian tories held so dear. In the first place, the culture accepted the doctrine of expediency and the value of empirical observation. Since the universe is ordered, rational, and mechanistic, and since this universe was created by God to promote human happiness and prosperity, therefore nature and order were means to an end. The bounty of nature should not simply be admired, but also developed to promote human happiness and prosperity. Nature and institutions, in effect, should be evaluated in two different ways: as elements in a divine system *and* in the light of the benefits they produce. Worth, at least in the latter sense, became a question of results. *Both* the church and the state, it is important to point out, justified the need for a religious establishment on the basis of the social benefits provided by an establishment[45] – religious truth and error was comparatively unimportant. Here was the fly in the tory ointment, for expediency was a social doctrine that could be used to attack the ideas and institutions that were at the centre of the tory universe. If an institution no longer provided the benefits it was supposed to produce or if those benefits could be realized more effectively in a different way, then the institution lost its reason for existence. The church was to learn the rigours of expediency when its opponents (and some of its friends) used this argument to attack religious establishments in the 1840s and 1850s.

Secondly, the environment of Upper Canada itself undermined the conservatism of this pattern of interpretation. Ideas organize and explain reality; in this case they explained and defended a rational and hierarchical world. But before a proper social, political, and religious order could be defended, it had to be established, and it took considerable imagination to proclaim the inherent harmony and order of nature and society at a time when the colony was still a wilderness devoid of hedgerows and well-kept fields, and when the institutions of church and state existed at best only in embryo form. For this reason social analysis had to be cast in the future tense: "Our argument," Strachan explained to the Rev. George Mountain, "is not what we are, but what we shall be if left unmolested."[46] In Britain the culture of order enjoyed the benefit of defending a social and religious system that not only existed but was so well established that it seemed to have become a part of nature itself. Conservatives in Upper Canada were not as fortunate; they had to defend what had not yet come to pass and transform what existed only in part into what ought to be. A pattern that was based in large part upon empirical observation and rational deduction had to ignore a whole world of empirical data; in Upper Canada an interpretation of the world as it was became a vision of what the world should become. Order, in effect, provided a blueprint for the Anglican millennium in the wilderness of Upper Canada: "for as the influence of Christian principles extend ... murmurs will give way to blessings and praise; and one-fourth of the human race being thus reclaimed, the remainder will gradually follow, and thus the whole earth become the garden of the Lord."[47]

It was this disparity between a hierarchical conservative vision and an unordered and seemingly egalitarian reality that so unnerved and frustrated the many critics of Strachan and the establishment principle. Where could one find the established church of Upper Canada? Where were its clergy and churches and schools; indeed where were all its adherents? How could one defend the beneficial results of something that was not yet in place? Dissenters were familiar with the texts on which the Anglicans and Presbyterians had built their case, they saw the inherent weakness in their position, and they used this weakness to attack what they regarded as an attempt to impose a host of unwarranted religious privileges on Upper Canada.[48]

The dissenting end of the religious spectrum also attacked the establishment vision of Upper Canada at a much deeper level. Men like Egerton Ryerson set out to rebut Strachan's specific charges, but, more important, they were determined to challenge the very culture that underlay the establishment position. In so doing they propounded an alternative to this culture that drew God and the world together in a different way. Christianity was not an abstract system of rational precepts, to use Ryerson's phrase, a series of "dry formularies";[49] the church of God was not one part in an elaborate set of social and political institutions. At the centre of this culture was a personal and immediate encounter with the spirit of a powerful and living God.

The first interpretation saw God as a divine rational intelligence conducting a learned discourse for humanity through the intermediary of nature. It treated Christ as a learned divine who had calmly explained the benefits of a virtuous life and presented his audience with a rational set of moral precepts for their guidance. Conversion, therefore, was a gradual process. It began as one restrained the passions and advanced slowly as one gained knowledge of the religious and social principles that helped one to lead a virtuous and rational life. The second culture began at a different point in the Biblical story and presented a very different image of God. Christ was not merely a teacher – anyone after all can be a teacher – he was the crucified and risen Lord. The physical pain he suffered became a model for all Christians: as Christ had suffered to save the world, so must everyone undergo an intense physical and emotional experience in order to save their soul.

If the first interpretation encouraged people to eschew passion and conform to the deeper rationality and order of God's creation, the second called on people to do just the opposite. It looked deeply, not into nature, but into the heart of the sinner; indeed it saw the physical world as an expression of the fallen state of humanity, which lives, not in a garden of order and happiness, but in a wilderness of sin and degradation. If people were to be saved, their feelings had to be roused, not restrained. Passion opened a door through which sinners could be pulled out of a fallen world. This was a religion, not of order, but of experience.

The official voice of Upper Canadian Methodism presented this contrast in the boldest terms. "True religion," the *Christian Guardian* explained, "does not consist in orthodox opinions, in the purest forms of divine worship, in correct moral conduct, or even in the combination of these things. 'The Kingdom of God is not in word, but in power.' However the Gospel may be admired, its great design is never realized but in the actual conversion and salvation of men. With whatever ability the word of life may be dispensed no sinner will be truly awakened, no heart will become broken and contrite, no polluted conscience will be purged from dead works, no impure mind will be sanctified, no human soul will be effectually renewed and comforted, unless the Holy Spirit descend in the plentitude of his love and power."[50] Here again we see the outline of a theological system that attempted to reconcile the secular and the sacred, but as the quotation suggests, it brought these two worlds together in a distinctive way. Orthodox opinions and proper conduct were not enough. To be "awakened," "broken," or "purged" a person had to feel the "love and power" of the Holy Spirit.

This interpretation rested on what one might call a theology of feelings. On an evening in 1738, John Wesley had felt his own heart "strangely warmed" by the spirit of God, and this event took on enormous symbolic importance for Methodists, coming to represent in their eyes a religious doctrine that distinguished them from all other religious groups. Theirs was an "experimental" religion that proclaimed the necessity of a direct religious experience with God. So important was such a religious experience that feelings became more important than reason. Early Canadian Methodism wore this badge of honour proudly. Most of the "religious world," the *Christian Guardian* explained, can "talk well upon the speculative points of Divinity, even reason accurately and quite logically on the attributes of God ... But who delights to dwell on Christian experience? Let us strike at the *infidelity of the heart*, and if we gain conquest there, our work is chiefly done."[51]

Though these theological discourses introduce the religion of experience, they do not reveal its inner character. In the early nineteenth century the concept of theology was not especially important to Methodists, whose theological training tended to consist of reading Wesley's published sermons and a few other texts.[52] In addition the extreme subjectivity of experience makes it very difficult to define this type of religion with theological precision. For the Anglicans experience confirmed the powers of reason and the principles of order, but for the Methodists the experience of meeting God was so unique, immediate, and overwhelming that it defied description and analysis. For these reasons we must turn to other sources. It is not what was written about the doctrines of Methodism but the style of worship created by the religion of experience that reveals the character and significance of this pattern of interpretation. When Egerton Ryerson responded to Strachan, he did not defend Methodism by debating theology and doctrine; rather he singled out the profound impact that Methodism had on hardened sinners. Uneducated itinerants might not understand theology, but they could lead hundreds of people directly to God. The means of conversion, in effect, reveals the beliefs that sustained the religion itself.

To understand the religion of experience we must turn to the revivals and camp meetings that were the hallmark of Upper Canadian Methodism in the early decades of the nineteenth century. This most distinctive style of worship had three essential features. According to contemporary accounts, revivals and camp meetings were distinguished by mass participation: "revivals and camp meetings bring a great number of sinners together." Secondly, revivals were able to isolate these sinners from the world and subject them to a continuous flood of religion: "there is much to be expected from the repeated attacks of divine truth on the minds of sinners at camp meetings, without the opportunity of bringing the pleasures of the world in contact with the impressions made thereby." And thirdly, this flood of religion was highly emotional, playing directly upon the feelings and passions of sinners. The result was an immediate and powerful conversion: "the animal sympathies of sinners are excited, under the influence of which they are placed in a hearing mood, and in this way often become truly convicted."[53]

The descriptions of revivals and camp meetings continually return to these three elements. Large numbers of people came together for a religious event that lasted for at least three days. They were isolated from the outside world, sometimes by nature itself, sometimes by specially constructed barricades.[54] In the enclosure preaching alternated with prayer and singing; mass participation was followed by a division of the people into small groups of penitents. The preaching was intense and emotional; the texts were drawn from some of the most highly charged passages of scripture.[55] In the language of revivals, the preachers had to "preach Christ crucified"; they had to "preach for a verdict," not to inform and instruct but to bring about an immediate conversion to Christ. This conversion experience was itself amazingly intense. As preacher followed preacher, as exhorters moved through the crowds, as the converted turned upon the unrepentant but wavering sinner, individuals would finally break under the weight of the revival, acknowledge their sinfulness, and accept God's saving grace.[56]

From the accounts of revivals and camp meetings we can begin to understand how this style of religion presented God and the world. Here again there was an essentially dualistic interpretation of reality – the recurring distinctions between heaven and earth, between the secular and the sacred. Indeed, the line between the two categories was drawn boldly, but this very separation of the two worlds made the movement from the one to the other all the more dramatic. People were sinners, suffering under the enormous weight of original sin, adrift in a world of evil without guidance or hope. Their souls were encased in a hardened shell that had become impervious to logic and reason; not only were they sinners, but they were even unaware of their own depravity. Only when these people had been forced to accept the enormity of their own sinfulness and plead for divine mercy could the sudden and overwhelming flood of God's saving grace shatter the defences of the world and set the soul of the sinner at liberty. In the flash of an eye, an awful transformation took place as the newly redeemed entered into a truly blessed existence.

God was not a distant and superintending rational intelligence; nature was not a mechanistic set of fixed and integrated relationships that when subjected to reason revealed the purpose of creation. God was an active and interventionist power who continually transformed people and the affairs of the world. The road to salvation was not through the intellect but through the emotions, and it was here that the revivalist could attack sinners and force them to acknowledge their depravity and cry for mercy. In the depths of the most profound feelings, people met their maker and secured their release from the bondage of the old and fallen world.

Such power and drama defied precise and adequate description, logic and reason could never penetrate this mystery. How could something that transcended normal circumstance, indeed something that overwhelmed the entire being, be defined and comprehended by people who still lived in a fallen world? This experience could only be described through metaphor and analogy, and it was in these terms that the language of revivals tried to capture and convey the essence of this religion.

Descriptions of revivals were redolent with images of power and violence. The words of a preacher were like "fire" and "lightning": God came down like a storm or in "showers of grace"; sinners were "broken" or fell "like a bullock at the slaughter."[57] Revivals were noted for their shouting and the physical convulsions that accompanied conversion. The extent to which such extravagances actually took place is a matter of debate; but the fact that conversions were described in these terms confirms the intensity of the experience that defined this interpretation of the nature of God and the world.

In essence religion became a search for experience: to feel God was now the central goal of existence. Other questions became less important; how one lived, either before or after such an experience, or the character of society were not matters of pressing concern. Not only was experience a religious goal, but it also demonstrated the very existence of God. Whereas others searched for

God in nature or, for that matter, in scripture, those who followed this religion looked into themselves. If they felt God, then God must be real. No additional proof was necessary when one had found God in one's soul. This explains why the personal search for experience forms the main theme in so many of the journals and autobiographies of Methodist clergymen in this period. Their words reveal both the self-doubt and anguish as they waited for the experience as well as the joys and raptures when it suddenly arrived.[58]

Those who conformed to the culture of order found this preoccupation with an overwhelming experience almost unfathomable. It was not experience itself that presented the problem, for after all experience that conformed to reason and revelation and led to humility and a virtuous life was a great aid to faith.[59] What they found so unsettling was the assertion that a genuine religious experience transcended a person's ability to understand it. "It is to be feared," Strachan preached in 1830, "that many suppose that the blessings of heaven consist in certain raptures and extacies of which we can form no conception in our present state ... But this is a great mistake – the foundation of our felicity in heaven is substantially the same as that which forms the foundation of the present world. [The individual] can enjoy no true felicity while he remains the slave of unruly passions and appetites."[60] In the culture of order, experience reinforced reason and helped to sustain the individual in the slow and peaceful progress towards salvation.[61] In the culture of experience, it overwhelmed reason and reality – it became self-sustaining, creating a world of its own.

The intensity and power of such a religious experience help to explain some of the important social and cultural aspects of this pattern of religious interpretation. Once again religion leads directly to culture: in defining a way of seeing God, this pattern also set out a way of understanding the world and acting in it. By equating, for example, religion and individual experience, this interpretation made experience the touchstone not only of religious truth but of truth in general. If religion had to be experienced in order to be genuine, then experience provided the standard for evaluating all elements of the world. In other words, if something was felt, it must be true. In this way religion sanctified a different and powerful criterion for evaluating thought and behaviour.

The enormous authority that religion gave to individual experience allowed many individuals and groups to follow the light of their own feelings to a wide range of religious and social destinations. In religious terms it opened the doors to various forms of antinomianism because salvation made newly minted Christians into their own social and religious masters, each one as good an arbiter of truth and error as any cleric or magistrate. It created a new environment where traditional doctrines, the law, and reason itself did not apply. Here indeed was a new world whose boundaries were as wide as the most fertile imagination. The saved could ignore their leaders and try to share in the sacred powers that the encounter with God seemed to place in their hands. They could walk on water, heal the sick, raise the dead, or predict the future.[62] Moreover, an untempered faith could easily loosen the bonds of moral and civil law. After all, the law had been set down to control sinners. Why then should it continue to restrict those who were redeemed and perfect? To paraphrase the first epistle general of St John, if one was saved then one could no longer sin, or what were sins for most people were not sins for the righteous. Sexual relations, for example, assumed a new meaning when this logic removed with one stroke the host of social and cultural prohibitions that sustained such institutions as marriage and monogamy.[63] The same logic could also lead to less extravagant instances of social antinomianism. If everyone was their own religious master, then everyone also had the power to judge all other aspects of life. Experience, in effect, internalized the sources of truth and imparted a truly marvellous self-confidence to social and political life.

Antinomianism is related to the religion of experience in much the same way that deism is related to the religion of order. The latter cultivated a dry intellectualism, in which God and the world worked according to a series of fixed and rational principles. How easy it was in this case to confuse the attributes of God with the sacred itself and simply to worship reason and nature. The religion of experience moved with the same logic to the opposite extreme. This was a religion in which God intervened continually in the course of human affairs, reshaping the world and its inhabitants. Logic and proportion disappeared in a world where anything was possible and where experience became the only standard for truth and action. Each heresy followed logically from the assumptions of its orthodox parent.

The religion of experience also encouraged a number of other distinctive social attitudes, for in this pattern a rigid division between the world of sin and the Kingdom of God encouraged a pessimistic attitude towards society. The material world was an obstacle to salvation and most certainly could not be seen as a reflection of God's benevolence. Moreover, the uniqueness of the conversion experience further undermined the authority of the world and social institutions. To induce a conversion experience, a revival pushed people to the very boundaries of their everyday existence. The religious experience had to be new and different so that sinners would realize the inadequacies of their old ways of life. By challenging the limits of the ordinary, the religion of experience challenged the social concepts and patterns of behaviour that sustained these individuals in their normal lives. The glorification of experience broke down the traditional distinction between normal and aberrant behaviour: the shouting and screaming that were unacceptable in everyday life were quite acceptable in religion, and once something received the blessing of God, how could it be restricted to only one area of life?

These social and cultural qualities of the religion of experience seem to suggest that it was closely tied to political radicalism, for neither accepted the existing social order or the dominant beliefs that justified the social system. Certainly, the Anglicans and the Presbyterians in the early nineteenth century often made this connection: those who were loose in religion were also loose in politics and society. But one must be careful not to overemphasize the radical aspects of this culture. To be sure, the experience of conversion did call upon the newly redeemed to abandon their former ways, but exactly where this call would lead was exceedingly difficult to predict. The direct experience of God inspired Mother Ann Lee and her followers to leave England and establish in America a thoroughly radical and wonderful community that rejected many of the social, political, and sexual beliefs and practices of traditional society.[64] An angel gave Joseph Smith a new gospel that in time carried him (in the company of many Upper Canadians) to Nauvoo and beyond.[65] One religious experience led David Willson to rebuild the temple of Jerusalem in the wilderness of East Gwillimbury; another struck down a young sinner, who fell down before the Lord and promised to stop wearing fancy shirts.[66] Experience might engender nothing more than a casual other-worldliness that after a short time faded away as the converted returned to their former ways. It might tear open the established norms of social action, but what this would produce was quite another question. At times the political divisions in Upper Canada clearly corresponded to the religious divisions of the colony;[67] at other times they did not. Although religion could encourage radical reform it could just as easily lead a person out of politics altogether. Experience was a singularly confusing light to follow.

III

Each of these patterns of interpretation is a composite picture drawn from a wide variety of historical materials. The diaries, sermons, forms of worship, and columns of the religious press contain a number of ideas and images that recur systematically and form a distinct pattern. The pattern drawn from the Anglican and Presbyterian materials is built on the virtue of order, the pattern drawn from the records of Methodism and other religious groups is built upon the virtue of experience. Each pattern then is an ideal type that sums up and integrates the ideas and beliefs of a religious culture, even though not all members of that culture conformed to every part of the pattern. The historical value of these patterns lies in their ability to throw a new light on the religion and the culture of Upper Canada in the early nineteenth century. Since they represent two general ways in which this society saw the world, they can help the historian understand the world that the patterns were trying to order and explain.

In the early nineteenth century these two cultures battled each other in the pulpit, the press, the legislature, and the fields, villages, and towns of the colony as they fought for the allegiance of people who had yet to form completely their ways of understanding and shaping the new world to which they had come. Although the two cultures battled each other intensely, they nevertheless had a good deal in common. What appear to be opposites often find ways of coming together. Rather than two distinct worlds, order and experience were in fact two parts of the same whole. They coexisted in the same historical setting, and by opposing each other they in fact attested to the reality and legitimacy of the other. Rather than being marked by massive ramparts built to withstand a long and arduous siege, the walls between them were low and contained many openings that allowed people to pass from one to the other.

The two protagonists of 1825 illustrate this process of cultural exchange. John Strachan betrayed a zeal for religion that seems at times decidedly Methodistical. For example, he reworked the parish structure of his church into a system of local itinerancy that transformed many of his missionaries into the Anglican equivalent of saddlebag preachers. He even encouraged the laity to conduct religious services by reading the lessons and preaching a sermon when no clergyman could be present, an innovation that was soundly rejected by his bishop.[68] A letter Strachan wrote to the Society for the Propagation of the Gospel summarized his attachment to both traditional religion and more popular forms of evangelism. There were two essential qualifications, he explained, for all prospective missionaries: they must be able to read the New Testament in Greek and know how to ride and care for a horse.[69]

Nor were Ryerson and the Methodists as unmindful of order as their Anglican critics so often asserted. Ryerson himself read Paley at an early date, and the Methodist clergy were far more subject to centralized control and discipline than the Anglican missionaries in the same period. Many Methodists still used the *Book of Common Prayer.* Furthermore, when the Methodists were challenged by other revivalistic sects, they defended themselves by appealing to order and reason. And, as we shall see in the next chapter, when Methodism began to redefine itself in the light of new circumstances and rejected at least some of the features of the old-style revivalism, it was Egerton Ryerson – the great champion of 1825 – who led the retreat from the religion of experience.[70]

Religious and cultural exchange was most prevalent at the frontiers of settlement. All religious groups complained about the frontier where, they argued, the generally sinful state of the colony reached frightening proportions. According to the traditions of Canadian religious history, Methodism enjoyed the greatest success in responding to this challenge because the itineracy of its ministry and the emotionalism of its religious practice were perfectly suited to the religious and psychological needs of a frontier community.[71] And yet the same people who seemed so caught up in revivals also demanded a number of religious offices that were very much a part of Anglican ways of worship. They demanded that an ordained clergyman baptize their children, church their women, and bury their dead. They were devoted to the almanacs and astrological guides that presented a symmetrical view of the universe very similar to the natural theology underlying the religion of order.[72]

The reproaches made to this frontier population by both the establishment clergy and the revivalist leaders describe the same process of interchange. When a revival drew off a large part of an Anglican congregation, the local missionary often railed against the evil excesses of religious enthusiasm, lamenting the lack of firm religious principles among his flock. If the people were only more rational they would not be caught up in such dangerous extravagances. At the same time, Methodist itinerants were continually frustrated by the regrettable tendency of the newly converted to "backslide" or fall away from Methodism after a revival had run its course. Where these backsliders might end up is not certain, but from Anglican accounts it is clear that large numbers of them simply drifted back to their former churches.[73]

The Anglicans attributed this mobility to a lack of firm religious principle; the Methodists, to the tendency of people to lose the power of the spirit. Set in a larger context, however, the movement back and forth between church and revival indicates the way people drew on both these religions and cultures. They selected, combined, and rejected ideas and styles in order to create a type of Christianity that in some measure satisfied their social, psychological, and religious needs. The ease with which people borrowed from both underlines the fluidity of the religious structure of Upper Canada in the early nineteenth century and the importance of both these religions in the life of the colony. In the pre-Victorian period, many people had yet to be institutionalized in a single religious body, and they borrowed from both religions precisely because both had gained a wide measure of support in the colony. Thus popular religion was an amalgam of order and experience.

The two were also joined together in another interesting way. From one perspective they opposed each other and occupied quite separate points in the religious spectrum. But the spectrum seemed to come back upon itself; the further one pushed at one extreme the more one approached the opposite end from the other side. The culture of order organized and explained the physical and social world, whereas the culture of experience spoke to an inner world and interpreted the myriad sensations that arose from living in a particular time and place. Each served different, and yet complementary, social and cultural needs: to find meaning and order in the world and to explain feelings and emotions. When the two were put together they seemed to complete the circle and encompass the culture of this society. In this sense each defined the reality of the other.

"Our senses and our reason," John Strachan wrote to John Elmsley in 1834, "whatever may be their imperfections, are our only guides, for by their means we arrive at all our knowledge, sacred and profane."[74] The culture of order was founded on reason and a very reasonable interpretation of revelation, but it never denied the existence of the feelings and the spirit. In a sermon that he first preached in 1821, Strachan gave particular prominence to knowledge "which hath been acquired by experience." Such knowledge, he admitted, "is by far more valuable" than knowledge "which hath been acquired from books and our teachers." He then explained the process through which experience is transformed into knowledge. Experience must be evaluated by reason; if it "be not reflected upon sifted and examined, if it is not made food for the soul, if it is not analised and separated into all its parts – that the proper lessons of improvement may be drawn from it we may rest assured that it never will ripen into solid knowledge."[75]

The culture of experience also accepted its counterpart. An experience might be unexpected and overwhelming; but the fact that experiences happened implied a need for order. Feelings had to be compared and interpreted, recorded and organized, and they had to be given a sense of order. But here the link between experience and order assumed a different form. Experience should not be tested by reason; reason should be tested by experience. "If the result of true faith be 'joy and peace in believing,'" the *Christian Guardian* explained, "and my experience bears testimony to the validity of this, what further proof can I wish of its divine origin and tendency?"[76]

Both interpretations also expressed an ageless quest to explain and understand the relationship between a life that is bound by time and space and a life that transcends all such limitations. They formed a bridge between the Bible and the world, and for this reason they shared in the authority that the Bible enjoyed. They were part of "the good," they were of God. Far from being two interpretations among a large number of tentative and arbitrary hypotheses, they set the standards to which other intellectual patterns had to conform. This sacredness allowed them to rise above the people and institutions who propagated them. Religion and culture interpreted and explained the world.

But the world, perhaps with a certain sadness, did not choose to follow the paths that religion and culture had set down for its guidance. If God had created the world and then rested, the descendants of Adam and Eve remained decidedly active. In nineteenth-century Ontario they proceeded to reorganize and develop the physical world and the character of the people who lived in it. The outpost of England that grew up on the margin of American civilization underwent a series of important changes that tore apart the old religious world of Catholic, churchman, and dissenter. These changes undermined the cultural patterns that explained the world; religion and culture pointed in one direction, while the world went another. The religions of order and experience began to lose touch with the reality that they were supposed to interpret and explain.

In the new world of the mid-nineteenth century these patterns of culture were transformed into new ones, which in their turn tried to explain the meaning of time and place. A complex series of social and religious changes destroyed the old dialectic of church versus dissent, of rational piety versus revivalism, of order versus experience. Strachan and Ryerson themselves also changed as they tried to confront this new world. Their old antagonisms seemed to recede as the course of history drew them together. Indeed years later, when they found themselves in the same coach on a journey from Kingston to Cobourg, they marvelled at how they now agreed on so many issues.

A new Protestant consensus was beginning to emerge. Within a few short decades, the debate over establishments and revivalism seemed to have become part of a distant past. When people looked at nature they no longer saw an apology for hierarchy, virtue, and a close alliance of church and state. When they described a religious experience they no longer referred to an overwhelming encounter with the spirit of the Lord; people no longer met their maker face to face along a back road in the wilderness of the old colony of Upper Canada. The old cultures were transformed into something new, the fusing of church and dissent, of order and experience, gave birth to the new culture of Protestant Ontario in the Victorian period.

CHAPTER THREE

The Tempering of Revivalism and the Transformation of Experience

Accommodation! When this word touches these
agencies, Methodism is no better than any other *ism*.
It is unchangeable in all its grand and saving essentials;
and whenever it is made anything but Old Methodism,
it becomes new heresy.

"Prepare for Camp Meetings,"
Christian Guardian, 21 April 1841

A study of the cultures of order and experience sets the debate between Strachan and Ryerson in a broader historical context and links this dispute in the obscure colony of Upper Canada to some of the central questions and controversies in the western world. The beliefs and assumptions of the culture of order would have been familiar to the elites of Georgian England or Federalist America who would have accepted almost without question the way this culture described the universe. Similarly, when Upper Canadian Methodists drew on the religion of experience, they were allying themselves with a religious and cultural tradition that encompassed a number of the Old Testament prophets, many leaders of the Protestant Reformation, and the passionate crowds and revivalists of the religious awakenings in eighteenth-century Britain and America.

Upper Canada was rehearsing a drama that was being played out on a number of stages. Immediately across Lake Ontario in upper New York State, religious revivals were tearing apart the religious structure of western New York and whipping up an excitement that ran through society for many decades.[1] In England the poet, artist, and radical, William Blake, confronted the same crisis that Ryerson faced in his battle with Strachan. The dominant culture, Blake argued, will always reject the ideas and assumptions that threaten its own dominance. The rulers of his society equated the religion of experience with insanity. Anyone who dreamed powerful dreams and had visions of new worlds could find no comfort in a society that worshipped the unholy trinity of Bacon, Newton, and Locke. For Blake religious experience broke through the barriers of reason and observation to unveil a new God and a new world. When order and experience collided in the wilderness of Upper Canada, was there not an echo of Blake's description of the last judgement? "When the sun rises, do you not see a round disk of fire somewhat like a Guinea?" 'O no, no, I see an Innumerable company of the Heavenly Host crying, "Holy, Holy, Holy is the Lord God Almighty."'[2]

In Upper Canada in the early decades of the nineteenth century the culture of experience gained enormous strength from its close association with Methodism. Although many individuals and groups – from Quakers to millenarians – drew upon the ideas and practices of this culture, to a large extent the history of the culture as a whole was the history of Upper Canadian Methodism, which not only proclaimed its ideas most loudly but also, through its distinctive religious practice and system of itineracy, carried them throughout the colony. The success of Methodism also owed a good deal to the way the ground had been prepared for its message by the culture of experience. People were ready to accept the religion of experience in general and revivals and camp meetings in particular because these religious phenomena reinforced the way they already saw the world. In spite of its claims, Methodism did not transform the way people understood reality; rather it crystallized beliefs that had already been implanted by the culture of experience. It gathered in a harvest that others had sown.

Methodism linked God and experience; it tied the culture of experience to the sacred. For many people the world seemed to conform to this pattern of interpretation, and this strengthened the authority of the culture and the religious group that proclaimed it most strongly. But even as Ryerson and his brethren preached about the true character of the world and religion, both the world and religion were changing. The world seemed to be moving away from the destiny that Methodism had prophesied, and the words and practices that at one time had moved mountains began to sound hollow and lose their power. The apparent harmony between world and explanation broke down, and the old ways of seeing and worshipping God could no longer sustain the life of organized Methodism. Against a backdrop of social and religious change the leaders of Methodism began to re-examine their beliefs and redefine the nature of Methodism, and in the process they gradually abandoned the standard of experience that had served them so well in an earlier age.

The relationship between social change, patterns of culture, and the history of Methodism is complex. For some people who lived through these events and shaped them, change was a sign of progress and growth. For example, according to at least Methodist tradition Ryerson won the battle with Strachan: after all, the issue on which Strachan had staked his whole design for Upper Canada – the creation of an Anglican religious establishment – was decided, at least on the surface, in Ryerson's favour. By the mid-1850s the state had removed the church from its midst, giving Upper Canada a religious system based on the voluntary principle which made no distinctions between churchmen and dissenters – the type of religious polity that Ryerson had advocated some thirty years before.[3]

Many people welcomed the changes that were taking place in the Methodist church. As revivals drew more and more people into the ranks of Methodism, the church had to create new kinds of religious institutions to accommodate the multitudes, and new styles of worship to meet the needs of new groups. The church no longer concentrated exclusively on converting sinners but now tried also to sustain and cultivate the saved. Moreover, the world had taken on a more pleasing prospect in the eyes of the church. Once Upper Canada began to fill up with more and more Methodists, how could one call upon sinners to come out of a fallen world? After all, the government of that world was no longer an Anglican preserve, and in the economic affairs of the new social order a number of Methodists and dissenters were now doing rather well. Success, from this perspective, was the mother of change.

This favourable interpretation of social and religious change encouraged a sense of optimism within Canadian Methodism that became especially strong in the 1860s and 1870s, when the effects of these changes had become clear. Methodism had emerged triumphant; church union was bringing a number of smaller Methodist bodies together under the Wesleyan banner and carrying the unified church from strength to strength. This rapid growth confirmed the belief that Methodism was peculiarly well suited to the circumstances of the developing Canadian community.[4] The Rev. William Morley Punshon, the president of the Conference of the Wesleyan Methodist Church in Canada and one of the most famous Methodists of the Victorian period, summed up these attitudes when he argued that Methodism had now replaced its old rival, the Church of England, as the real Canadian establishment.[5] Without any special favours it had become the leading Protestant denomination in the new Dominion; even though it was not established by law it was nonetheless the new national church of Protestant Canada.[6]

Such confidence was matched, however, by a sense of unease and fear because the rhetoric of future glory could not disguise the serious reservations that many people had about the present. Upper Canada was a colony not only on the edge of empire but also on the edge of the Industrial Revolution, a revolution that was transforming almost every aspect of Canadian life. Though some of the most dramatic features of this process were yet to come, the impact of economic change on political and social relations was becoming increasingly evident by the middle decades of the nineteenth century. Many Methodists questioned whether their church could control the new world that was growing up in mid-nineteenth-century Ontario. To meet the challenge of what Neil Semple has aptly termed a "new urban environment"[7] the church was forced to undergo many institutional and administrative changes. But these "reforms," as Semple has so skilfully shown, were induced by fear as much as hope. If the church did not change, society would pass it by and Methodism would become little more than a historical curiosity.

The new environment forced Methodists to alter not only their administrative structures but also the way they worshipped their God. If the old ways could not satisfy new needs, then Methodism must abandon many of the religious beliefs and practices that had identified it in the past. Methodists began to redefine the religion of experience; indeed, the very concept of a religious experience changed dramatically as the church sought a more moderate interpretation of the relationship between God and creation. That most Methodist phenomenon, the old-style camp meeting, fell victim to this cultural redefinition as God was brought indoors and institutionalized in a church.

Many Methodists refused to give up their old culture and fought tooth and nail to defend their religious connexion from what they saw as the inroads of the secular world. Furthermore, as Methodism changed it found that old enemies became new friends while old friends became new enemies. Methodism moved towards the centre of the religious structure, where it met the Anglicans, who for a number of reasons had left their old establishment position. At the same time, the vacuum created by the departure of Methodism was filled by several sectarian groups which drew upon the cultural traditions of the old-style religion of experience and attacked the new Methodist Church. They captured the guns of the old-style religion and trained them upon the group that only a short time before had commanded this very position.

This chapter analyses the process of religious and cultural adaptation. How did Methodism change? How did the way in which it responded to a changing world alter the culture through which it interpreted and presented the world? What was the effect of these changes on the religious structure of the colony? To answer these questions we must try to reconstruct the religious world of Upper Canadian Methodism. The Methodists of that day did not interpret social and religious change in the modern language of economics and sociology. Rather, they discussed their problems in the language of revivalism and conversion that their culture provided, and central to their religious discourse was an issue that preoccupied them for a number of years: what is the place of the religion of experience in a changing church and a changing world, and how could they solve the problems that had become so apparent in their religious culture and yet still maintain the distinctive features of Canadian Methodism? As might be expected, in a time of crisis Methodism first had to examine the world in relation to the way it saw itself.

In time the Methodists formulated a new culture for a new world, and some of those who lived through these changes were able to see, if only darkly, the character of this cultural transformation. By the 1860s a number of writers had come to regard the previous decades as a watershed in the history of Canadian Methodism. In fact, the Rev. John Carroll, the most famous and prolific historian of Methodism in Canada, adopted this dramatic change as the central theme of his massive historical canon. The very titles of his works attest to this overriding concern: *Past and Present, The Canadian Itinerants' Memorial*, and *The Old Style Canadian Itinerant*.[8] For Carroll and others the world of the revival and the itinerant was disappearing rapidly, and they wrote their histories in order to keep at least its memory alive.

In a curious and instructive way the sense of time that these works of history embody is a measure of the social and cultural changes that had taken place. The events that these historians described had occurred only a few decades before, well within the collective memory of their audience. But the pace of change and the advent of new ways of seeing the world had pushed them almost beyond the memory of the present generation. Carroll treated the world of camp meetings as something that was part of another age, so far in the past that it could only be rescued by the memorializing of historians. History provided the epitaph to the old culture of Methodism that had recently passed away.

I

The religion of experience presented a clear and distinctive interpretation of the relationship between God and the world. By their very nature people were sinners in desperate need of salvation. Once they recognized their sinful state, confessed their sins completely and unreservedly, and called upon the Lord for forgiveness, God responded directly and immediately. The spirit of the Lord descended into their very being, releasing them from anguish and freeing their souls. Each stage of this spiritual progress was marked by intense emotion. Sinners struggled under the weight of sin; God struck them directly in the heart, overwhelming them with a powerful wave of uncontrolled feelings, while shouts of joy and rapture greeted the release from bondage.

Did all of these things actually take place? Were thousands won to Christ in this manner? Perhaps such descriptions demand a certain scepticism, and it is easy to challenge the authenticity of this type of conversion. The words and phrases used by the writers seem artificial and highly stylized. They have a shorthand quality that obscures what must have been a very complex religious process. People gathered together, they called upon the Lord, who came in "showers of grace,"[9] hundreds, nay even thousands, were won for Christ.[10] The events seemed to fly in the face of common sense – we are told that sinners fell to the ground and did not move for three days before returning to life as new people. It is tempting to agree with the Anglicans and Presbyterians of the day and attribute all this physical and emotional excess to human rather than divine agency. When the Bishop of Montreal saw two women "in the raptures," he quickly pointed out that the object of their emotion was not the Lord's blessing but the attention of the two young soldiers who were watching their gesticulations.[11]

Such criticisms, however, devalue the beliefs of the thousands of people who participated in these events. The highly stylized descriptions of camp meetings suggest strongly that people were so familiar with revivals that only a few phrases were needed to capture their essence. It was easy to fill in the blanks. Similarly, the language might have been excessive and overstated because the events went so far beyond what was normal. Excessive language fitted the occasion; how else could the drama and power of an emotional encounter between a sinner and God be described?

Did salvation actually take place? Were thousands saved at camp meetings? To answer these questions an empirically minded historian will have to wait upon a latter day for solid data about who did and who did not attain this blessed state. May then one of their number – who for professional reasons must remain behind – count the souls of the blessed as they rise up to heaven.

In the meantime we must leave this as an open question and accept the wisdom of a reasonable historical perspective. The fact that so many people described their lives and experiences in this way testifies eloquently to the fact that they saw salvation in these terms. They accepted the framework of reality provided by this pattern of religion and culture and led their lives accordingly.

The religion of experience deeply coloured all facets of Methodist religious life. The diaries, newspaper accounts, and autobiographies of the period describe in glowing terms the way God spoke directly to people. As one might expect, conversion experiences received pride of place in this genre, as people went to great lengths to describe their own conversion as well as those of others.[12] But the life of the spirit did not end with salvation, for in many cases conversion was only one episode in a continuous and highly personal dialogue with the Lord. God came in a remarkable dream to the Rev. Joseph Gatchell, who saw himself trying to rescue a woman who was being ravished by the devil. In his diary he described these events. "I saw also the vision of the devil as a roaring Lyon and he in great fury took hold of the woman as if resolved uterly [sic] to destroy her and while he was thus in great rage making every effort to destroy her I was moved by the Holy Ghost in my dreams to go to her relief and to deliver her out of the hands of the devil."[13] The encounter with the devil and the Holy Spirit led Gatchell to become a preacher: "I was fully convinced that it was my indispencible [sic] duty to go out into all the world and preach the Gospel to every creature."[14] In a similar, if less visionary encounter, the young William Case, fearful of his shortcomings as a preacher, threw himself on God's mercy. The Lord answered him while Case was riding through the forest. He fell to the ground as if struck by lightning and rejoiced in both the goodness of God and the assurance that he would be equal to the tasks before him.[15]

Many aspects of Methodist worship were designed to encourage such a spiritual encounter, to bring about an immediate and emotional union of sinners and God. The emotional language, the skilful use of large numbers of people, the dramatic alternation of the general charge and the personal attack, the combination of ceaseless preaching and powerful exhortation were all means to a single religious end. Camp meetings are the fullest embodiment of this religious style, but the same pattern runs through all aspects of Methodist life. Revivals of religion might occur, and indeed must be encouraged, at all times and in all places. The sermon preached by the American Methodist bishop, Enoch George, in 1817 at Elizabethtown, Upper Canada, is a stunning example of both the emotionalism of this style of worship and the way the experience of God overwhelmed whatever stood in its path. An eyewitness, the Rev. Charles Giles, wrote such a vivid description of the event that his words have often been repeated; they deserve to be quoted once again:

Near the close, as he was bringing the strong points in his discourse nearer together that their united strength might impress the assembly effectually, he produced a climax the most bold and thrilling I ever heard. He ascended from thought to thought in his towering theme, like an eagle soaring and winding up the distant sky.

I heard with admiration, and almost trembled to see him rising to such a fearful eminence. Several times I imagined that he could go no higher, but he would suddenly disappoint me. At the very point where imagination fixed his return, he seemed to inhale new fire, and soared away on wings of thought again; then higher still, till it seemed his inspiration would become his chariot, and, by the grasp he held on the enchained assembly, would take us all with him to the third heaven.

Some of his hearers appeared as motionless as statues, absorbed in thought and charmed with the grand scene before them, while strong emotions were rolling in waves through the excited congregation; and as the man of God was about to descend from his lofty elevation, thrilling shrieks burst out from the awakened crowd in the gallery. Immediately some of the preachers who were acquainted with the place pressed through the multitude to conduct those sighing penitents down to the altar, and soon they were weeping and trembling, and urging their way along to the consecrated spot, where a prayer-meeting was immediately opened, and ardent supplications offered up to heaven in their behalf. The time was well improved, and it was a season of power and glory. Some, I believe, found the great salvation before the exercise was closed. It is believed that more than *one hundred souls were awakened during the session of the Conference.*[16]

This sermon and the reaction it provoked also reveal the inner logic of revivalist religion. Although this style of religion was highly emotional, the techniques used by the revivalists had their own rationality. The preacher ascended to exalted height; the people burst into shouts and tears; the preachers responded immediately with prayers and supplication; people were saved. Viewed in this way, revivals were systematic and well conceived. They set out to achieve an emotional encounter with God, and they used the most effective means to do this end. That explains in large part why Methodists argued that revivals, in spite of their emotion, were well-ordered and well-managed affairs. There was a certain order within the seeming chaos of emotional religion.

There were other features of revivalism, however, that both its opponents and supporters found unsettling. When camp meetings and revivals are seen through the eyes of witnesses who were not Methodists and did not accept the assumptions of the religion of experience, some of the very real problems inherent in this type of religious practice become apparent. Here the primary evidence must be treated with caution. The point of view of the people who wrote these accounts is especially important. If Methodist accounts of the revivals could be ritualized and unanalytical, so too could the descriptions by the critics of revivalism. Anglicans and Presbyterians could attack camp meetings and describe their many shortcomings in detail without ever having seen one. What one group defended, the other attacked; what was one person's chaos was the next person's delight. But the eyes of another can also see different things – what a Methodist leaves out, others might include. It is this discrepancy that provides new insights into the phenomenon of camp meetings and revivals.

In 1833 a Scottish traveller to the new world, Patrick Sherriff, attended a camp meeting in the western part of Upper Canada. A Presbyterian and no friend of religious enthusiasm, he not surprisingly framed his description of the event in the standard enlightenment critique of revivalism. He was a witness to bedlam and disorder and wrote scornfully, "I could not believe the sect was addressing the same Deity."[17] But in spite of these assumptions (or perhaps because of them) his account reveals a number of important and largely neglected features of this type of event.

First, Sherriff readily acknowledged the emotional power of revivalism. He described the large crowd, the high-pitched preaching, and the stirring exhortation to come forward and be saved. Even though he mistrusted revivalism, he was undoubtedly moved by the events he witnessed. His own heart was so "strangely warmed" by the revival that he had to stand back from the event – "I arranged to meet my friend in half an hour, and retired from the multitude."[18] Second and more important, his account highlights features of revivalism that seemed to have escaped the notice of those who praised camp meetings. For example, his account makes it clear that the leaders of the revival had great difficulty controlling the pace and direction of the event. When the preacher called upon the repentant to come forward, only a few came. On another occasion the singing of a beautiful young woman interrupted his sermon, and much to his dismay, the crowd ("either old men or young women") followed her voice rather than his own as she changed the course of the revival without warning. In Sherriff's eyes the "nymph of the gipsy bonnet" seemed to understand the dynamics of revivalism better than the preacher himself.[19]

Sherriff's account is also a fascinating commentary on some of the most highly valued techniques of revivalism. A popular story in the history of Methodist revivals in Upper Canada tells how one of the first revivalists, the Rev. William Lossee, responded to an instance of unruly behaviour. While in the midst of one of his "impassioned, voluble, fearless, and denunciatory"[20] sermons, Lossee was confronted by a young man named Joseph Brouse who was "in the act of making derision." Lossee suddenly stopped his sermon, "lifted his eyes to heaven and cried out smite him, my God! My God, smite him!" At that very moment, we are told, Brouse "fell like a bullock under the stroke of the butcher's axe, and writhed on the floor in agony, until the Lord in mercy set his soul at liberty."[21] The story became famous and was often retold by historians.[22]

There is no need to speculate on the salvation of Joseph Brouse; whether the story is literally true is less important than what the episode reveals about an important revivalist technique. The preacher suddenly stops his discourse, turns all his attention (and the attention of the crowd) to one person, and then calls upon God to strike down a hardened sinner. The technique presents in microcosm the structure of the whole revival – an emotional force brings about the direct experience of God's saving grace. Bourse is not only cut down (and then saved), but his dramatic conversion also confirms the power of the preacher and provides a way of moulding the behaviour of all those who are taking part in the revival.

Sherriff's account, however, raises questions about the success of this technique. He described how a participant in the revival tried to use much the same technique to rebuke an outsider who was ridiculing the event. Raising his voice, he turned to the offensive youth and called upon the Lord. But, unfortunately, nothing seemed to happen, and worse still, the unrepentant sinner returned the fire by engaging his accuser in a long and inconclusive argument that further disrupted the camp meeting. Sherriff also suggests that far from being alone, this disruptive youth was part of a large group that Methodist commentators once again had the regrettable tendency to overlook. Sherriff found a large number of onlookers standing outside the enclosure, making fun of the revival. He treated them as a distinct group and described the interplay between them and the people who were caught up in the revival, noting especially a number of young men in the group who seemed to regard the revival as simply an opportunity for harmless but interesting sport.[23]

Other eyewitnesses confirmed Sherriff's observations. In July 1839, William Orde Mackenzie, a British army doctor stationed in Canada attended a Methodist camp meeting near the village of Brighton in the eastern part of the province. His diary contains perhaps the most detailed account of a religious revival during this period.[24] Although Mackenzie did not share in the enthusiasm of the events he recounted, his observations are exceptionally perceptive. He began by describing in considerable detail the arrangement of the grounds. A ring of trees formed a large circle within which two sets of benches (one for men, the other for women) faced an elevated preaching platform. On one side of the platform along the edge of the circle stood roughly built structures for sleeping: on the other, a large "sheepfold" for those who were moved to seek salvation (see Figure 1). Like Sherriff, Mackenzie recounted the now familiar rituals of revivalism – the succession of preachers, the call for prayer, the exhortation to come forward. He also described a preacher who singled out one of the unrepentant – in this case a young woman leaving the campground – and attacked her moral character. Once again the technique met with little success.

Mackenzie, however, was struck most by the inability of the leaders of the revival to control the emotion they had generated. A preacher took off his jacket, rolled up his sleeves, tied a handkerchief (by custom a red one) around his neck, and called upon the multitude to come forward to the sheepfold. He separated the men from the women, gave out a psalm that was led by "a fine but dirty looking fellow acting rather out of tune as precentor," and then called the people to fall down in prayer. "And now," Mackenzie explained, "arose a scene which I can not intelligibly describe." These techniques had brought the people to a fever pitch, and then the revival took a course of its own. Bowled over by emotion, the people in the enclosure flew about like skittles. "Among their men, a new set of 'inspired' poured forth their effusions with all sorts of gestures and in time so loud, so disagreeable and apparently so heart-rending, as completely to put a stop to all the rest, and to cause a great sensation among the

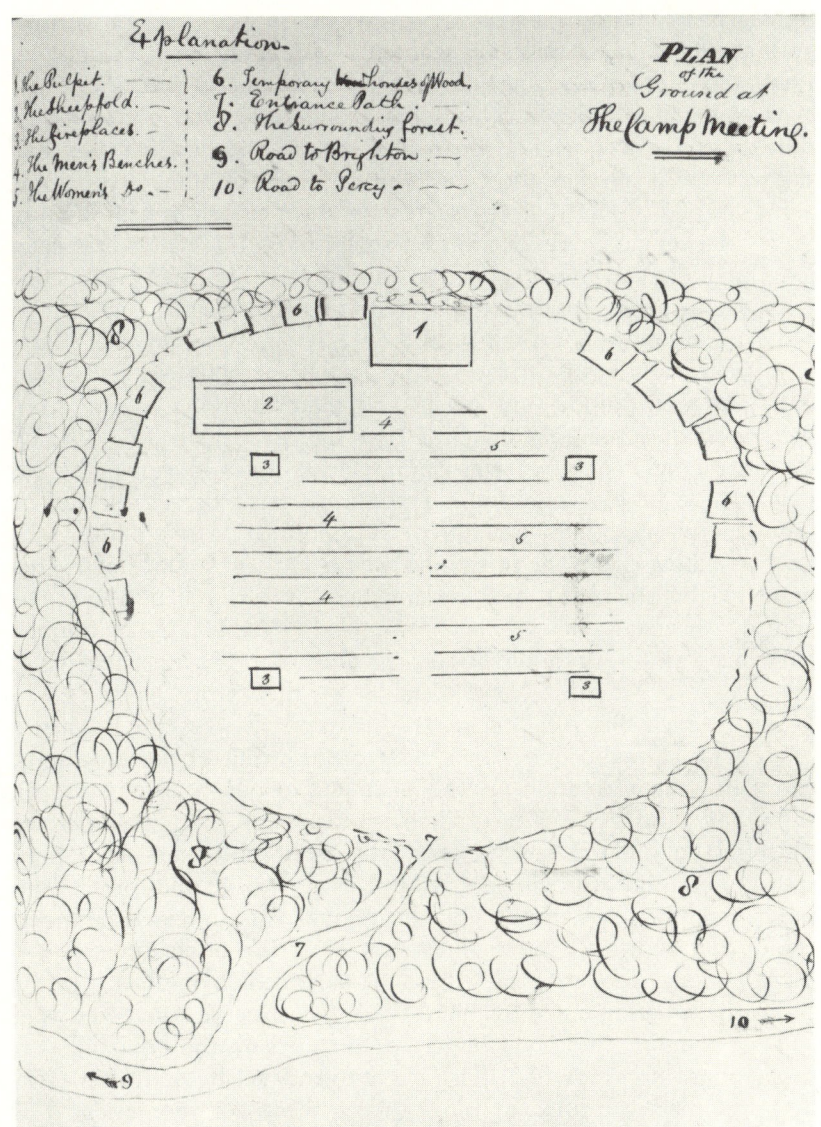

Figure 1 "Plan of the Ground at the Camp Meeting" from Dr Mackenzie's Canadian Diary, 1839–43. (Courtesy University of Toronto, Thomas Fisher Rare Book Library)

female part who now exchanging sobs for screams, began to howl and cry in a most pitiable manner ... Several were obliged to leave the place screaming, or to be carried out in hysterics."[25]

The next day Mackenzie and the friends who had accompanied him debated the question of how to interpret the events they had witnessed. As one might expect, given their original disposition, some argued, "All we have seen was sheer affectation and humbug." Mackenzie however, after reflecting upon the events at greater length, offered a revealing explanation. From his own perspective it was clear that "undoubtedly hypocrisy was legibly written in the face of many of them," but he also understood that those who were caught up in the revival saw their actions very differently. In their minds and hearts the manifestations of the spirit were real; they honestly believed they had experienced God's saving grace. Such a belief was so powerful it could cause the believer to do almost anything. "There must have been," Mackenzie argued, "many others (of the most ignorant classes I allow for they are always the victims) who worked up to a state of excitement by the Denunciations contained in the sermon, by the scene, and by the marvellous effects produced in some, the extraordinary invocations of others, were capable of believing themselves inspired to do anything and touched by the spirit."[26]

Like Patrick Sherriff, Mackenzie hit upon two essential features of revivals. On the one hand, they could bring about an almost complete transformation in the character of the participants; on the other hand, they were unstable and it was hard to anticipate the effect of all the techniques. Crowds of onlookers (like him) could scoff and ridicule just as easily as they could praise and pray; and once the emotion of the revival was unleashed no one could control it and the revival took on a life of its own.

Methodists were extremely hesitant to acknowledge publicly the problems inherent in revivalism. Revivals, after all, were the soul of their religion, and they preferred to dwell on the amazing successes that often crowned these events. And yet if Methodist writings are read carefully in the light of these commentaries, it is clear that the church was becoming aware of these problems and was searching desperately for ways to deal with them.

Although Methodists protested at length that their revivals were well-controlled, the precautions they took to maintain order – banning beer and cake dealers from the grounds, building high fences around the camp, and patrolling the perimeter with what one observer called "a strong 'watch,' a sort of camp-meeting police" – strongly suggest that they indeed recognized the problem. At a recent camp meeting in Kemptville there had been "no rioting, no obscenity, no impropriety of any kind," but just in case the "ruffians grouped round at a distance" decided to attack, there was "an active magistrate on the ground, backed by an efficient corps of watchmen, ready at a moment's warning to inflict summary punishment on transgressors."[27]

Many Methodists were also aware of the other problems mentioned by commentators like Sherriff and Mackenzie. Emotional techniques might bring about wonderful results, but they were also unreliable and difficult to control. The Rev. George Ferguson, who recorded many dramatic conversions in his journal, was keenly disappointed as he watched the newly converted lose their spiritual conviction. He described a man who had suppressed his sins for so long that he could not even pray for mercy. With Ferguson's help the man finally overcame this obstacle and underwent a profound conversion, even seeking out the person he had wronged and begging his forgiveness. But unfortunately this newly redeemed person soon lost the power of the spirit and slid back to his former ways. "Alas!" wrote Ferguson, "he got overcome again, and went back into Egypt. How mutable and fallible is man!"[28]

All these incidents point to a problem that continually plagued revivalistic religions in Upper Canada. However hard Methodists tried to develop precise techniques for generating emotion or channeling it towards specific religious goals, emotion had a life of its own that no one could control. This problem manifested itself most clearly in two closely related issues. The first was essentially the one the Rev. George Ferguson encountered so often. Though the power of revivals won countless souls for Christ, far too often these souls returned to their sinful ways. How then could the church achieve and maintain a level of intensity that could keep former sinners walking along the path of righteousness? The second problem, which represents the other side of the same coin, was to control and even limit the intensity of religious feeling. If some cooled too quickly, others remained too hot; emotion carried the converted too far. In the revivals that Sherriff and MacKenzie had witnessed, the leaders could not control the people who had "got religion" and set out on their own. How then could the enthusiasm of the newly converted be moderated so that they would walk along the *proper* path of righteousness?

The first problem was one that all religious groups had to face. Anyone – be they Anglican, Presbyterian, Methodist or even Catholic – might cast off their faith and return to the ways of sin. Revivalistic religion, however, raised this problem to new heights because mass conversion created the possibility of mass defection. A camp meeting brought hundreds of people together and as the itinerants preached and prayed and exhorted, large numbers were won for Christ in the most dramatic fashion; but when the itinerant preachers returned a short time later, many of the saved had disappeared almost without a trace. It seemed as if the revival had not even taken place. The famous Father Corson, who led a series of revivals on a circuit in Durham County, lamented at the end of the year how "sifting" and "backsliding" had reduced the number of Methodists, not only in his own area but for the connexion as a whole.[29] In an article entitled "Hints for Helping a Revival," the *Christian Guardian* addressed the same issue directly: "Twenty, thirty, perhaps forty or fifty have been brought out of darkness during a meeting; but owing to the omission of an immediate and constant culture of the plants of piety, before the year rolled round, few have remained to need culture."[30] Both these examples highlight a fear that lurked in the minds of many Methodists. What good were revivals if they could not sustain salvation? What good was it to convert Anglicans or Catholics into true Christians only to see them fall away into a life of irreligion? If so many people fell away after receiving the Lord, might revivalism not be a way out of religion rather than a way into it?

For a religion so firmly committed to experience, the only solution seemed to be to increase the intensity of emotion. Since all the techniques of revivalism tried to effect an immediate and highly emotional encounter with God, failure could be attributed only to a lack of emotional intensity. More emotion was needed – so much emotion that the sinner would be completely won over to Christ. If some emotion was good, then more was even better; if the weeping of one or two sinners was a sign of God's favour, let the Lord hear the cries of hundreds or even thousands. The Rev. W. C. Walton, following the logic of revivalism to this conclusion, called upon his brethren *not* to comfort the repentant sinners too quickly, but to let the full force of emotion wash over them, because the more intense the emotion the more lasting the conversion. "If they have been thoroughly convinced of sin; if they had under this conviction, realized that they were justly condemned and lost sinners, and from that awful condition been snatched by the hands of mercy: all this would have made an impression upon their hearts which they could never forget."[31] The intimacy of the love feasts that often concluded revivals and the demand for personal confession at class meetings[32] were designed to sustain the depth of the religious conviction of the newly won convert. Distinctive ways of speaking – the use of "thee" and "thine," and "brother" and "sister" – and the wearing of simple clothes gave the convert a group identity that emphasized the uniqueness of the conversion experience.

Unfortunately, this way of solving the crisis of backsliding aggravated the second part of the general problem that plagued the religion of experience. In many cases the emotion of the religious experience was so strong that it threatened to undermine the entire structure of Methodism itself. A religious experience often made people so secure in their faith that they felt perfectly at liberty to determine for themselves the religious course they should follow. The direct and personal encounter with God gave the saved enormous power and authority. Since they had experienced God they did not need an advocate with the father and could make their own decisions. The "nymph of the gipsy bonnet" who took control of the revival described by Sherriff had such power, but she was by no means alone. Revivals were continually being disrupted by people infected by the spirits – what Methodists often referred to as "wild-fire." As the term implies, this disease was highly contagious, and once the spirit had caught hold everyone could quickly be consumed.

This problem occurred dramatically during a quarterly meeting of the Bay of Quinte circuit in 1797. The presiding elder, the Rev. Darius Dunham, had retired with the official brethren for their quarterly meeting when "the power of the Most High seemed to overshadow" the people gathered in the adjoining room. Soon there was "groaning for full redemption," some people shouted in praise while others lay prostrate upon the floor.[33] When Dunham saw these things he was astonished and, falling to his knees, "began to pray to God to stop 'the raging of wild-fire'." After a time, however, he became convinced that the spirit was genuine, and he too fell to the floor and "received a baptism of the very fire which he had so feelingly deprecated as the effect of a wild imagination."[34] Although in this instance the "wild-fire" proved to be the spirit of God, the frenzied behaviour of this leading religious figure betrays the horror with which many Methodists greeted such spontaneous outbreaks of uncontrolled religious emotion.

The intense power of the spirit could also generate more organized and sustained threats to Methodism. The experience of God could lead whole groups of people to try to transform their own vision into a living reality. New religious sects and new utopian communities flourished in this religious atmosphere. Experience was so powerful that it undermined traditional social norms and values. Since their experience assured their salvation, these groups no longer needed to obey the old moral law, and consequently they were free to reinterpret the meaning of love and marriage in startling ways.[35] Others, convinced by their encounter with the spirit that the Kingdom of God was at hand, called upon the people to come out of an evil world (which included the Methodist Church) before the awful moment of Christ's return.[36] Here one catches a glimpse of the "hot-bed" perfectionists, millenarians, and religious visionaries who followed the religion experience to the far end of the religious spectrum.

The religion of experience was a two-edged sword, which could cut through the flesh of friend and foe alike. It was a useful weapon against the religion of rationality and order, but it was difficult to control. It might save thousands of sinners, but it could turn others away. Some lost the spirit too quickly; others followed their own sacred light to destinations unknown. On the one hand revivalism was a half-way house on the road to irreligion; on the other it was a half-way house on the road to antinomianism and sectarian extremism. People left Methodism by the front door as well as the back.

All these problems might have remained largely hidden had Methodism in Upper Canada remained a revivalistic sect. After all, there is a certain logic that leads the religion of experience to ignore those things which do not pertain directly to the actual experience of salvation. If the single and all-absorbing goal of religion is a direct encounter with God, everything else is less important: once such an encounter takes place then the work of religion is essentially complete. After a person had wrestled with the devil and then felt the flood of God's saving grace, how could a mere human being try to alter the course of this divine encounter? The Rev. J. Scott, a leading Methodist in the Niagara Peninsula, understood the logic of revivalism very well: "Emotion knows nothing of law. If a man cry aloud, he is to be allowed to cry. If he cry long terminate not his cry. If a new born soul be incoherent in prayer, place no interdict on him ... What policy shall limit its designs – what rules better its operations – what bounds circumscribe its expansiveness?"[37] Emotion was the working of the spirit, and it was unthinkable for any Methodist to challenge the workings of the spirit.

But as the social and religious structure of the colony began to change, Methodism found that it could no longer ignore the problems inherent in the religion of experience. Revivalism had gained strength from the power of its enemies and was most effective when it faced an adversary that denied the value of emotion and experience. By the 1840s, however, the religion of order and the society of elites and establishments were on the defensive. The issue had become how many different churches should benefit from the largesse of the government, now that the forces of a single Anglican establishment had been driven from the field. Once the establishment principle had been lost, the old religious structure quickly fell apart, and with its collapse the old revivalist rhetoric lost its force and meaning.

Society was also assuming a more pleasing prospect. Now that the corrupt alliance of church and state no longer controlled society, it was not necessary to call on people to come out of a fallen world. The old Anglican elites were losing power and many Methodists were assuming important positions in the new society. Once again the social criticism that was central to the religion of experience lost its meaning for want of a ready target. Social change, in effect, provided an opportunity for Methodism to enter a world it had once rejected, and it leapt at the chance. But to do this it had to re-examine itself in the light of this new religious and social environment, and it was precisely at this point that the problems inherent in the old-style revivalism became acute.

Many Methodists began to reassess the place of emotion and experience in their church, concluding that some emotion was fine, but that too much frustrated the work of conversion by making camp meetings into outlandish spectacles and hardening the souls of those who had become accustomed to revival techniques.[38] Methodists also worried that the love feast and the class meeting did not provide enough guidance for Methodists who lived most of their lives in the secular world. These old badges of distinction were no longer sufficient, and the church itself began to question publicly its old assumption that emotion, separation, and distinctiveness were essential for the survival of Methodism. In fact some of the most clearly identifying marks of old-style Methodism became the subject of ridicule. Methodist preachers were now asked to dress in a more becoming and conventional manner, restrain their gestures, tone down their emotional oratory, and refrain from using quaint forms of language. The traits that had once defined Methodism as a distinct movement now limited both its appeal and the prospects for growth and expansion.[39]

In retrospect it seems obvious that these problems called for an institutional response. If emotion and separation no longer worked,

Methodism had to make an accommodation with the world it had once rejected. Preachers had to explain rather than exhort, the church had to stop relying on sudden conversions and instead nurture the faith of Christians by creating a moral environment of churches, Sunday schools, and voluntary organizations. The wisdom of this response seems beyond doubt, for did not the history of the next half century demonstrate both the inevitability and the wisdom of such a course?

History may have anointed this response, but its apparent inevitability did not diminish the genuine difficulties of such a course. To exchange emotion for reason, to replace mass revivals with a host of religious institutions threatened the very essence of Upper Canadian Methodism. Methodism was a religion of the spirit; how then could it control and limit a force that was by definition uncontrollable and without limits? The encounter between God and humanity could not be bounded by time and space. The world of reason and religious institutions was the very world that Methodism had once attacked so strongly. As Methodism moved into the future, it had to keep one eye on the problems it was trying to solve and the other on the history and the culture that had given it such strength. It had to meet the needs of a new religious and social world and yet maintain some continuity with the religion of experience that had defined Methodism in the past. It is this tightrope that marks the path of Methodism in Upper Canada over the next thirty years.

II

During the middle decades of the nineteenth century Upper Canadian Methodism underwent a number of important changes. The connexion was growing very rapidly; new churches were built, educational institutions and religious societies were established, and circuits were expanded and regularized under more effective bureaucratic control. The ministry was also changing. Exhorters and lay preachers lost much of their former importance, and the saddlebag itinerants were now better educated. The Methodist laity also began to assume a more important place in the church. The administrative and financial ability of this group increased its influence at the local level and on a number of influential conference committees. The expansion of religious newspapers and journals not only marked in itself an important change in Methodism but also provided a vehicle for explaining these changes to the growing Methodist membership.[40]

All these changes helped the Wesleyan Methodist Church to meet successfully the problems of a developing society. Success, in turn, helped the church consolidate its dominant position among other Methodist groups that had either grown up in the province or entered it with the more recent waves of British immigration. Consequently, when Methodism was unified in the 1870s and 1880s, the religious and administrative structures developed by Wesleyan Methodism during this earlier period provided the framework for church union. Other Methodist bodies adapted themselves to Wesleyan norms: to a large extent church union was a process of benevolent absorption.[41]

These changes can be explained in a number of ways. Most historians have emphasized the influence of external social forces in the transformation of Methodism. The development of new administrative structures, for example, was a response to changes in Upper Canadian society. Having become more settled and mature, the colony was now demanding a religious organization better suited to the new social and economic environment.[42] According to some historians, social progress brought with it new concepts of middle-class respectability which forced the leaders of the church to reject their rather tacky past and conform quickly to more refined codes of social and religious behaviour.[43]

These external forces however, are only one factor in a very complex process, and although they help to explain why and when religious change took place, they cannot explain why religions responded to these forces as they did. When social change forces people and institutions to change, they interpret those forces and shape their responses in relation to the existing cultural framework: the way a group sees the world shapes the way it responds to changes in the world. In sum, external forces must be seen in relation to the internal culture in order to understand social and religious change.

The issue of "respectability" illustrates the interplay between external and internal forces. The external process of class formation undoubtedly spurred the drive for respectability – the concept became an important part of the ideology of the middle class, who used it to shape the world in its own interests. Yet respectability is a relative term that only acquires a specific meaning in relation to the norms of a particular group at a particular time. For Methodists in the early years of the nineteenth century, it was quite respectable to fall to the ground and shout to God, though other more "rational" groups found this much less becoming. By the mid-nineteenth century, however, a number of changes were taking place within Methodism that redefined the meaning of respectability; new patterns of belief and new styles of religious practice gave respectability a decidedly more refined meaning. The issue is not only the impact of an external code of respectability on Methodism but also how codes of respectability changed within Methodism itself. Social change provided the occasion for the growth of this middle-class cult, but the values and ideas that this cult put forward can only be understood in relation to the internal dynamics of religious change. In fact, respectability may well have been a result of religious change rather than the other way around.

A Methodist who witnessed the growth of this cult offered a fascinating commentary upon the relationship between social and religious change. A strong supporter of camp meetings, he attacked unmercifully the changes that were taking place in the church and the way the advocates of change were justifying their cause: "We have no alliance – nor do we wish to have – with those who say, the religious knowledge and habits of the colonists, are so matured, and their intellectual refinement so palpable, [that] camp-meetings are superseded by the ordinary means of grace, and forbidden as vulgar and rustic by the usages of respectable life and the dictates of good taste." Methodism, he argued, must not change: "Accommodation! When this word touches these agencies, Methodism is no better than another *ism*. It is unchangeable in all its grand and saving essentials; and whenever it is made anything but Old Methodism, it becomes new heresy."[44]

This defender of "old Methodism" was fighting the forces of respectability and accommodation, but history was not on his side and, in spite of his warnings, Methodism became more respectable and reached an accommodation with the world. But the intensity of his admonitions makes it clear that some Methodists did not accept the changes that were taking place, and this division occasioned intense debate within the church. The defence of old Methodism also suggests how this debate focused upon a number of religious questions. In effect, the problems that had grown out of the emotionalism of the old-style religion raised the question that this particular Methodist addressed so passionately, namely the place of revivalism and camp meetings in this new social environment. The uncompromising stand that Methodists such as this writer were prepared to take set important limits on the type of cultural change that could take place. Religious and cultural beliefs can be very resistant to change, and the new Methodism had to take this fact into consideration: if it changed too quickly it could tear itself apart. Some continuity with the past had to be maintained.[45]

The subtle but important changes in the basic forms of revivalistic religion from 1835 to 1860 illustrate the process of religious and cultural adaptation. From one perspective these decades mark the high point in camp meetings and revivals in the Methodist Church. According to Arthur Kewley, the leading authority on camp meetings in Upper Canada, Methodism laid the foundation for revivals and camp meetings in the 1820s and 1830s and then built on these foundations and expanded revivalism throughout the province during the 1840s and 1850s. By Confederation, however, the number of revivals and camp meetings had fallen off dramatically as new religious practices became popular. In Dr Kewley's words, "the established congregation had come into its own with a practical stress upon the week by week growth of the Christian."[46] The importance of revivalism declined as churches and Sunday schools became more numerous.

These changes, however, raise another set of questions. The popularity and growth of the new forms of worship strongly suggest that important cultural changes were already taking place. Church building gained speed because Methodists had already begun to reject revivalism and accept the cultural assumptions embodied by the new styles of worship. As early as the 1840s, for example, a number of changes were taking place that made the old-style revivalism into a more moderate and controlled style of worship. In early camp meetings the people at large had an important influence on the course of events. As the spirit moved among them and they cried out for salvation, the revival passed out of the control of the clerical leaders, who were forced to follow the lead of others. Revivalism was in large measure a popular event.[47] By the 1840s, however, revivals were becoming increasingly subject to strict clerical control. The succession of events became more standardized, and the church tried to restrain outbreaks of popular emotion and to channel the emotion that did break out towards the specific religious goals defined by the church. Methodist leaders took greater precautions against the external threats to camp meetings; they built fences and gates and monitored admission to the camp grounds very carefully.[48]

The church also tried to moderate revivalism by linking revivals to the quarterly meetings of each circuit. These meetings had served a number of functions: they brought together the travelling and lay preachers, dealt with the general business of the circuit, and acted as a court in matters of disputation and discipline.

They also provided an occasion for prayer meetings and love feasts.[49] In the 1830s these quarterly meetings were extended into "protracted meetings," which often continued for several days and produced a large number of emotional conversions. Evening revival services, often held during the winter, were also becoming very popular.

These "new measures" are in many ways reminiscent of the older styles of revivalism,[50] and they drew upon the rich tradition of religious revivals that was still very strong in the colony. At the same time, however, protracted meetings and evening revivals mark a number of important changes in Upper Canadian revivalism. In the first place, these services were intended primarily for people who were already Methodists rather than the people who might become Methodists. For this reason, they tried to refresh and sustain the spiritual life of the converted rather than awake the souls of hardened sinners. Secondly, revivalism moved indoors. Circuits built one meeting house that was large enough to accommodate all who came to the quarterly meetings, and this church replaced the forest meadow with its towering trees and glowing fires. In addition, the people did not remain together for the entire revival. Protracted meetings stopped for the night, and the people who came from a distance boarded with local Methodist families.[51] In evening revival services the participants came from the immediate neighbourhood and were able to return home after each service. Thirdly, there was a change in the religious services themselves, as the pattern of worship became more regular (again reflecting stronger clerical control) and now proceeded through a series of short and well-planned religious observances. One description set out the following schedule: begin at 9.30 with prayers, hymns, a short sermon, a brief exhortation, and a prayer meeting; take an hour's intermission for lunch; and then repeat the program in the afternoon until 5.00 p.m. "By this quick succession of services," the writer explained, "there is an interesting and profitable variety. With long sermons and prayers a day's meeting can not well succeed."[52] Quite clearly, then, these new measures rejected some of the premises of the old-style revivalism, no longer demanding that the people be completely isolated from the world and subjected to an unceasing barrage of religious events.

Preaching was also changing, although it is difficult to determine precisely the extent and pace of this change. At this time the *Christian Guardian* began to attack the very style that early Canadian revivalists had made famous. How often, wrote the of-

ficial voice of Methodism, had people "been disgusted by the sin-
gularity and eccentricity of the preacher."[53] The paper took particular aim at the preacher "who commence[d] an out-pouring of
vituperation against [the people] saying hard things of their supposed errors, and charging them with vice and wickedness."[54]
Now Methodist preachers were told to present a more pleasing
appearance, employ refined manners of speech, and always keep
the tastes and character of their audience in mind. Had the Rev.
William Lossee read this, he would surely have been at a loss for
words! Similar demands were now placed upon the congregation.
Hymn singing should display greater decorum and harmony.[55]
People should all face the minister, they should say a short prayer
upon entering and leaving the church,[56] and they should avoid
that most expressive revivalist phenomenon – the continuous shouting of "Amen.". The word was not to be said "with insincerity,
rashness, and irreverence, but reverently, appropriately, and earnestly. It is a devotional act and should be characterized by spirituality and solemnity; yet with humble confidence of importunity."[57]

It is clear that the central authorities of Methodism were also
trying to challenge the stature of revivalism in the church in
general by stressing the importance of other forms of religious
worship. Revivals might be useful, but they were to be regarded
as "extraordinary means" of grace. They might occasionally produce good results, but they should never be allowed to detract
from the "ordinary" pattern of regular Sabbath services, class meetings, Sunday schools, missionary endeavours, and the day-to-day
duties of leading a Christian life.[58] There was only one type of
revivalism that received the blessing of the central authorities of
Wesleyan Methodism: the relatively new phenomenon of the religious meeting conducted by a professional revivalist. During this
period a number of these revivalists passed through the province;
in January of 1852, for example, the Rev. James Caughey, the
author of *Earnest Christianity*, led a large revival in the Richmond
Street Church in Toronto.[59] The character of these revivals, however, simply confirms the direction that religious change was taking. Professional revivalists were well known and reliable; their
revivals took place for the most part in church buildings, were
carefully controlled and lasted for only a few hours; nor did they
threaten the work of the resident ministers, who could continue
to look after their regular religious obligations.

These changes in Methodist worship did not pass unnoticed:
indeed they generated considerable and widespread opposition
from a number of clergy and laity who at almost every turn tried

to defend the old ways. The opposition to the drive for moderation came from the local level and especially from older itinerants in those parts of the province that had a strong revivalist tradition, such as the eastern part of the province, the Bay of Quinte, and the Niagara Peninsula. The forces for moderation, in contrast, were strongest at the centre, especially among the younger and better educated clergy.

During the mid-1840s the battle was especially acute. The pages of the *Christian Guardian* were filled with an intense debate over the place of revivalism in the Methodist Church. Especially revealing were a series of letters from a minister who had once conducted mass revivals but now questioned the need for such practices. Writing under the Hebrew letter "YOD," he repeated all the criticisms of revivalism that are now so familiar. Though revivals had been a great help, they had also done "much harm and injury to the Church."[60] They encouraged too much emotion and were difficult to control. People became impervious to revivalism: they "now understand it and begin to fortify themselves against every attempt at their feelings and passions."[61] Too often revivals were like whirlpools, growing in emotional intensity and consuming so much time and energy that both ministers and people began to ignore the ordinary means of grace.

These letters certainly stirred up the pot. Many indignant ministers and laymen wrote to the *Guardian*, defending revivals and protracted meetings.[62] Their response once again attests to the persistence at the popular level of the now somewhat unfashionable religion of experience. Salvation, they argued, was the true goal of Methodism; to be saved one must have an emotional encounter with God. Religious revivals were necessary to bring about such an intense religious experience. The quest for such an experience should not be limited by turning Methodists away from revivals and camp meetings. The fires should be allowed to burn until the world is consumed by God's power and glory. "May He make his ministers flaming heralds," a local preacher in Prince Edward County exhorted in the old oratorical style, "and may salvation go forth as a lamp that burneth, and Zion put on her beautiful garments, and the world be gathered into the fold of the Redeemer."[63]

The debate between "YOD" and his critics allowed the *Christian Guardian* to state its own position on the question of protracted religious meetings. In a long editorial that appeared on 31 December 1845, the official voice of Methodism reviewed all the arguments in the case and tried to bring this contentious debate to a satisfactory resolution. It balanced the strong points on each side: although revivals and protracted meetings had been effective, they had also created problems; though they had brought people into the church, they had also pushed others out. What first appeared as a middle position, however, turned out to be a justification for the moderate party. The editorial concluded that protracted meetings were *not* divinely instituted, that too often they took ministers away from other important duties, and did not achieve their religious objectives. The arguments that the *Christian Guardian* attributed to a "Presiding Elder of the Conference" undoubtedly summarized its own position: "Ministers better succeeded in the objects of the Gospel by scrupulously attending to the regular duties as given in chapter vii and ix of the Discipline, than by adopting new means requiring much time and labour, and especially when engaging in the extra work might prevent the due and prompt performance of regular duties."[64] The editorial concluded that such revivals should be allowed to continue but only under strict control and only if they did not detract from the normal activities of the church.[65] The official organ of Wesleyan Methodism had come down squarely on the side of tempering revivalism.

These changes in worship went hand in hand with a number of important cultural changes. As revivalism became more systematic and controlled, and as the authorities of Methodism tried to limit its place in the religious life of the church, the intellectual basis of revivalism also began to change. Methodism began to reshape the way it interpreted the nature of God and the world. More moderate worship was part of a more moderate culture.

To sustain all these religious changes, Methodism had to redefine the meaning of a religious experience. In the Methodism of the old style, experience was an intense and overwhelming event: God struck suddenly and dramatically at the heart of the sinner; saving grace broke the hard shell of sin and set the soul at liberty. The physical manifestations that accompanied this event marked the intensity of the experience itself. The new understanding of experience, however, was decidedly more moderate and much more compatible with the institutional character of the new Methodist Church.

Once again the new culture had to work with the materials at hand. Methodism could scarcely abandon its commitment to the necessity of a religious experience. Wesley himself had attributed the beginning of his own spiritual awakening to the exact moment when he felt his heart "strangely warmed" by the presence of God. The doctrines of an "experimental religion" distinguished Methodism from other religious bodies and had served for many years as a rallying point when the connexion had to defend itself. Consequently, Methodism continued to defend the value of religious experience – especially when attacked by the Anglican press [66] – but at the same time it transformed the concept into something new and different.

Official Methodism now introduced the ideal of reason to temper the extremes to which emotion and feelings so often carried the unwary and unthoughtful. In a sense, Canadian Methodists now remembered that Wesley himself had tried to limit the authority of religious experience. If emotion went unchecked by reason, the mind flew wildly towards antinomian extremes. It "soars into rapturous flights, leaving behind prudence, discretion, and sound judgement; [this] may be called enthusiasm in the least excellent sense of this word."[67] Only those feelings that were consistent with reason came from God – those that failed this test were "evidently the effusions of an enthusiastic brain."[68] Methodism also tried to control religious experience by pointing it towards safer and more practical goals. Too often the people who had "got religion" followed their experience as it led them out of the Methodist Church towards, as one itinerant had put it, "a strange compound of semi-Pelagianism and hotbed Perfectionism."[69] To combat this contagion, Methodism tried to link the experience of salvation to another set of religious obligations. Preachers were not only to preach "Christ crucified," they were to push people beyond the initial conversion experience to seek complete sanctification. "Whoever has secured that gift," explained the *Christian Guardian*, "ought to appreciate it as a pledge of something which God proffers to him to increase the salutariness of his influence. Without it there cannot be the sympathy for souls which evangelical measures adopted for their welfare involve."[70]

The specific ways of increasing "the salutariness of his influence" are also instructive. In the early decades of the nineteenth century sanctification carried with it the goal of separating oneself from society. One should try to live piously according to the principles of Methodism and stand apart from the cares of the secular world. By the mid-century, however, the demands placed on Methodists had become much more worldly and activist. "Holiness is the guarantee of distinguished usefulness,"[71] stated one Methodist writer. And being "useful" meant helping to promote Methodist religious causes in the world. Missions, temperance, Sunday schools, and sabbatarianism were causes often recommended to the faithful. Nor did the assurance that one was saved mean that one could neglect the need to do good works in the church. The more religious one became, the greater the obligation to lead a moral life and do good deeds.[72] Rather than drawing people out of the world or out of Methodism, the experience of God should serve to strengthen the institutions of the Methodist Church here on earth.

The attempt to limit and redirect the implications of a religious experience led inevitably to a much more moderate description of the conversion experience itself. Here too the history of Methodism made it difficult to reject outright the importance of sudden and dramatic conversions, but as in the case of revivals, the central authorities of Methodism tried to limit the power and authority of this representation of the relationship between God and sinners. They did not rule out sudden conversions; they simply said they were infrequent and relatively unimportant. For example, when the official newspaper of the United Church of England and Ireland launched one of its many attacks on Methodism, the Rev. Matthew Richey, a leading Methodist and the principal of the Upper Canada Academy, sprang to the defence of his church. But he did not spring very high or quickly, and his defence shows the extent to which Richey and the church were trying to reduce the power of the old-style conversion experience. The critique of sudden conversions that *The Church* presented followed the lines that one would expect: impulses can too often be mistaken for a true conversion; such "conversions" can disappear as suddenly as they arrive; and gradual conversion "is much more likely to prove genuine and permanent than one which has been suddenly begotten."[73] To all these points Richey offered almost no defence. He could only argue that sudden conversions *might* occur and for this reason should not be rejected completely. He admitted that they happened infrequently and had to be carefully examined and evaluated in the light of scripture and the good works they produced.[74]

The new emphasis on gradualism and good works also led Methodism to a stronger doctrine of the church. Revivalism of the old style saw the church as essentially a means to an end. As the name implies, Methodism was essentially a method of finding God: itineracy, class meetings, and revivals were instruments that helped to bring about a religious experience, and their value lay in the ends they helped to produce, not in their inherent character. By mid-century, however, Methodism saw the church as a good deal more than something that helped people to reach a certain religious goal. To the uninitiated it might appear that Methodism was beginning to indulge itself in a little bit of Popery, for now the church was presented as the very embodiment of the spirit of God, a part of the Kingdom of God on earth. The church was "the conservator of our piety, and was designed to be the almoner of the world."[75]

The new Methodism emphasized moderation, gradualism, and the central place of the institutions of a well-established church in the religious life of the individual. A religious experience was no longer seen primarily as a sudden conversion which was followed by a life of separation from the world. Methodism became more standardized and lost the intense individual introspection of an earlier age. When Nathanael Burwash, one of the leaders of the new Methodism, described in his journal the recent decline in the importance of the old class meeting, he captured the essence of these changes. Class meetings, he pointed out, still persisted in many congregations. "But with the greater objectivity of modern church life centred round the ideas of practical Christian activity, organization, and service, the older subjective methods have fallen somewhat into the background."[76]

III

Methodism reshaped old ideas and old forms of worship until they became something new, finding in the process a new way of describing the relationship between God and the world that helped to solve the internal problems that had grown out of the old culture. Now emotion and feelings did not pose such a threat to the institutional structure of the church. Indeed the new culture spurred on the growth of Methodism by channelling religious feelings directly into church affairs, where they sustained not only the individual, but also a host of religious and educational institutions. The entire span of the religious life of the community was now encompassed by the life of the church. The new culture also helped Methodism respond to the demands of the secular world. Methodism began to occupy a more central position in the religious structure of the colony and to take a more active interest in the world it once rejected. The new religious institutions it created provided the means for Methodism to address the social and moral issues that preoccupied the church in the mid-Victorian period; while the new and more moderate culture brought Methodism into a broad Protestant alliance that tried to confront the new sins of the new age.[77]

In the new culture Christians must still undergo a religious experience, but it was an experience that differed markedly from a religious experience of the old style. Instead of being an intense emotion that brought a person directly into contact with God, experience was now a more temperate force that refreshed and sustained Christian life. The new Christian was not struck down but raised up. People listening to a great sermon did not shout 'Amen!' but rather felt the words and phrases of the preacher in their souls. So, moved by this event, the new Christians set off to do great deeds in the name of Christ. "Christian experience" the *Christian Guardian* declared, "is a right state of affections which directs us to the high and holy on earth and heaven, and causes us to love it ... The life of God in us is the full discharge of all the duties which our high and commanding position renders obligatory."[78] Experience was now clothed in the rhetoric of inspiration and heroic individualism. The religion of experience had become a romantic evangelicalism.

No longer were Christians urged to abandon the world. Inspired by the "high and holy" they should devote themselves to solving the problems (and especially the moral problems) of the world.[79] It was in this connection that the *Christian Guardian* praised the words of the Rev. John Strachan, now the Bishop of Toronto. The official voice of Methodism was anxious to point out that Strachan had distinguished carefully between two meanings of the "world." On the one hand the world was evil and reflected the sinfulness of human nature; in this sense the world was an obstacle to the progress of the church. This usage was quite familiar to Methodists, having been one of the staples of the old-style revivalism, which had exhorted sinners to come out of the world and be saved. But at the same time the world had a second meaning, which Methodists had too often forgotten: "It signifies our field of duty, – our place of probation where, in humble imitation of our beloved Master, we must fulfill the work which has been given us to do."[80]

Moreover, the type of sin that Christians should fight against in the world was also changing. Religion, of course, has always been preoccupied with sin, although Protestants might lay claim to greater familiarity with the character and extent of sin than other religious groups. What is interesting to observe here is the way sin began to acquire a more social meaning. The rising materialism of nineteenth-century life began to emerge as one of the central preoccupations of the Methodist Church. "The prevailing sin of the age," the Rev. William Case explained in 1855, is "the love of gain."[81] The love of profit was coming to dominate the world and pull people away from the church. At one time great religious debates had raged over what type of Christian one should be: Arminian or Calvinist, voluntarist or establishmentarian, churchman or dissenter. The new world had shifted the terms of this debate; now arose the prospect that materialism would undermine the religious character of society as a whole[82] and that large numbers of people might not enjoy the benefits of any religion. In the light of that possibility the former religious conflicts became much less important; secularism became the common and omnipresent enemy.

In this way the new culture provided Christians with a new way of interpreting the world. Inspired by a powerful religious feeling, they caught a glimpse of a glorious future: they then sacrificed their own wealth and ambitions to take up the cause of Christ, and turn their talents to the moral reform of society. Filled by the spirit of God, with the banners of Methodism fixed to the standards of the faith, Christians set out upon a life-long quest to establish the Kingdom of God on earth. The old revivalist had become an evangelical romantic.[83] Indeed these important religious changes were marked by a new romantic style: Methodists began to sing their hymns differently, their ministers preached their sermons in a new manner, and they built their churches according to a new set of aesthetic principles.[84]

Another important measure of this transformation was the way they interpreted these developments. How a society interprets change is an important commentary on change itself. In this instance contemporaries marked these changes by separating the recent past from the present. In the 1850s Wesleyan Methodism began to describe its own history in terms that emphasized change rather than continuity. The *Christian Guardian*, for example, published a number of "traditionary recollections"[85] that matured into a formidable host of Methodist histories, the greatest of which were the works of John Carroll.[86] Almost every page in these works was written to preserve a past that men like Carroll felt was disappearing very rapidly. In this sense history was a memorial to the world that these changes had destroyed. In another sense, however, these histories also revealed the types of cultural changes that were taking place. The sensibilities of the new romantic Christianity were woven subtly into almost every page of every story. The old past was reconstructed in the new vocabulary of romantic evangelicalism. History became romantic fiction, transforming a patchwork of events into a distinctive mythology in which the early nineteenth century was the heroic age of Canadian Methodism. In those days there were giants on the earth.

The early revivalists – Case and his cotemporaries – were more than simple preachers: they now became knights errant. Inspired by the Godly vision of a world redeemed, they had forsaken all else and set out on a religious quest in the spiritual and physical wilderness of Upper Canada in an age long past.

CHAPTER FOUR

The Alliance of Church and State: Dissolving the Religion of Order

[The church] is yet a blessing to the land overshadowed
by her wide-spread branches; and right honourably
had she adhered to her obligations in the civil compact.
But has a like fidelity been evinced by the state in
discharging its share of the mutual compact?

The Church, 5 September 1845

The Methodists were not the only group who had to go through the process of institutional and cultural change in the first decades of the Victorian era. At precisely the same time, the establishment side faced a series of crises as the Anglicans and Presbyterians tried to come to grips with the religious implications of a new social and economic environment. Again two kinds of change took place. First, there were revolutionary changes in the institutional character of these churches. The close alliance of church and state, which had been the *sine qua non* of the establishment position, broke down completely, forcing the churches to find new ways to survive. Secondly, there were important changes in the culture of order. As their institutional structures broke down, so too did the way these religious bodies understood and described God and the world. They had to pick up the pieces of their past and build new cultural forms from the remnants of the old.

On the Presbyterian side of this story the changes in Canada were closely bound up with events in Scotland, where in 1844 the Rev. Dr Thomas Chalmers led the Free Church out of the old Kirk. Though the specific issues that occasioned this disruption were not directly relevant to Canada, the larger question raised by the disruption, that is, the proper relationship between religion, the state, and society, was of enormous concern to Canada in the mid-1840s. For this reason, the disruption in Scotland led to a major division in the Presbyterian church in Canada as the Free Church left its supposedly contaminated parent and in time carried Canadian Presbyterianism as a whole towards an evangelical and voluntarist position very similar to the one that Methodism was coming to occupy at almost the same time.[1]

The Anglican part of the story is much more complicated. By temperament, history, and practice the United Church of England and Ireland was closely tied to the colonial and imperial state. The state supported and to a considerable degree controlled the church in the colony, while the church accepted, indeed glorified, the close relationship that these ties created. Both institutionally and culturally the principle and practice of establishmentarianism were vital to the life of the church. Consequently, the Anglicans suffered acutely from the events of the 1840s and 1850s, when a number of disparate forces combined to destroy the apparatus of a religious establishment. The way in which the colonial church responded to this crisis (again at both an institutional and a cultural level) changed it almost beyond recognition. All this in turn reshaped the religious structure of the colony even more dramatically, for once the establishment had disappeared, the old battle between church and dissent had little meaning: former enemies became allies, if not friends.

The process of religious and cultural reorganization is a complicated story in which many characters and themes appear, but this complexity indicates the historical significance of the changes themselves. It is also a story that many historians have overlooked, but in the long run the changes that took place on the establishment side of the old lines of battle were just as important as those that were taking place on the sectarian side.

For the establishment churches the link between religious reorganization and social, political, and economic change was direct. The Presbyterians, and especially the Anglicans, began their journey from a point in the religious spectrum that tied them very closely to the world of Upper Canadian politics: they were not "other-worldly" sects determined to separate themselves from the affairs of the world. For the leaders of the "official" church in the colony, the close alliance of church and state defined the role the church must play in society and provided the revenues that were essential if the church was to follow an aggressive program of expansion. In the eyes of the state *and* the church, religion and politics were closely related: "A Christian nation without a religious establishment is a contradiction."[2]

For these reasons, when the state reorganized Canadian society, the church that had tied itself so closely to the old state system found itself at the centre of a social and cultural revolution. While the Methodists were drawn slowly away from the other-worldly extreme by the powerful but distant magnet of social change, the Anglicans were so close to the state that they had to withstand the full impact of these forces. The gap between the old ways of interpreting the world and the new world that was emerging in the province became so unmistakable that the necessity of religious and cultural adaptation was overwhelming.

The dispute that took place in Upper Canada over the proper relationship between the church and the state was also part of a larger drama being played throughout the English-speaking world. During the first half of the nineteenth century a number of jurisdictions redefined the relationship between the state and religious belief. In almost every case, as the British historian E.R. Norman has pointed out,[3] the forces of religious pluralism and expanding nation-states dismembered a number of religious establishments (whether they were Anglican, Congregational, or Presbyterian) and transferred what had been religious jurisdictions to a non-denominational (but broadly Protestant) state. The religious and political leaders of Upper Canada who were very aware of this, kept a close eye on what was taking place in America, Britain, and other British colonies, and indeed the international setting often influenced events in Canada directly.

Yet, no matter how the events in Upper Canada were shaped by the international forces of religious and social change, the Canadian story can stand on its own. The first canon of Canadian historiography may well be the doctrine that important things happen elsewhere, that Canada receives from Clio only those things that are dull and second-hand. But the events witnessed by Upper Canadians during the early Victorian period drew local and external forces together in a way that did not happen elsewhere, and their conjunction brought the larger currents of international affairs into a specific and singular environment. The consequences were genuinely important and perhaps unique. The transformation of the old establishment created an essential component of the new Protestant alliance that gave this region a truly distinctive character.

Certain parts of the general story of church and state are well-known. The politics of disestablishment, for example, have been analysed in considerable detail by historians who have carefully documented a story Byzantine in its complexity. They have explained the political events that led to the removal of the church from the provincial university in 1849; the forces that modified, changed, and eventually in 1854 brought about the secularization of the famous clergy reserves; and the development of a system of public education that was divided along religious lines. In the process they have outlined the impact of these events on the growth of political ideologies such as liberalism and nationalism. The "state" side of the crisis of church and state is reasonably well known, and this analysis relies upon the excellent scholarship that has illuminated these parts of the story.[4]

The "church" side of the crisis of church and state, however, has not received the same scholarly attention.[5] The words and ideas of the reformers who attacked the establishment have been examined, but the church's defence of its so-called privileged position has remained a dark and unexplored mystery. Perhaps the fact that the defenders of establishments lost the battle has devalued the currency of their beliefs; perhaps the rather silly notion that Britain imposed a religious establishment upon an unwilling colony and that such an establishment was somehow unnatural in North America has caused people to assume that the arguments in defence of such an "anachronism" were also contrived and artificial.[6]

The defenders of church and state should be heard for a number of reasons. First, what they chose to support was by no means an out-dated imposition upon the freedom-loving people of Upper Canada. The established church was embedded in the British state, part of the fabric of the nation, and in a British colony one would expect to find such an establishment as a matter of course. Nor was the imperial state the only one to advocate public support for religion: the people themselves petitioned the government to set aside land for religious and other social purposes.[7] Secondly, the Anglican commentary upon the political and economic events of the day offers a perspective on the process of secularization that is not provided by the standard accounts of the period. The United Church of England and Ireland began the century as a part of the state – it drew its revenue from state sources, and the state controlled many aspects of its life. By mid-century this connection had been broken, and the church faced the world as a denomination of Christians much like any number of others. This position at the centre of events gives a special value to the way the church interpreted its own history. The forces identified by most historians – the struggle for religious equality and the voluntary principle – have only a small part in Anglican accounts. At the core of their arguments was a sustained and often bitter critique of the new type of state that was emerging at this time. What should have been an ally was becoming an adversary; the institutions that should have cultivated the garden of the Lord in

Upper Canada chose instead to promote railways. By looking at the process of change through the eyes of the church, we can read an important commentary on the transformation of Canadian society and the Canadian state.

The establishment perspective also illuminates a number of important cultural changes taking place in the colony. The new secular state pushed the church out of the political polity of the nation, forcing it to create new administrative and financial structures to meet the problems that the new state created. Cultural change went hand in hand with this process, and the culture of order fell victim to the same events. The church had to find a way of defining itself that did not rely on the institutional and financial framework of an establishment or on the cultural assumptions that secured the establishment position. The church responded to this cultural crisis so successfully that when the time came to sever the few remaining bonds holding the church and the state together, the final blow was struck by the new church.

The old adversaries – churchmen and dissenters – moved in concert. The forces that caused the Methodists to abandon the sectarian extreme also pushed the Anglicans and Presbyterians away from the establishment position. The removal of Anglican privileges cut down one of the last barriers to Protestant co-operation, while the retreat from revivalism made such co-operation much more acceptable in Anglican eyes. As a result of events and circumstances, the two sides now saw themselves and the world in a similar way.

I

To love and venerate order was the first commandment of the religious and social teachings of the old establishment. Order was an attribute of God: did not the structure of the world reveal so clearly the handiwork of a rational intelligence? Order was also the measure of a proper and virtuous life. Since order and hierarchy were inherent in God's creation, happiness could only be attained by accepting the same principles in society. Freedom and liberty grew out of social order; without order there could be no society and therefore no freedom.[8] Scripture and revelation confirmed the lessons of the natural world and imparted to the love of order an even richer and more majestic purpose by demonstrating that order and virtue not only provided immediate pleasures in this world but also led to the joy and happiness of the life eternal that Christ had promised to those who accepted his teachings. In the culture of order there was no boundary between social and religious values; order drew together God and the world, religion and life.[9]

The glorification of order also explains why this culture placed so much importance on that most contentious of issues, the close relationship between the church and the state. Regarded by many as nothing more than a curious anachronism, the assertion that the state must recognize, protect, and support a single religious institution followed logically from the assumptions that permeated this culture. Indeed, when the leaders of *both* the church and the state in Upper Canada defended the necessity of religious establishments in general and the Anglican establishment in particular, they returned invariably to a single logical sequence: order was essential to the existence of society; religion (and religion alone) could inculcate and sustain this crucial social ideal; therefore the state must support the church.

Other arguments developed this syllogism further. It is the goal of religion to bring salvation to the world, but salvation (or the type of salvation the church presented) was both a religious and social doctrine. As people moved closer to grace they also led more ordered lives and became better subjects of the crown. The church cultivated these ideals with kindness and generosity, seeking to admonish and convince rather than threaten and punish. Consequently its teachings were accepted more readily and were therefore all the more effective. The charitable and philanthropic works that grew naturally from religious virtue created a system of public welfare that forestalled social disorder, since people who accepted the comforts of religion were not likely to take up arms against the state. And finally the church did all of this efficiently and at very little cost: after all, a host of clergymen comes much cheaper than a standing army.[10]

The same preoccupation with social order also informed the historical arguments often used to justify a religious establishment. Although all reasonable people agreed that the state should demand obedience to the civil laws of the nation, history had demonstrated that at a number of times in the past, civil strife had been generated by religious causes. The Puritan revolution and the Jacobite rebellions, for example, demonstrated beyond doubt the close link between political disorder and unorthodox religious belief and led to the inevitable conclusion that the state must also enforce the religious laws of the nation. The rebellious American colonies and the horrors of the French Revolution brought the same lesson home with a vengeance and gave an urgency to those who defended the tie between public order and public religion in the Canadas. The corollaries of this theorem confirmed the same conclusion. If disorder were to occur – if, for example, the colonial society of Upper Canada were faced by rebellion or invaded from the south – then the state needed the clergy of the established church as the advance guard of the forces of the counter-revolution. As John Strachan said, "They are the only teachers over whom the government has any control."[11] Onward Christian soldiers! All these arguments began with a vision of a well-ordered Christian society and then turned quickly (and logically) to questions of social utility, mutual benefit, and expediency. A religious establishment was the keystone of this structure, because without an establishment order was impossible and without order there could be no society.[12]

When the leaders of the colonial church justified a religious establishment by listing the social benefits it provided, they were grafting a set of well-established concepts and ideas onto the body politic of Upper Canada. The leaders of church and state in England used not only the same ideas, but almost the same words to defend their own establishment. The leaders of the church in England and Canada were part of the same institution, and they interpreted that institution in the same way; by birth, training, and habit they shared the same culture. In addition, the political theory on which Upper Canada was founded reinforced this trans-Atlantic association. According to the leaders of the colony, Canada was the reincarnation in the new world of an ideal Britain and as such enjoyed the very image and transcript of the British constitution.[13] An established church was an integral part of this constitution and therefore part of the British inheritance in this new land. Furthermore, the church in the colony relied heavily on the British state and the British church. Consequently, the colonial church used the ideas and arguments that were most appealing to the centre of religious and political power. The leaders of the church in Canada were well aware of what was happening in Britain, where state support of religion was also under attack, and more often than not it was this British cultural and political situation that helps to explain the course taken by the colonial church.

It was perfectly reasonable for the leaders of the colonial church to adopt the standard British arguments for religious establishments; nevertheless these arguments created a number of problems for Canadian churchmen, who, unlike their British counterparts, did not have the advantage of defending an established church already in existence. Although there was no reason to assume that an establishment could not be created in Upper Canada and even less reason to assume that the attempt should not be made, it took considerable imagination and intellectual nerve to assume by the logic of one's arguments that an establishment did in fact exist in Upper Canada. And it took even more imagination to wax eloquent upon the benefits that society received from something that did not yet exist.

These problems point out an important cultural tension. Cultures provide ways of explaining the world, but the world does not necessarily conform to these cultural interpretations. Upper Canadian churchmen based their arguments on ideas and principles that were perfectly reasonable in England, and formed their alliances accordingly. But these ideas and values did not carry the same authority in the colony. It is precisely the tension between rhetoric and reality that helps to explain the part played by the church in the cultural drama that took place in the first half of the nineteenth century, and to understand this tension we must now examine these ideas and the world they attempted to describe.

The arguments used by Upper Canadian churchmen to defend their position were drawn from the works of a number of British authors who had developed by the end of the eighteenth century a clear and coherent theory of the proper relationship between the church and the state. Like so many fathers of the Canadian church, these men worked in a highly rational and abstract world, and it almost goes without saying that a preoccupation with social and religious order ran through their writings. In general, these ideas defined the relationship between church and state in contractual terms, as an alliance between two independent institutions. Both the church and the state entered into the alliance for their own benefit, each believing that it allowed them to achieve certain goals that they could not achieve alone. The specific details of the alliance – the terms of the contract – were described at length in 1736 by Bishop William Warburton, whose book *The Alliance Between Church and State, or the Necessity and Equity of an Established Religion and a Test-law, demonstrated* was the basic text on this question for at least a hundred years. The other authorities to whom Canadians appealed, such as Edmund Burke and William Paley, built upon the framework that Warburton established (although in different ways).[14]

Bishop Warburton began his treatise on a purely abstract plane, claiming to ignore entirely the course of British history and the needs of the present day. It was the duty of any state, he argued, to protect liberty and property from disorder and chaos. To do this a state must enforce a number of laws. But the law was not completely effective. It relied upon the fear of being punished, and yet many crimes never came before the courts, and even when they did criminals often escaped punishment. At this point religion came to the aid of the state. A belief in God instilled in all people a personal desire for order and virtue by promising the joy and happiness of eternal salvation. Thus, people led ordered lives not out of fear alone but in hope of heavenly reward. Religion could do what the law could not. In Warburton's phrase, religion provided "the sanction of rewards which society wants, and hath not"; and for this reason the church was "absolutely necessary to civil government."[15]

A similar line of reasoning explained why the state was so important to the church. The primary goal of religion, unlike that of the state, was "to procure the favour of God, and secondly, to advance and improve our intellectual nature."[16] But even though the state pursued different goals it was nonetheless an ally of the church, providing the social tranquillity that was so necessary for religion to flourish, protecting the church from other religious groups that threatened its mission (and by so doing threatened the stability of the state), and most important, providing the financial resources that enabled the church to carry its religious message to every corner of the kingdom.

For those reasons the church and the state entered into "a politic league and alliance for mutual support and defence."[17] On its part the church surrendered a measure of its freedom and independence to the state – the chief magistrate became the head of the church, and the church agreed to advance the interests of the state by teaching people to venerate order. In return the state protected the church from social and religious violence, supported the church from the revenues of the nation, and allowed certain religious leaders to participate in the national legislature. The terms of the compact, like those of any good alliance, were mutually beneficial: the church received financial support while the state enjoyed the social order that only a national church could secure.

This was then the basic article of the alliance: "that the church shall apply its utmost influence in the service of the state; and the state shall support and protect the church."[18] Warburton concluded his long analysis by descending rather gloriously from the abstract realm of pure reason to everyday life. His arguments, he claimed, were "formed solely on the contemplation of nature, and the invariable reason of things." But oh what joy to find that his own country conformed perfectly to the ideal he had deduced so rationally from nature! What is, it turns out, is what ought to be, leaving the Bishop to marvel at "the uncommon excellence of our happy constitution."[19]

Other British authorities to whom Canadian churchmen often appealed followed the same line of defence: church and state must be joined together in order to achieve social order. In his famous *Reflections on the Revolution in France,* Edmund Burke drew heavily on Warburton's ideas, although he tended to base his argument on history rather than on an abstract analysis of the nature of a church and a state. While he alluded to alliances and contracts, his church and state were so thoroughly mixed together within his glorious constitution that it was difficult to distinguish the independence of the bodies that had at least in theory originally entered into the compact. For Burke church and state were like a pleasing scene in the English countryside, and the beauty created by their happy union was a sign of God's superintending Providence. To defend the glories of England and the British constitution was to defend the unity of church and state. It is the established church that imparted a moral and reverential quality to the leaders, the people, and the institutions of the nation and saved England from the horrors that were taking place in France. Burke embedded the church so deeply in English life that its very independence seemed to disappear, but in doing this he emphasized even more strongly the close tie between religious establishments and social stability.[20]

The question of church and state was also addressed by the Rev. William Paley, one of the true fathers of Anglican thought in Canada. He too was deeply in Warburton's debt, so heavily in fact, that he simply took the alliance of church and state as a given and concentrated on the characteristics of establishments and the social functions they should serve.[21] A religious establishment, he argued, had three essential features: it relied upon a group of people who devoted their lives exclusively to religious affairs, it received by law a sufficient financial provision for its maintenance, and it enjoyed the exclusive favour of the state. Without these features, an establishment could not successfully perform its religious and social functions. The learned and rational nature of religion demanded a well-educated and professional clergy; without state support religion became the prisoner of private interests, unable to meet the religious needs of the nation as a whole; and if the state supported many different religions, there would be no consistency of doctrine and the church would not be able to preserve social stability.

These arguments were standard fare. Social utility was, after all, a most Anglican doctrine: the church defended state support by appealing to the many social benefits that were provided by an establishment. Above all, establishments were useful things. Nonetheless, Paley added an important element to the establishment position. By raising the doctrine of social utility to such heights he defined a series of propositions that would have a profound impact upon Upper Canada. By setting down the criteria that justified the existence of an establishment, he also provided the arguments that could be turned against an existing religious establishment. If the church met these tests, it was an establishment, but if it did not then the establishment should be overthrown. An establishment, for example, should appeal to all the people; it should seek to include dissenters rather than turn them away. To include as many people as possible, its creeds and confessions "ought to be as simple and as easy as possible."[22] But this breadth of vision raised the important question of what would happen if the established church did not embrace the majority of the people. Paley's logic was clear, consistent, and even predictable. If the church and the nation were not one and the same, the establishment lost its social utility and therefore its reason for existence. In a phrase that must have sent shivers up and down the collective spine of the colonial church, he concluded, "If the dissenters from the establishment become a majority of the people, the establishment itself ought to be altered or qualified."[23] Social utility would indeed be a cruel master.

The cultural importance of these ideas and assumptions cannot be overemphasized, for they expressed the basic outlook of the church in Upper Canada and, moreover, defined in practical terms the character of the church and the course it should follow. The United Church of England and Ireland saw itself as an ally of the state and willingly accepted the terms of this alliance, surrendering its rather theoretical independence because it believed it would receive a number of benefits in return: if the church performed its duty by promoting loyalty and order, then the state was obliged to provide the protection and financial support that the church so desperately needed. The church also accepted the institutional implications of such an alliance with the state. To perform its social and religious duties the church must become embedded in the very fabric of Upper Canadian society:[24] it must have a well-trained missionary in every parish, a schoolmaster in every schoolroom, higher officials in the legislature, and ministers in every district and town. Above all the church must win and maintain the allegiance of the people by leading dissenters back into the fold and persuading the uncommitted to worship at its tables.[25] When the church called on Methodists to return to the church and indulged in the fanciful practice of including "all others"[26] in the Anglican column, it was only acting out the role that its position and cultural assumptions had given it.

The same body of ideas and assumptions also reveals one of the most vulnerable points in the position of the colonial church. Though an alliance with the state held out great promise for the church, contracts and alliances have the regrettable tendency to be broken. If the state did not help the church or if the state came to believe that social order and loyalty could be brought about by other means,[27] the alliance would soon lose both its legitimacy and practical necessity. What social utility had joined together, comparative advantage could easily put asunder.

Since the colonial church saw itself as the Canadian establishment, it conducted its life according to the rules that such a belief defined. In a curious manner the way in which other religious groups treated the church tended to confirm this exalted status. Both the Presbyterian arguments in favour of a co-establishment and the demands of dissenters to disestablish the church implicitly acknowledged the Anglican Church as the Canadian establishment. But was the church's image of itself accurate? It is one thing to act as if one were an establishment, but it is quite another to enjoy this status at law and to exercise the power that comes with it. Was the United Church of England and Ireland in fact the established church of Upper Canada? The answer to this question reveals a good deal about the character of the church and the course of history that it had to follow.

The legal status of the church in Upper Canada has occasioned a good deal of debate;[28] indeed neither contemporary nor more modern commentators have been able to resolve the question satisfactorily. No one is quite sure what being an establishment actually entails, let alone whether the colonial church actually met these standards. The lingering antipathy to the very idea of an establishment[29] and the fact that the Anglican Church both in England and in Canada was changing rapidly during the early decades of the nineteenth century have added to the confusion.[30]

The study of canon law commends itself to the historian who wants to understand this important cultural issue. If the early nineteenth century saw the relationship between church and state in contractual terms, perhaps the terms of the contract offer the best point of departure for analysing this complex question. The church, as we have seen, was supposed to surrender its independence in return for protection and financial support. In Upper Canada, at least one side of the agreement seemed to be in place: the state exercised a good deal of authority over the church, from the power to appoint colonial bishops to the power of the colonial governors to present incumbents to rectories. The other part of the agreement, however, was not as clear. The church enjoyed few of the laws and institutions that in theory protected it from abuse. Church courts, for example, which still enjoyed considerable (if declining) power in England, had not been reproduced in Upper Canada – probate, to cite one case, fell under the purview of the temporal courts.[31] The religious tests that prohibited Catholics in fact and dissenters in theory from enjoying certain offices did not apply in Canada, and the monopoly of the church to solemnize matrimony (a perfectly reasonable practice given the fact that all ratepayers, whether churchmen or dissenters, had the right to demand this, and other, church offices) did not survive for long in Upper Canada.[32] Similarly, the tithes that provided a sizeable measure of support in England were legal in Upper Canada but were never collected, and in 1823 they lost even this worthless status at law. The attempt to integrate the church into the fabric of local government met with only limited (and very short-lived) success. The system of local government based upon the parish meeting, church wardens, and church rates fell quickly into disuse as the quarter sessions became the basic forum for the administration of local affairs.[33] The place of senior ecclesiastical dignitaries in the colonial government also had a very short life. Although the first Bishop of Quebec entered the government ex-officio, as did the first Bishops of Nova Scotia, the Bishop of Toronto earned his place in the Legislative Council as a reward for outstanding public service, and in the Maritimes the right of bishops to sit in the Legislative Council was specifically rejected for Hibbert Nova Scotia by Earl Grey in 1851.[34] The Constitutional Act, which set out the political structure of Upper Canada, is strangely silent on the matter of bishops in the Council, although the fact that the clergy were prohibited from sitting in the lower house implies perhaps that their interests were to be served and protected by allowing certain of their number to sit elsewhere.[35]

Another part of the bargain, the obligation of the state to provide financial support to the church, is also difficult to decipher. The Constitutional Act empowered the crown to create and endow rectories "according to the Establishment of the Church of England,"[36] and when the crown exercised this authority in 1836 it undoubtedly strengthened Anglican claims to be the Canadian establishment. The same Act also created the famous clergy reserves "for the maintenance and support of a Protestant Clergy."[37] This provision led first to the problem of defining Protestant clergy and then to a crisis of political will that bedevilled Upper Canada for half a century. In the end the reserves only confused the question of establishment, for if financial support from the state made a religious group into an establishment, then not only the Church of England and the Church of Scotland, but also the Methodists and even the Church of Rome had to share this glory.[38] From this perspective then, it seems clear that the Anglicans were claiming something that they did not in fact enjoy, or that they enjoyed only in a very attenuated form.

There are, however, two other briefs on the question of church establishment that must be considered. First, the same documents that might have failed to establish the church *at law* reveal that it was the clear and explicit *intention* of the imperial government to create a religious establishment. The instructions sent out to General Murray in 1763 concerning the government of Quebec contain a number of articles defining imperial policy on the use of the *Book of Common Prayer,* the school system, marriage, the authority of bishops, and land policy that were, in the words of the document, "to the End that the Church of England may be established both in Principles and Practice."[39] The Quebec Act of 1774 included provisions for the Church of England which were defined in more detail by the instructions given to Carleton in 1775.[40] The American Revolution seemed to strengthen the resolve of the British government to create an Anglican establishment. In the minds of many the failure to create a proper religious establishment explained why the revolting colonies had risen up against the crown. For this reason the Canadas needed a constitution that gave sufficient weight to the proper forms of religious observance. When William Knox wrote to Charles Jenkinson, the future Lord Liverpool, he stated this necessity in words that surely were drawn directly from Warburton:

The Influence of Religion on the Opinion, Temper and Conduct of Mankind – its Tendency to promote the Internal Peace of Society, when under proper Regulations; and how capable it is of being made an Engine of Discord and Sedition – are matters too well understood, and generally acknowledged, to require any Proof in this Place. The National Religion of any state may be presumed to be best adopted to the Civil Constitution of the state, hence it claims the Countenance and Support of the

Civil Magistrate, which should be considered not only as a Matter of Piety and Prudence, but of the utmost Necessity in a Political View, being connected with the Peace and Welfare of the Community.[41]

But all these documents simply underline the discrepancy between intent and practice, between the reasonable expectation that the church was about to be established and the failure of the state to carry out such a policy. This created a serious problem for the church and helps to explain some of the crucial religious decisions it made in this period. Given the fact that the state had proclaimed its desire to create an establishment, how then could the church encourage the state to do its duty? Within the terms of the alliance that Warburton and others had described, the answer to this question was clear: the state would respond favourably to the legitimate claims of the church only if the church could show that it was fulfilling its part of the bargain. The church had to emphasize continually the practical benefits of an establishment, especially the stability so essential to society. But it could only tell the state what it *would* do if it received enough support. This revealed an important fact: when the church described itself as an establishment, it was not trying to defend a privilege, but to acquire one. It was admonishing the crown to make good its intentions so that the church might fulfil its part of the bargain even more completely.[42]

There is another aspect of this "partial" establishment of the church in Upper Canada that also helps to explain some of the church's seeming peculiarities. Though the establishment in Upper Canada was incomplete, the colonial church was nonetheless a more reformed and potentially more effective religious organization than its British parent. First, the fact that certain parts of the English establishment were not reproduced in Upper Canada could be seen as a blessing in disguise. Church courts, for example, were of questionable value. In England they were subject to prohibition by the temporal courts, had a reputation for delay and high fees, and were rapidly losing their status and power.[43] Lay patronage was another problem that did not burden the colonial church to nearly the same extent as in England, where patrons enjoyed almost absolute control over their livings and used their power in ways that were very damaging to the church.[44] Secondly, the colonial church enjoyed certain privileges that the church at home did not. The creation of rectories and clergy reserves for example constituted a reform of great magnitude. If these sources could provide a consistent and reasonable return, the church in

Upper Canada would not have to rely upon two sources of support – church rates and tithes – that were being challenged in England. The reserves would also allow the church in Canada to avoid the abject poverty that existed among the lower ranks of the English clergy.[45] From this perspective then the desire to defend (and complete) the colonial establishment took on an even greater urgency.

The church approached the events of the early nineteenth century in a unique and somewhat incongruous position. Its ideology, however rational and coherent, conformed only in part to the circumstances in which it found itself, for what it most desired – a close alliance with state – was far from complete. But to complete the establishment the church had to use arguments that seemed at odds with its position and to emphasize unceasingly the social benefits that a proper establishment would produce. The promise that such an establishment held out, however, reinforced the almost messianic zeal with which the church approached this task. In time Upper Canada might indeed become the garden of the Lord.

II

The discrepancy between what was and what ought to be shaped Upper Canadian Anglicanism and in the course of time undermined the position of the church and the culture of order. In retrospect it seems clear that the leaders of the church were never able to reconcile the world they wanted with the world that was developing in the early Victorian period and were forced to reconsider a number of elements that had defined their church in the past. In a remarkable about-face the group that had nailed its colours to the mast of church and state became a leading force in dissolving that very alliance, and by the middle of the nineteenth century the church had acquired a new administrative structure and a new way of interpreting God and the world.

Cultural changes of such magnitude are not shaped by the winds of change that blow across the face of the world but rather by the practical problems and tensions that affect the daily lives of people and institutions. As we have already seen, cultural change for Upper Canadian Methodists resulted from the problems inherent in the way they worshipped their God. For Upper Canadian churchmen, cultural change grew out of a number of financial, political, and administrative problems. As the church grappled with these problems, it had to cast aside the ideas and assumptions that could no longer speak to a changing world and reshape old ideas and beliefs into new cultural patterns that could explain the world more coherently.

The question of church and state once again permeated the process of cultural change, and once again it was the practical aspects of this relationship that determined the course of events. Although the leaders of the church were interested in the general issue of church and state, they were more concerned with the tangible and specific benefits that the alliance was supposed to bestow upon their church. Two very practical issues were central to the life of the church in the first half of the nineteenth century. The first was how the church should evangelize Upper Canada. What should it be doing to promote the religious happiness and welfare of the people? Which religious practices and institutions should be transplanted from the old world, and what should be modified or created afresh to meet new needs and circumstances? The second issue was a financial one. How could this religious program be paid for? Who should underwrite the Kingdom of God in Upper Canada? There was no easy answer. The church had to turn to a number of different sources in order to meet its considerable needs, but almost inevitably it had to return to one of the central tenets of its culture: given the alliance of church and state, it was the duty of the state to protect and support the church. It was precisely at this point, however, that the state began to question this request seriously. The state was changing, and as it changed it began to reject the very idea of an alliance with the church. When the church called, the state refused to answer. The alliance that had defined the very nature of the church fell apart, and the church found itself alone in a world it neither appreciated nor fully understood.

The apparent conservatism of the Anglican vision of Upper Canada tends to obscure the scope of the church's program for the colony. Though the church spoke as if it were preoccupied with protecting its privileges, in fact it had little to protect because it had to create a proper religious and social system before it could protect one. The church's program was wide-ranging and ambitious, and its specific details followed directly from the way the church understood the nature of religion and the tasks that it had to perform within the close alliance of church and state. It simply would not do for the church to send out a gaggle of poorly trained itinerant preachers who excited the emotions of the people, pronounced them saved, and then passed out of their daily existence. Conversion was a gradual affair in which reason slowly overcame the passions; therefore, proper religion demanded a system in which the clergy lived with their people continuously so that they would be present to preach the Gospel, administer the sacraments, baptize the young, solemnize marriages, and bury the dead. The rational character of religion also demanded that the clergy be well-educated and free enough from other responsibilities to devote themselves entirely to the duties of religious instruction in the church and the local school. Religion was a professional vocation, not a seasonal job to be taken up by someone waiting for permanent work.[46]

The social roles that went hand in hand with religious office increased the demands on the clergy. Because the clergyman was one of the few educated men in the area, he would be called upon as a matter of course to look after a whole range of issues. His very presence in local affairs forestalled any threats to public order and raised the general tone of society. The records he kept of births, deaths, and marriages provided a primitive system of social and religious service, and the crucial place of the parish in the system of local government further strengthened the position of the clergy and wove the church into the fabric of society.[47]

The religious and social goals of the church constituted a detailed and extensive religious program.[48] There was to be a system of rural and urban parishes containing churches, parsonages, and schools. In each parish there was to be a resident clergyman who was trained to serve as pastor and teacher to the community and who was willing (and had the wherewithal) to devote himself unceasingly to the duties that his position demanded. The Anglicans set out what was in effect a complete way of life; they demanded that their missionaries perform a number of roles in conditions that were at best extremely primitive. Sustained by an almost millennial vision of their calling, they took on the wilderness with an extraordinary sense of dedication.[49] Though many triumphed and looked back on their lives with joy and satisfaction, others failed. Some of the letters and journals of the early missionaries tell of adversity and misfortune overcome, but others tell all too often of moral breakdown, alcoholism, and insanity.[50]

The Anglican program was also extremely expensive. Church buildings, parsonages, and schools cost a good deal of money, as did the administrative structure of bishoprics, deaneries, and theological colleges that sustained the basic parish system. Salaries, pensions, and support for widows and orphans added to the growing list of financial demands. In these circumstances the leaders of the church learned from practice to recite a common refrain:

they could do so much if they only had sufficient resources.[51] But this was a substantial qualification. As the leaders of the church pressed ahead with their plans, they found their way continually blocked by several financial constraints; as they exploited traditional sources of revenue and sought out new ones, they encountered one financial crisis after another. In meeting these crises the church slowly transformed itself from an eighteenth-century establishment into a Victorian denomination.

To finance its activities, the church could appeal to its own members, it could appeal to the state, or it could appeal to great English Church Societies – the Society for Promoting Christian Knowledge and the Society for Propagating the Gospel in Foreign Parts. Each of these sources, however, created almost as many problems as it solved, and none was able to provide the steady and reliable revenues that the church so desperately needed.

The laity of the church, at least in retrospect, seemed to offer the most promise – it presented few administrative problems, and had the advantage of cost-effectiveness and general equity, since those who attended the church and received the satisfaction of its ministrations would pay for their cost. But "voluntarism," as the system of self-support came to be known, presented practical and theological problems. Like all other groups in colonial society, the laity of the colonial church had little ready money. They might donate a bit of land (the common and rather debased currency of the colony), buy a pew to help defray the cost of building a new church, or pay stole fees for baptisms and marriages, but beyond this the church could expect very little. Churchpeople in England offered perhaps a better prospect, and their donations certainly helped the colonial church on many occasions. But appeals to England, even for specific projects, were very expensive undertakings, and the colonial church was not able to translate English generosity into a steady income.[52]

There were also serious theological objections to the voluntary system. If it became the only (or even dominant) source of revenue, it would weaken the hierarchical principle that was at the heart of the establishment system. Once the clergy were paid by their parishoners, they became the prisoner of local interests and relied upon the very people over whom they were supposed to exercise spiritual guidance. Voluntarism, in the words of Strachan, was "at variance with the nature of an establishment" and "inconsistent with the respectability and independence of the clergy."[53] His conclusions were shared by his friend, the Rev. Thomas Chalmers, who at this time was becoming a prominent leader of the Church of Scotland. Voluntarism, Chalmers argued, was a form of religious free trade that worked on the heretical principle that individuals could make religious decisions based on their own self-interest. It assumed that success and failure should be decided by a religious open market: the churches that people chose to support would win out while those that the people did not support would fail. But religion was not an item of trade. Although it was in everyone's interest to be religious, the depravity of human nature made people very poor judges of their own religious needs. Indeed those who needed religion the most – the poor and the unbelievers – were the very people who were least likely to seek it out and provide for its maintenance. Under the voluntary system religion became a blessing for only one part of the commonwealth, and the ideal of a Christian nation was lost forever.[54]

Perhaps then the church should turn to the state, since given the alliance of church and state, it was surely the duty of the state to help the church carry out its program. The state, at least initially, seemed willing to help. The first Anglican clergymen in Upper Canada received their salaries directly from the state (indeed from a number of different sources within the state), and the state made gifts to the church, endowed rectories with land, and provided the church with the revenue from the famous clergy reserves. But the state never seemed to be prepared to carry out its obligations to the full. The church wanted to have endowments because, as Strachan explained, "subscriptions are transient and unsatisfactory, and while they continue [they are] a source of frequent trouble and estrangement; but get a parish once endowed and it continues for many generations."[55] But this was exactly what the state would not do. It waited until 1836 to act on the provisions of the Constitutional Act to endow rectories (and then present clergymen to these livings), and the legal questions that were raised about this action left the matter hanging for some time.

The clergy reserves which held out such promise also led to one problem after another. Before the 1840s they generated very little revenue, and when a reasonable revenue finally did arrive, Anglican claims were disputed by many different groups. Here the basic problem was so simple that many historians have failed to grasp its significance: the reserves were *not* church lands. They were *crown* lands whose revenue was dedicated to the support of a Protestant clergy. They were never owned or even controlled by the church. They were not a mortmain, although some feared (while others hoped) they might become one.[56] The implications of this fact must be drawn out clearly; crown lands are subject to the will of the state and open to political pressure from those who disagree with their intended purpose. What the crown giveth, the crown taketh away. In effect, state support proved to be just as precarious as support from the laity.

For all these reasons the prospects of the colonial church were tied more and more closely to the enormous beneficence of the great English church societies, especially the Society for the Propagation of the Gospel in Foreign Parts.[57] Founded in 1701 to support missionaries in the old American colonies, the Society had grown in scope and power, and with the appointment of one of its former missionaries, the Rev. Charles Inglis, to the new colonial bishopric of Nova Scotia the Society became the leading missionary organization in the church. In Upper Canada, where its rival the Church Missionary Society was very weak, the hegemony of the SPG was virtually unchallenged.[58]

The Society was truly generous in its support of the church in Upper Canada, paying the salaries of most of the clergy, helping to build churches and endow them with land, providing financial support for theological colleges, and making many small donations to a wide range of projects. It also served as a channel for special gifts from the British laity. The church in the colonies was deeply in its debt. Such financial support, however, gave the Society a strong voice in the affairs of the colonial church, and although the Society was careful to consult local ecclesiastical officials before making its decisions, it was nonetheless prepared on a number of occasions to use its power as the exchequer of the missionary enterprise in Upper Canada to impress the importance of its own views upon the colonial church. When the time came, the SPG played an important part in reorganizing the financial structure of the church in Upper Canada.

The SPG became directly involved in the complex story of financing the church in Upper Canada in 1813.[59] In that year the imperial government set out to rationalize the payment of clerical salaries by transferring this task from a number of different government departments to the SPG. In return for an annual government grant the Society agreed to organize and pay Anglican missionaries in the colony; the amount of this grant increased from £3,600 in 1814 to £16,000 in 1828. Under this arrangement the SPG selected the missionaries, chose their location (in consultation with the Bishop of Quebec), and paid their salaries, generally at the rate of £200 per annum.

This system was altered drastically in 1832, when the British Parliament responded to calls for economy and what it saw as a general hostility to the annual grant to the Society by proposing to reduce the grant by £4,000 a year until it ceased altogether in 1836. The Canadian church faced the prospect of having to rely totally on its own meagre resources. Under pressure from the SPG and the English bishops, however, the government reconsidered its position and reached a compromise that came to be known as the "1834 arrangement." The church in Lower Canada was hit especially hard by this compromise, which cut off grants to schoolmasters[60] and reduced the salaries of the clergy by about 15 per cent. Upper Canada was treated differently: the crown agreed to guarantee a sum of about £7,000 a year to meet the salaries of the clergy who were in the colony at that time. This money was drawn from the revenue of the clergy reserves, but since the reserves at the time could not meet this charge, the government undertook to make up the shortfall from the crown's casual and territorial revenue. This policy was designed to meet the crown's obligations to the missionaries who had come out before this date. If they died, or left Upper Canada for other reasons, the revenue that had been paid them was lost to the church. The 1834 arrangement also reduced the stipend of missionaries from £200 to £175 a year. All these changes lessened the influence of the SPG in the affairs of the church in Upper Canada and tied the local church more closely to the colonial government. The Society, however, agreed to assume the financial responsibility for any new missionaries sent out after this date at a salary of £150 per annum. Although the church survived these changes, the new arrangement severely strained the relationship between the SPG and the colonial church: the Bishop of Montreal threatened to resign, and the "official " newspaper of the church in Upper Canada attacked the Society in language that for such a rational institution was quite unbecoming.[61]

Within a few years, however, the Society reasserted its position in the colonial church. In 1837, it resolved "to take into special consideration the state of the church in the Canadas," and during the next two years the secretary of the Society, the Rev. A. M. Campbell, wrote to the Bishops of Montreal and Toronto offering to increase dramatically the support from the Society by providing a salary of £100 per annum for a large number of new missionaries.[62] Between 1841 and 1847 the Society spent over £42,000 in the Diocese of Toronto alone, and by the latter date was supporting about fifty missionaries in this diocese.[63] Although these missionaries were under the general authority of the local bishop, they reported annually to the Society, which in effect made many of the most important administrative decisions.

The influence of the Society on the colonial church became quite clear after 1840. In an attempt to solve the political problems that had bedevilled the pre-rebellion era, the government introduced a new formula for dividing the revenue from the reserves as part of the general political reorganization of the colonies of Upper and Lower Canada in 1841. The existing obligations of the crown to the clergy who had arrived before 1834 were once again protected, but now the new revenue from the reserves was divided according to a complex formula between the Church of England, the Church of Scotland, and at least in theory several other religious groups. All this was supposed to protect the finances of the church by "solving" the reserve question. At the same time the measure introduced an important new element into the financial structure of the church. The Act entrusted the revenue from the surplus in the reserve fund *not* to the local church but to the SPG, which assumed responsibility for deciding how this revenue should be used.[64] In effect the SPG was given the power to reshape the administrative and financial structure of the colonial church.

When this long awaited surplus actually arrived, it raised a storm both inside and outside the church. For a group of older clergy whose salaries had been reduced in 1834, the prospect of new money was a chance to make up for lost time. Even Bishop Strachan had to retain his salary as rector and archdeacon because there had been no provision in 1839 for a suitable episcopal stipend. A number of these clergy now petitioned the SPG for what they claimed to be their arrears, that is the amount of the 1834 reduction times the number of years it had been in effect. When the SPG failed to offer them satisfaction they carried their grievance to the local legislature (after all they assumed they were an establishment). Strachan had enormous difficulty keeping his clergy in line, a difficulty to which he undoubtedly contributed by winning his own appeal to the SPG for arrears and receiving an episcopal salary calculated retroactively to 1839.[65]

More important in the long term was the way the SPG itself regarded the surplus. At this time the Society was hard pressed to meet what were now world-wide obligations; consequently it decided to shift its expenditures from the better-established regions of the Empire, such as the Diocese of Toronto, to those that needed funds more urgently.[66] The Society itself had come to rely heavily on the voluntary contributions of the laity of the church in Britain, especially as Parliament had reduced its support. Having done quite well under this system, it was determined to teach the colonial church the benefits of this arrangement. The Society had always encouraged local bishops to call on the laity for financial support,[67] but now it decided to institutionalize this obligation. In a series of regulations drawn up in consultation with local ecclesiastical leaders, the Society stipulated that the surplus was to be used in the first instance to support theological colleges that could train Canadian clergy and pay the salaries of new missionaries in frontier areas. Then the Society set down a new formula for paying the rest of the clergy. Instead of providing a fixed stipend, it would only match the level of local giving up to £100. Additional resolutions specified that as vacancies occurred in more settled areas these parishes would lose even this matching grant.[68] Strachan was able to modify some features of these regulations, adding a clause that allowed the lower-paid clergy to transfer to the new system only with his approval. He could not, however, change the essentials of the new policy.[69] Indeed he now grasped the need to make the church less reliant on external sources of support. "The period has therefore arrived," he explained in his primary visitation in 1841, "when the parishes and congregations must be appealed to on the necessity of contributing towards the support of their respective ministers. And I trust there will be no backwardness in answering such an appeal."[70]

By the mid-1840s the church in Upper Canada was surrendering an important part of the establishment position as it accepted, however grudgingly, the inevitability of voluntarism. But it was not the legions of dissenters who railed against Anglican privileges that forced this change on the church. The Society for the Propagation of the Gospel in Foreign Parts, the institution that had saved the colonial church in so many times of crisis, turned the church in this new direction. It is also somewhat ironic that the Society used the revenues from the state to help the church give up the principle that the state should finance the Kingdom of God in Upper Canada. In effect the revenue from the clergy reserves made the church more reliant on voluntary support. Well before the reserves were confiscated in 1854, the church was already being instructed in the virtue of financial independence.

The SPG was not, of course, the only force pushing the church towards the voluntarist position. The colonial state, with much less grace and consideration, was also demanding that the church stand on its own, and once again the inherent logic of establishmentarianism shaped the course of these specific events. Having looked at the establishment, the state concluded that the benefits the alliance was supposed to provide had not been forthcoming and that these benefits could be obtained more easily by other means. No longer needing an alliance with this church (or indeed with any church), it set out to dissolve the alliance of church and state. The specific timing of this decision was instructive. The new arrangements of 1842 and the growing surplus in the reserve fund held out the promise that the vision of a well-endowed colonial church establishment might yet come to pass. The church was expanding rapidly and drawing heavily on the revenue being generated by the sale and leasing of reserve lands. Its goal seemed within its grasp. But unfortunately, the arrival of the surplus coincided almost exactly with the election of the great reform ministry and the announcement that there were no longer any good crown lands available for agriculture in Canada West.[71] These political events spelled the demise of the Anglican dream of a state-endowed church establishment in Upper Canada. Over the next decade the alliance between church and state was irrevocably broken.

Two events mark the end of the old alliance: in 1849 the state removed the provincial university from the control of the church, and in 1854 it secularized the revenue from the clergy reserves. The general history surrounding these events is reasonably well known and needs to be recounted here only in outline form.[72] The university question was quite straightforward. Strachan had been the driving force behind the creation of a provincial university, and in response to his efforts the University of Upper Canada received a royal charter in 1827, although the institution, which was now named King's College, did not open its doors until 1843. Both the original charter and its amended version were extremely liberal for their day: although the university was under Anglican control, there were no religious tests for either students (except those studying divinity) or staff. In 1849 the great reform ministry did away with these few elements of clerical control, and King's College became what is now the University of Toronto.

The clergy reserve issue was much more complex. The compromise of 1840 divided the revenue from the reserves according to a complex formula that in effect changed the system from a single-church establishment to a plural establishment. The Church of Scotland was already receiving government support as one of the established churches of the Empire, and other religious groups had received government aid from time to time (although not from the reserves). Now all of these groups could share in these revenues.[73] The church reluctantly agreed to accept this arrangement as a "final solution" to the reserve question.

This compromise, however, did not hold. During the late 1840s and early 1850s the debate shifted from the question of how to divide the revenue among the different religious groups to one of removing the revenue from religion altogether and using it for purely secular purposes. Then in 1854 a moderate conservative government, in which the young John A. Macdonald was a prominent figure, secularized the reserves. The revenue from the reserves underwrote loan funds that the new municipalities could draw on to finance local improvements. This legislation and the judicial decisions that first rejected and then sustained the legality of Colborne's endowment of the rectories mark the end of the establishment question as a contentious issue in Canadian politics. They also mark the end of the hope that the state would finance the Kingdom of God in Upper Canada.

Why did the state abandon the church? Why did it reject the old axiom that public order demands a degree of conformity to a specific set of religious beliefs? Many people at the time and many who have looked back on these events attribute the actions of the government to the growth of liberalism and reform. Disestablishment has been treated as one of the main events in the grand and majestic story of political and social reform in which the principles of liberty and equality triumphed over vested interests and special privilege. The separation of church and state, responsible government, and the movement towards independence led the colonies from the dark ages of their history into the warming light of liberty and political self-determination.

In one sense this interpretation is accurate. Religious privileges were good game for the reformers to hunt, and by attacking this issue they attracted a wide range of groups to the reform standard. In addition, simply the fact that these reforms came to pass seemed to demonstrate the inevitability of the forward march of liberal ideas. This explanation, however, has also obscured the importance of other factors that influenced the course of these events. Beneath the specific political issues of the day ran a deeper current of forces that were reorganizing the religious and political life of Upper Canada. To put the matter as succinctly as possible, the alliance of church and state broke down because the state decided it no longer needed the church; the state rejected the old axiom that public religion was essential to public order because it had found a new formula for creating order and happiness.

Nowhere are these changes in the basic nature of the Canadian state revealed more clearly than in Lord Durham's famous *Report*. This document, as every student of Canadian history knows, responded to the rebellions of 1837 by proposing certain changes in the structure and practice of imperial and colonial politics. These changes have been seen as the first important steps in a series of liberal reforms leading to responsible government and eventually national autonomy. But if one reads the *Report* carefully it becomes clear that "reform" was a relatively unimportant item on Durham's political agenda, or to put the matter a slightly different way, "reform" for Durham meant a good deal more than constitutional change. Reform was a means to an end: Durham's allegiance was not to a set of abstract liberal principles, but to the social and economic goals that these principles were supposed to realize.

In fact, Durham's *Report* began by arguing against the very liberal principles that historians associate with his memory. "I expected to find," Durham wrote in one of the most quoted but least read passages of the document, "a contest between a government and a people: I found two nations warring in the bosom of a single state: I found a struggle, not of principles, but of races." Perhaps a fascination with bosoms and races has distracted historians from grasping the real meaning of this passage. Durham expected to find a traditional battle between an oligarchy and a people; if he had, he would have applied his liberal principles (such as responsible government) to the Canadian problem. But he found racial conflict, and this led him to *reject* a program of liberal reform. "I perceived that it would be idle to attempt any amelioration of laws and institutions until we could first succeed in terminating the deadly animosity that now separates the inhabitants of Lower Canada into the hostile divisions of French and English."[74] The racial problem had to be resolved before he would even consider liberal reforms.

The "racial" conflict reveals the real intention of the *Report*. Durham and his entourage were preoccupied with economic development. He set his *Report* against a backdrop of political, social, and economic disorder, and all his recommendations were designed to stimulate economic growth and prosperity. But two main obstacles stood in his way. In Upper Canada the Family Compact monopolized offices and denied power and reward to aspiring social and economic groups. Still more alarming was the political power of the economically irresponsible French majority in the lower province. Durham's racism is a matter of debate, but what is beyond doubt is that he defined "race" (and history and culture and art) in materialistic and economic terms. When he described the social condition of this "race" he did not refer to their inherent physical traits; rather he assessed how well (or in this case how badly) they adapted to the new economic forces that were shaping the world. "They remain," the *Report* concluded, "an old and stationary society in a new and progressive world."[75] Historians have been troubled by what they see as contradictions in this part of the *Report*. Durham proposed great reforms, but in the next breath he excluded the French Canadians from enjoying these privileges.[76] But if the economic thrust of the *Report* is recognized, then the recommendations become consistent and logical: the political (and hence economic) power of the state had to be placed in the hands of those who would use it properly, and the French did not meet this standard. The union of the two colonies would reduce the power of the French, while responsible government would break the hold of the Family Compact. Both recommendations had the single consistent objective of giving power to the economically progressive groups in colonial society.

Central to this program was an essentially materialistic and developmental understanding of politics and the state that simply cast aside the old principles of hierarchy, restraint, and order. Instead of dividing political power between various groups in order to balance monarchical, aristocratic, and popular elements, the *Report* argued that political power must be concentrated in the hands of men of property, men who wanted to develop the resources of the colony. By using political power to pursue their own self-interest this group would promote the prosperity of the entire colony, and prosperity would solve the problem of social disorder and political instability that had occasioned Lord Durham's procession to the colony.

The developmental vision of Canada and the materialistic assumptions about the state and politics on which the *Report* so clearly rests are in many respects more important than the immediate fate of Durham's specific proposals. Responsible government was not granted simply because Durham had recommended it, but when it arrived it contributed to the type of society that the *Report* had envisaged. The history of the union period confirms the accuracy of Durham's appraisal of the relationship between political power and economic self-interest. When given power, this class of people used it to develop the colonial economy. Too often remembered only as a period of intense sectional rivalry and political deadlock, the pre-Confederation decades enjoyed a general consensus among all groups on the necessity of rapid economic expansion. Political parties may have disagreed about where railways should run and where their terminals should be, but almost all agreed on the need to build railways.[77]

The Family Compact and the established church fell victim to this process of "reform." Although the Compact had strongly supported the economic growth of the colony, especially the Welland Canal,[78] their vision was essentially an agrarian one in which prosperity was supposed to secure the position of the landed gentry, who, along with an established church, were the cornerstones of a stable and hierarchical social system. The groups who replaced the Compact also used the state to promote economic development, but their goals were quite different. Land, for example, no longer carried any social and religious obligations; it was simply an instrument for creating capital and a large pool of wage labour.[79] The Compact had shown how useful the state could be; now others turned this lesson to their own ends by using the power of the state to restructure Canadian society in capitalist terms.

The same developmental ethos cut down the religious establishment. In fact Durham and his fellow travellers turned the assumptions of the old alliance against the colonial church. Warburton and Paley had argued that the state must support the church because religion helped to sustain social order. Durham judged the church by the same standards and concluded that the establishment had become the source of the disorder it was supposed to dispel. The reserves were "the great practical question" of Canadian politics, and a "prompt and satisfactory decision of this question [was] essential to the pacification of Canada."[80] The church was now the problem rather than the solution; the establishment, in effect, had lost the social utility that justified its existence. Expediency, which after all was both a religious and a political principle, demanded the disestablishment of the colonial church.

At the same time Durham offered a new political prescription for social stability: economic development. If the economy was moving forward the people would be happy. Durham's analysis of Canada's relationship to Britain illustrates the way he tied stability and order to economic growth, arguing that British North America would not remain part of the empire unless it enjoyed the economic prosperity of its American neighbour. To achieve American prosperity Canada must adopt American political practices by making the state and society an arena for the free play of economic self-interest. The old belief that the loyalty of Canada rested upon reproducing in British North America the very image and transcript of the British constitution was no longer tenable. In the new Canada, prosperity and progress would assure social stability and order; for Canada to remain British, Britain must allow Canada to follow the American economic example.[81] Progress was to replace religion as the new opiate of the masses.

All these changes were summed up in the way the clergy reserves were secularized in 1854.[82] The revenues from the reserves were now used to fund a large number of municipal projects. Instead of sustaining religion, they underwrote economic development; instead of financing the Anglican vision of the garden of the Lord, they promoted the building of railways. In the light of this change one may marvel at the mysterious ways in which the Lord passed judgement on these events, for within a short time a number of municipalities had used their new-found wealth to speculate themselves into bankruptcy.

The church responded to this new world in a number of ways. It reshaped the financial structure of the church by establishing the Church Society of the Diocese of Toronto in 1842.[83] Modelled in large part on the organization of the SPG with a central board and local committees, the Church Society was set up to raise money for clerical salaries, missionaries, church buildings, parsonages, insurance, pensions, special missions to Indians, theological education, and a Cathedral endowment.[84] Its creation acknowledged the precarious state of the reserves and the necessity of shifting the burden of support to the individual congregation. Just as important, it brought the laity of the church directly into the administrative structures of the church. Here the parallel with the Methodists is striking, in both cases finance being the door through which the laity entered the inner courts of the church.

These reforms helped to prepare the church for the loss of the reserves in 1854. From an early date the church had realized that the income from the reserves was neither safe nor permanent. Since the reserves could never escape the vicissitudes of provincial politics, the SPG decided "to expend in each year the whole annual income,"[85] putting as many missionaries onto the fund as possible so that in the all too likely event that the reserves were lost, the salaries of the clergy would "be placed within the protection of the calculated regard to vested rights."[86] The church was well served by these precautions, for when the reserves were secularized the Act recognized and protected the "vested rights" of the clergymen who had been supported by the reserves (at this point the list included Anglicans, Presbyterians, Methodists and Catholics). It then allowed these clergy to commute their salaries for a lump sum that was to be paid to an ecclesiastical corporation, which would then assume the obligation to pay the salaries of the clergy who had drawn upon the fund. The clergy of the Church of England agreed to this provision for commutation, and the state paid the Church Society of the Diocese of Toronto about £245,000 as a final settlement of this long and complicated dispute.

In effect the church received from the state the type of endowment that it had always wanted, although the amount was considerably smaller than it had hoped for.[87] The SPG came forward and covered the projected shortfall in the endowment and then began to withdraw from the area. It agreed to support a few missionaries in the new dioceses of Huron and Ontario that were established in 1857 and 1861 respectively. This level of support, however, was far below what the Society had contributed in years past, and in 1878 the Society that had done so much to shape the colonial Church withdrew officially from the old Diocese of Toronto.

Finance, however, was only one of the ties that had bound the church and the state together. The alliance was based on a whole series of reciprocal relationships: in return for financial support, the church surrendered its administrative and legal independence to the state. The secularization of the university and the reserves now placed the church in an anomalous position, for although it no longer received financial support from the state, the state nonetheless continued to control the church. The state, for example, still had the power to present clergymen to the rectories Colborne had endowed in 1835; indeed with the arrival of responsible government this patronage fell to the leader of the government party! In addition the state in England still exercised considerable control over the colonial church, especially in the nomination of colonial bishops.

Certainly this was the worst of all possible worlds. As long as the state was nominally Anglican (or at least Christian) and provided to some degree for the financial needs of the church, then state control was reasonable and proper. But now the church enjoyed none of the benefits and all of the disadvantages of the establishment position. It was at the mercy of those who demanded an end to the financial support but were unwilling to give up the political power that the old alliance had left in their hands:

"We feel that we are now as a church not merely deserted by the Imperial Government, but it lends itself to our oppression and gives readily to Romanists and Dissenters privileges and benefits which it denies to us." The conclusion Strachan drew from this assessment points towards the final steps in the long march towards institutional and cultural independence: "henceforth we must depend upon ourselves."[88]

Only a few short years before, the church was prepared to defend the principle and practice of establishmentarianism at almost any cost; now it was the church rather than the state that was most anxious to cut the final ties binding the two together. When the state dismissed the church from the provincial university, Bishop Strachan created another (his third). Trinity College was a thoroughly Anglican institution, but it was Anglican in the new sense rather than the old – independent of the state and firmly under the control of the clergy and laity of the church. When Strachan (who was now in his early seventies) went on yet another fund-raising tour of England, he no longer used the language of establishments and social order, but based his case on the principle of general equity, calling on the state to extend to the church the rights already enjoyed by other independent religious denominations.[89]

To break the hold of the state and make the church independent, Strachan created a new administrative body, the diocesan synod. He was well aware of how synods had helped the American church replace the ties to the crown that had been broken by the late war.[90] The idea of holding clerical conventions had been discussed in Upper Canada as early as 1832 and had gained considerable support, although the idea of including the laity met with a decidedly cool reception in England. Informal meetings of the clergy of the Diocese of Toronto began in the 1840s at both the regional level and for the diocese as a whole through the bishop's triennial visitations.[91] The Church Society, as we have seen, brought the clergy and the laity of the church together, but its mandate was restricted to financial matters. Since the Society had no power to discipline the clergy or enact canons it did not threaten the traditional and ancient structure of the church *per se*.[92]

The events of the 1850s made the problems of administration and authority much more acute. In 1851 Strachan invited the laity to attend his visitation, which became in effect the first diocesan synod. The second diocesan conference, which met in 1853, approached the question more directly by simply declaring itself a synod and assuming the power to regulate and administer the affairs of the church. It was the first synod with lay delegates held in the British Empire.[93] In fact Strachan had moved before he had the clear legal authority to initiate such reforms. The legal opinions he had solicited on the question of synods in 1850 pointed out the prohibitions against clerical convocations but encouraged him to consult with his clergy informally and petition the crown to remove any prohibitions that might exist against more formal synodical meetings.[94] The British government, however, was wary of granting such a request, primarily because of its implications for the church in Britain. Nor was it certain it even had the power to do anything in this regard since responsible government had transferred many of the rights of the crown to the local authorities. Once again the church faced a crisis: the state that had cast the church adrift financially refused to release the church from its grasp.

In 1855, however, the British government finally gave royal assent to an Australian bill, known as the Victoria Church Act, that tried to strike a compromise between colonial religious independence and the rights of the British crown. On the matter of the election of colonial bishops, the issue that was of particular concern to the church in Canada, the Act went to great lengths to remain silent by including a long clause that said in effect that nothing in the Act would affect this question.[95] The British government recommended the Victoria Church Act as a model for Canada and asked Strachan to accept a practical compromise in which synods would propose a candidate to the crown, which would then act on this advice.

Strachan rejected the proposal and persuaded the Canadian legislature to pass a short bill (it had only two clauses) that cut through all the qualifications and compromises of the Victoria Act by giving the synod the power to do whatever it wished in church affairs. Whitehall, which objected strongly to what it quite correctly believed to be a challenge to the prerogatives of the crown, submitted the bill to the Judicial Committee of the Privy Council. The Council, however, upheld the legality of the colonial legislation, pointing out that the new principle of responsible government had given the colonial legislature the authority to act in this area.[96] In this nice turn of events, the church in Canada was able to use the new political ideology to its own advantage. The principle of responsible government that had undermined the old alliance of church and state now came to the aid of the new type of church that was emerging in the British dominions of North America.

The final opposition to these changes came from the English bishops who did not welcome the idea of colonial self-government in religious affairs. Led by the Archbishop of Canterbury, they tried to keep the colonial churches under the control of the local legislatures and protect the royal supremacy by making all holders of clerical office take the oath of supremacy.[97] Strachan rejected this course, and his own bill severely limited the power of the mother church. "I am not surprised at the measure," Archbishop Sumner explained to Henry Labouchere, the Secretary of State for the Colonies. "The Canadians think that they do not obtain much from the church here, and have never forgiven us for abandoning the clergy reserves."[98] The Canadian church continued to oppose the attempts by the British church to assert (or reassert) its authority. When Archbishop Archibald Campbell Tait suggested to the colonial bishops that Canterbury be given a special position in the Imperial church, the Canadian bishops greeted his suggestion with something less than enthusiasm. Complete independence, they maintained, was the best bond of union, and they looked forward to a world of "free and unfettered [churches] such as under the blessing of God has been organized in this Province of Canada."[99]

The long and complex process of disestablishment transformed the old eighteenth-century United Church of England and Ireland into a Victorian denomination that could work with other Protestant denominations in a number of common causes. The Anglicans were joining the new Protestant alliance, but they were not the only group in English Canada that had to face the problem of disestablishment. The Church of Scotland, which also lost a number of privileges, had to respond to the impact of religious, social, and cultural change. Although the Presbyterian side of this issue is not nearly as complex as the Anglican one, it nonetheless enriches the story and especially illuminates the formation of an important part of the new Protestant alliance.

The two establishment churches had a good deal in common. Both were part of the Upper Canadian establishment, both accepted the highly rational universe of the culture of order, both attacked the superstitions of Rome and the enthusiasms of sectarianism with the same passion, and both reacted to events in a similar fashion.[100] Much has been made of the fact that Strachan himself had a Presbyterian past and only "converted" to Anglicanism after failing to receive a call to an important Presbyterian pulpit in Montreal.[101] This conversion, if it indeed occurred, belies the fact that Strachan saw little difference between the two institutions. He certainly kept an eye on events in Scotland and used Presbyterian models on more than one occasion; even his synod had a very Presbyterian character, clergy and laity joining together to administer and discipline the church.

At the same time the Presbyterians approached the whole issue of church and state from a very different position. The Church of Scotland in Canada was not integrated into the colonial state to nearly the same degree as the Church of England, and consequently it could deal with the problems of disestablishment much more easily. In addition, since the Presbyterians already had a synodical form of government that included the laity of the church, they were not forced to create new administrative structures. A long synodical tradition also gave the church a strong spiritual independence from the state that the Church of England, which had not met in convocation for centuries, did not enjoy. For those reasons the Presbyterians did not have to take the same long and tortuous journey as the other part of the Canadian establishment.

At the same time the Presbyterians had serious problems that the Anglicans were able to avoid. In spite of the massive changes taking place in the Church of England, the church remained reasonably united and was never fragmented into smaller bodies. Schism and disruption, however, graced the progress of the Church of Scotland at every turn. During the early decades of the nineteenth century, Presbyterianism in Upper Canada was divided into at least three principal groups, which tended to agree on most points of doctrine but went their own way on questions of religious practice (American Presbyterians were revivalistic) and the relationship between church and state.[102] Most Presbyterians accepted the idea of a state church, but many were voluntarists. In effect, groups of Presbyterians could be found at a number of different points along the religious spectrum of the colony.

The most important Presbyterian church in the colony before 1840 was the Canadian offshoot of the Church of Scotland. Since this church was part of one of the established churches in Britain (and Canada was a British rather than an English colony), these Presbyterians pressed the government to recognize their claim to be an established church in the colony. In time they won their case and began to receive the financial support that went hand in hand with the establishment principle. The settlement of 1840, for example, recognized a dual Protestant establishment in the colony and gave the Presbyterians a sizeable share of the revenue from the reserves. The prospect of greater financial support from the reserves and the encouragement of the government helped the

Presbyterians achieve a degree of church union at this time, although the United Secessionist Presbyterians, who refused to compromise their voluntarist principles, remained outside the union.[103]

It is against this background of union and division, of establishmentarianism and voluntarism, that the events of 1843 and 1844 can be best understood. At that time the church in Scotland was suffering the "great disruption," as Strachan's old friend, the Rev. Dr Thomas Chalmers, led the evangelical wing out of the Scottish establishment and founded the Free Church. His actions were not so much an attack on the doctrine that the state should support religion as an attack on the control the state was trying to exercise over the church. Chalmers believed the state must acknowledge religious truth and the headship of Christ by providing the church with financial support to carry the faith into every corner of the realm. The state must not, however, try to determine either the character of that truth or the way it was propagated. But now, he asserted, the state was violating these principles by recognizing the authority of lay patrons to decide who should receive a call to a church. In the eyes of many this decision struck down the spiritual independence of the Scottish establishment, and Chalmers took his leave of the manse, believing that the state was obliged to build it but had no right to determine who should dwell therein. When the leaders of the Anglican Church in Canada faced the same problem, they solved it in much the same way withdrawing their church from its alliance with the state in order to assert its independence as a sacred institution. Chalmers, in fact, was a guiding light for many Canadian Anglicans who followed events in Scotland closely and strongly supported Chalmers' critique of state interference.[104]

The great disruption in Scotland altered Canadian Presbyterianism and the place of Presbyterianism in the religious structure of the colony. Since lay patronage was not a serious problem in Canada, many Presbyterians, especially those east of Toronto, did not feel compelled to sever their connection with the old Kirk. The Presbyterians who were more sympathetic to the succeeders, however, argued that the church in Canada was contaminated by its parent; consequently they left the old church and established Free Church congregations and presbyteries. But the Free Church in Canada did *not* abandon the principle that the state should support religious truth. Indeed its strong evangelicalism confirmed its belief that the state must support the moral reform of society.[105] For this reason the proposed union of the Free Church and the strongly voluntarist United Secessionist Presbyterians could not be consummated: the Free Church clung to the ideal of state support, even though it had opposed the terms on which such support had been offered.

Once again the course of the secular world realigned this constellation of religious bodies. When the opportunity arrived for the Free Church to enjoy the financial benefits of its adherence to the principle of state support, the church refused to accept its share of the revenue of the clergy reserves. As before, the way state support was being offered was at the centre of the problem. Instead of supporting evangelical truth, the state was offering support to almost every religious group in the colony, including the Catholics! The state was not doing its duty to God but merely paying off its friends.

The Free Church found itself being pushed into a voluntarist position as it realized that the ideal of a moral state supporting an aggressive evangelical church was not attainable. Now the church alone had to lead and finance the great moral crusades, for which it became justly famous. Evangelicalism and voluntarism were joined together in what soon became the largest Presbyterian body in the colony, and as the dissolution of the reserves withdrew state support from all religious groups, including the old Kirk, the Free Church position became the gathering point for Canadian Presbyterianism in general and the basis for the eventual union in 1875 of all the major Presbyterian groups in Canada. The Anglicans, Presbyterians, and Methodists had in effect reached the same position.

III

Cultural change went hand in hand with religious reorganization. The financial and administrative crises of the early Victorian period forced religious groups to modify not only their institutional structures, but also the way they interpreted the meaning of God and the world. Once again it was the Church of England that changed most dramatically. The culture of order that expressed so clearly the values and assumptions of the establishment position lost its power. As the world of establishments and compacts began to break down, the church had to search for a different way to explain the new realities of Ontario life.

In the midst of this crisis the official newspaper of the Anglican church published a long and at times bitter analysis of the history of the church in Canada that marks an important shift in the cultural attitudes of the church. The analysis summarized the beliefs that had sustained the church in the past, outlined the weaknesses in this position, and indicated the new culture the church would develop in the following decades. The article began by reiterating the doctrine of the alliance of church and state (with clear references to Burke, Warburton, and Paley): "A certain form of Christianity has been interwoven with the framework of the British Constitution. The state, in the way of equivalent for the advantages it derives from such an alliance, has provided, in this manner, a solemn and abiding memorial of its religious duty, – an article of which duty is, to shield the church from injury and aggression."[106] Here was indeed the culture of order. At this point, however, the article asked the one question that undermined that culture. "[The church] is yet a blessing to the land overshadowed by her wide-spread branches; and right honourably has she adhered to her obligations in the civil compact. But has a like fidelity been envinced by the state in discharging its share of the mutual compact?"[107] The question is phrased in the language of compacts and alliances, of reciprocal duties and mutual benefit, but the inevitable answer destroys that very culture. If the state had not lived up to its part of the covenant, it was time to dissolve the alliance. But what then should take its place? How could the church survive in a cultural sense without the values that the alliance embodied? The terms of the alliance perhaps offered an answer to these questions: since in ages past the church had surrendered its independence in order to gain certain benefits from the alliance with the state, did not the church regain that independence once the state had failed to fulfil its obligations?

In the early nineteenth century the culture of the church reinforced a clear social and constitutional position. The rational world of premise and conclusion was in perfect harmony with the principles of an establishment. Since society must have order, there must be an established church. To a considerable extent the social benefits provided by religion demonstrated the divine character of the church. But this world and the intellectual assumptions that had sustained it were no longer tenable. Without an establishment the church could no longer defend itself in the old language of order and social utility. Now, turning the argument around, the church proclaimed itself a sacred institution in a secular world. Social utility did not make the church sacred; rather the sacred character of the church gave it an important role to play in society. The church was a church because it was a church.

This important cultural shift is illustrated by John Strachan's sermons, of which over four hundred survive, a rich testimony to a life in Canada that spanned the entire period from 1800 to 1867. In the first decades of his career the sermons integrate the church and the state so thoroughly that there is almost no distinction between social and religious ideals. Questions of church polity, like any questions of social policy, are judged according to their expediency. The doctrines of the church are correct because they produce the best results – they promote human happiness and social order. The church, in effect, was a means to an end. After 1840, however, Strachan's concept of the church changed dramatically.[108] In the later sermons the church stood on its own and was the channel through which God spoke to the world. Divine Providence was no longer tied to nature and the structure of society and the state, but institutionalized within the church. Not only did the sacred independence of the church become a major theme in Strachan's sermons, he seemed to preach on little else.

This cultural transformation is also illustrated by the relationship between the colonial church and the Oxford Movement. This movement was perhaps the most important development in the Anglican Church in the nineteenth century, and its impact on the church in Britain and throughout the world was far-reaching. The leaders of the church in the Diocese of Toronto, however, drew on the movement very selectively, accepting certain elements that helped them deal with their cultural crisis but rejecting others, especially those that might contaminate the colonial church with any Popish associations. In a curious way the colonial church tried to Protestantize the Oxford Movement.

Strachan, for example, had nothing but praise for the way the Tractarians cut through the old (and now corrupt) world of rationalism and Erastian practices, what *The Church* referred to as the "easy and intelligible doctrines" of Locke, Paley, "and certain Scottish writers."[109] The leaders of the church praised *Tracts for the Times* for trying to return the church to "first principles" and for putting the church on a foundation that was independent of the state. They were especially thankful for the new emphasis on the doctrine of apostolic succession, because the assertion that the church enjoyed an unbroken link to the primitive church gave the colonial church what it was seeking – a sense of itself that did not rely on the state and could justify the independent course the church was now pursuing.

At the same time, however, the Tractarians, by so strongly emphasizing the Catholic nature of church doctrine, threatened to drive a wedge between the Anglican Church in the colony and the main Protestant denominations. Strachan was determined to avoid this course of events at all costs by quarantining his church from any form of Romish superstition. Methodists and Presbyterians regarded Tractarianism as only one step removed from Popery (and all the more threatening for that reason). Strachan, who shared their fears, regarded Newman's departure for Rome with contempt, unable to understand how any intelligent person could become a Roman Catholic. When others followed Newman, he saw them as part of a Roman conspiracy bent upon undermining his church. They were "new enemies" who had issued from the "bowels" of the church.[110] The colonial church accepted with open arms the attack that Oxford had launched on the world the church had abandoned only a few years before, but it would not allow the movement to threaten the Protestant character of the church in Upper Canada.

Another measure of cultural change is the new language that the colonial church began to adopt. In the early period the discourse of Anglicanism was rational and deductive. As befits an institution dedicated to reason and order, Anglican thought was organized around premise, deduction, and conclusion. Sermons were carefully ordered to appeal to reason, and the articles in the Anglican press were often models of rational discussion in which one person (an Anglican) inevitably convinced the opponent (a dissenter) through the power of careful argument of the perfect reasonableness of church doctrine.[111] Now, however, the church was not only talking about new things but it was talking about them in new ways. As it proclaimed the doctrine of apostolic succession and emphasized its unbroken ties to the church in ages past, it expressed these doctrines in a style that complemented the new historical orientation. When Strachan, for example, called on the laity to support the church he reconstructed a romantic age of Christian belief, arguing that this ideal from the distant past should guide the church in the present. He appealed to history rather than reason, alluding to medieval Christianity and the primitive practice of the Church of God:

We may consider ourselves in primitive times, when the Bishop sent out his missionaries from the cathedral or principle church ... If the inhabitants of any district or settlement said, "Here is a house to live in – a glebe to furnish provisions – and an endowment to rent for the supply of other necessities – abide with us, and be faithful not to us but your bishop, and to his master and your master" – a parish became established. In this way arose the parochial system in Great Britain and over the whole continent of Europe, and thus must it arise in this diocese.[112]

Strachan's words on this occasion foretell a change that soon overwhelmed the church as history and romanticism quickly coloured almost every facet of Anglican life.

The internal divisions that began to develop in this period also indicate the new character of the colonial church. In the period before disestablishment the church tended to divide on financial rather than theological issues; matters of stipends and arrears rather than doctrine and churchmanship took centre stage. After disestablishment, however, the battle between high churchmen and evangelicals raged without pause for many decades as a wide variety of issues, from the election of bishops to the use of candles (either lit or unlit), led to bitter confrontations between two clearly defined parties. These new divisions, however, grew out of the type of institution the church was becoming. In the early nineteenth century, doctrine *per se* was not especially important. Because establishments must try to appeal to everyone, it was best to avoid rubrics that excluded people from joining the church. As Paley had argued, if establishments did not have a genuine breadth, they could not perform their social function and therefore lost their reason for existence. But once the church began to present itself as an independent and sacred institution, it inevitably had to reconsider the way it justified its existence. By appealing to the sacred, it had to define the sacred, and doctrine and practice quickly became important issues. Whereas some sects were becoming more church-like, this church began to debate what had traditionally been a sectarian question, namely, the nature of true religion.[113] The romantic appeal to a golden age in the past both pulled the church together and divided it in new ways.

The doctrine of the church, the emphasis on historical continuity, and the new language of romanticism all point towards a new representation of the church and the world. Whereas establishmentarianism had emphasized the links between the church, society, and the world, the new culture pulled the church away from society and the state and constructed a counterworld of the sacred that stood against the values and beliefs of the new secular society. In Strachan's words, the church was "like a city on a hill ... one august, incorruptible and glorious verity, shining with celestial light over the ocean of uncertainty and change."[114]

All these changes had a profound influence on the colony as a whole. In the 1820s the church had seen itself as an ally of the state, protecting society from sectarianism on the one extreme and Roman Catholicism on the other. As the establishment position began to erode, the church realized that what it shared with other

Protestant groups was becoming more important than what had kept them apart. Their new common ground was fittingly marked by the very man who thirty years before had been so anxious to emphasize the distance that separated the church and dissent. In 1856, Bishop John Strachan, who was now close to eighty, acknowledged the existence of the new religious structure in the province and adjusted the goals of his church accordingly. Rome was still an enemy, but dissent had been replaced by "a worse foe," which he called "open infidelity." Realizing that the resolution of the reserve question had removed the last major obstacle to Protestant co-operation, he called upon all groups to join together to fight the Church of Rome and the secular society: "I do not feel that the progress of the church can be much impeded by the efforts of Protestant Dissenters, now that our temporalities have vanished and ceased to be a source of contention. I trust that a conciliatory spirit will take the place of former bitterness between us; and unless they are determined to patronize and favour unbelief rather than Christianity, they must come forward and assist us."[115] The specific issues that he put on the agenda of this new alliance summarize many of the moral questions that would dominate the social thought of Ontario Protestantism for the rest of the Victorian era: the development of Sunday schools, the use of the Bible in public education, a common crusade against the encroachments of Popery, and the creation of the Ontario Sunday – "the proper observance of the Sabbath to keep it holy."[116]

These issues also suggest the way this Protestant alliance would approach society in general and the new state in particular. At one time the establishment had tried to use its alliance with the state to influence the very structure of society. Establishments worked from the principle of integration: the church was an integral part of the hierarchical social structure. Now the church questioned the character and motives of its former ally, practical experience having taught it to fear the power of the new state. Other groups reached much the same conclusion. Although the disestablishment of the church made the state much less an Anglican preserve, the materialism that the state encouraged made it highly suspect. And yet religion could not abandon either the state or society; religious groups needed the state in order to realize their institutional and moral goals, they needed the power of the state to incorporate religious institutions (such as universities and synods) and enact the laws that advanced the many moral crusades launched by the Protestant alliance. On the one hand the Protestant alliance feared the new state and the new society; on the other, it needed the state to help it transform the new society into a Protestant garden.

This ambivalence was captured in the concept of division and integration that began to characterize Victorian culture as a whole. People, institutions, and society itself were given two natures. "The church and the world," said Strachan, "although consisting of the same human beings, exhibit two societies as distinct from each other, as if each of the parties composing them were of different natures."[117] The sacred was a distinct world, even though it was filled with the same people who lived and worked in the secular society. It was this idea of separation that gave religion such tremendous social power. From the high ground of the sacred, the Protestant alliance turned to the task of drawing the two worlds together and transforming the secular into the sacred. If it could no longer work in concert with the state, it could use its position as an independent sacred force to reshape the world through a massive program of moral reform. It could work to create a moral atmosphere that would inspire Canadian Christians to keep at least one eye on the kingdom of God as they struggled through the hazards of a materialistic world. In its enthusiasm for material progress, the secular state had helped to shape Ontario Protestantism by pushing religion into a separate sphere. Now the moral imperatives of Ontario Protestantism attempted to address the social and ethical problems created by the same state.

As older cultures broke down, they were replaced by a new culture, which divided reality into secular and sacred worlds, held out the vision that the secular would eventually be transformed into the sacred, and called on the power of a strong set of moral norms and values to bring about this transformation. These elements formed the basis of the common Protestantism that impressed its authority upon Ontario society in the mid-nineteenth century.

As always the new culture drew upon the old. The emotionalism of the sectarian tradition gave energy to the great Protestant crusade, and a moral earnestness became one of the most distinguishing features of Ontario religious life. The establishment tradition also made an important contribution to the new culture. Central to the concept of an established church was the ideal of the Christian commonwealth. State support, the establishment had argued, was essential because it allowed the church to carry the message of salvation into every town and village in the Kingdom. For writers like Edmund Burke it was the glory of the British constitution that religion was prominently displayed in the very fabric of the nation.[118] Although the secularization of the state destroyed the institutional and financial foundations of this ideal, it did not destroy the ideal of a living Christendom.[119] If a conscience could not be found in the structures of the state, perhaps it might be found outside the state. Perhaps the new Protestant consensus itself held the power to transform Upper Canada into the garden of the Lord. By joining the moral imperatives of romantic evangelicalism with the sacred independence of a new Anglicanism, now clothed in the rich fabric of a revived medievalism, it might be possible to forge a powerful religious world that could counterbalance the growing materialism of the Victorian age. Out of this union of church and dissent was born the new forms of the Protestant culture of Ontario. Now this new culture had to perform its appointed tasks. Born out of the failure of older patterns to explain the world, it had to define for Ontario Protestants a sense of place and time that would allow them to participate in both the secular and the sacred worlds.

CHAPTER FIVE

Epics in Stone: Placing the Sacred in a Secular World

In these buildings we have as a people, both French and British ... epics in stone, revealing to us not only universal beauty and inspiration, but emblematic of our common ideal, our common artistic sense, our common ancestry, and our common Christianity.

Wilfred Campbell, *Canada*

When the old religious structure of Upper Canada was destroyed by social and religious change, the groups that had been drawn into the new Protestant alliance had to find answers to the basic cultural questions that the older systems could no longer answer. More specifically, the breakdown of the culture of order and the culture of experience raised two questions that are central to all cultures,[1] and for this reason they provide a framework for analysing the new culture that was emerging from the old. The first question addresses the meaning of place; put most simply, it asks how a society interprets its environment. The second question, which will be taken up in the next chapter, concerns the meaning of time: How did the new culture define the course of events that shaped its life? How did it interpret the present, the past, and the future?

Place is an important cultural construction. All cultures organize their environments in a particular way, ascribing special attributes to certain parts of the environment, which then become reference points for giving meaning to the physical world. Religions, for example, associate certain places with the sacred – this land is of God – and by doing so divide the world into the sacred and the secular. Here then we must try to understand how the new culture organized its environment, where it found and proclaimed the sacred in the world.

The answers that the older cultures of Upper Canada had offered to these questions once again set the new culture in its proper historical context. The Methodism of the old style defined the sacred as an immediate and omnipresent reality that intervened directly in the affairs of the world. Its God was a spirit without limits, unbound by rules and laws. At the same time the other-worldliness of this culture drew a strong line between God and the world; sacred space and secular space were distinct, although the omnipotence of God could transform the latter into the former at any moment. Place was defined very differently by the religion of order. Although its God was a rational being who worked according to certain principles and did not choose to disrupt the course of human events, it did not draw such a clear line between sacred and secular space: the two were joined together in nature, the social system, and the institutions that sustained society. Order, virtue, and reason were at once attributes of the divine and practical guides for living in the world.

As these older answers lost their authority, the culture had to find new ways of explaining God and the world. This new sense of place that came to dominate Ontario Protestant culture is revealed most clearly in the way Protestants worshipped their Lord. In all societies worship is the primary act that binds the people and the sacred. It is also in large measure a public act that relies heavily upon visual rituals and public symbolism that define the meaning of place for society as a whole.

At this time the style of worship was changing in Protestant Ontario. As the religious structure of the province changed, so too did the way people approached and represented the sacred. On a grand and public scale these changes were summed up and proclaimed in a new style of religious architecture. In the mid-nineteenth century all the denominations in the new Protestant alliance rejected their former assumptions about the nature of a church and began to build their places of worship in the revived medieval manner. Indeed the revival of the Gothic and Romanesque was so extensive that these romantic forms defined (and perhaps continue to define) how a church should appear. The new medieval church, which occupied such a prominent place in almost every village and town, became the most powerful and enduring symbol of the Protestant culture of Ontario.

The study of architecture and worship offers a number of important insights into Ontario Protestantism. First, the very extent of the revival of medieval architecture is a measure of the new type of religious structure that was developing in the province. During the mid-nineteenth century Anglicans, Methodists, and Presbyterians all began to pay considerable attention to church architecture, setting up committees to consider questions of church design and offer guidance to individual congregations.[2] The Presbyterians even sponsored an architectural competition to develop a series of standard church designs for new churches throughout the Dominion.[3] Groups that had used different architectural styles, or for whom style had not been important, now began to compose their own variations on the same medieval theme. Churches in Ontario began to look like one another, confirming visually the growing unity of Ontario Protestantism itself.

Secondly, the aesthetics of the revival offer a number of insights into the new culture that was coming to dominate the religious life of Ontario. Every work of art, be it a building, a picture, or a work of literature and history, embodies an aesthetic principle, a way of organizing and explaining the world. Giving form and structure to the world is the most human (and divine) expression of life; all form has meaning. In this instance the relationship between form and meaning was made in the strongest terms. The advocates of the new style both in Canada and abroad set out with an almost messianic zeal to popularize a body of aesthetic and architectural principles that explained not only how churches should be built but also how they should be seen, especially in relation to the surrounding world. By building these churches Protestant Ontario was making an important cultural statement about the place of God in the world.

Thirdly, the study of architecture and worship helps to explain how the new church and the new culture became such a dominant feature of Ontario life. To be effective, a culture must be integrated into the life of a society; forms and symbols that remain at a distance from the people who use them quickly lose their power. The new Gothic churches and the cultural assumptions of romantic art had to be developed and adapted to meet the specific needs of Ontario religious life and Ontario society. Architects had to keep one eye on the aesthetic and architectural principles of the revival and the other on the spiritual needs of many different groups. The ability of a number of gifted architects to meet this challenge helps to explain how a revived medievalism became the Ontario style and the romantic form became so embedded in the consciousness of society.

I

During the mid-Victorian period, Ontario Protestants built churches in great numbers. The statistics of church building, especially when examined in relation to the growth of the major denominations, attest to the optimism with which these groups approached the future. Between 1851 and 1881 all the major Protestant denominations either matched or exceeded the rate of increase in the population as a whole, and quite remarkably, church building outpaced even the rapid rate of denominational expansion. In this period the Anglicans almost doubled their number of adherents, while they trebled the number of their churches. The Presbyterians (taken as a whole) and the Baptists grew a little more rapidly than the Anglicans, and they too trebled the number of their churches. The Methodists were even more prolific builders. While the number of their adherents trebled (again taking all the Methodists together), the number of their churches increased by a factor of five. Even in a period of exceptional denominational growth, there were far more Protestant churches per capita in Ontario in 1881 than thirty years earlier. In fact, these denominations built so many churches that they actually reduced the average size of their congregations. Anticipating that their rate of growth would soon fill all these new buildings, they were building for the future.

The smaller Protestant groups faced exactly the opposite prospect. Although they managed to increase the number of their churches by a factor of 1.9 (a rate that was slightly less than the rate of population growth), the actual size of this group as a percentage of the general population declined quite sharply. Consequently, in 1881 they had fewer churches per capita than they had had thirty years before. The average size of their congregations also decreased, but the decrease simply confirmed the fact that these groups were in decline. They were left with half-empty churches and little hope of filling them.[4]

Undoubtedly the extraordinary growth in the number of churches in Ontario was partly due to the material development of the province. New churches were expensive, and as external sources of funding became more and more tenuous, all the denominations had to appeal to the generosity of their own members, whose wealth was tied to the rise and fall of the local economy. Each congregation had to call on those who had prospered in the new economic order, and their benefactors are still acknowledged in the hundreds of memorials that grace the churches they helped to build. Many religious leaders readily acknowledged that the business cycle had become an important religious consideration.[5] Without considerable affluence Ontario could not have sustained such a rapid pace of church construction.

The close tie between wealth and church building, however, should not lead to the conclusion that the growth of Protestantism and the increase in church building can be understood in exclusively economic terms. Although the expansion of the economy and the growth of Protestantism ran concurrently, the relationship between the two was complex. Economic development may have generated the capital to finance new churches, but economic development in itself cannot explain the decision to invest so much wealth in a religious sector that was hardly known for its secular dividends. A vaguely conspiratorial interpretation that focuses on the ability of religion to keep the masses in their place might give such investment a higher economic rationality; but this is a reductionist theory, and it strains the limits of reason and the doctrine of rational economic action itself. More important, it ignores the way society at that time tried to understand the relationship between economic and religious life. Many people in fact argued that religion should not justify the materialism of the modern age, but challenge it at every turn.

In the early nineteenth century the ecclesiastical architecture of the colony did not conform to any single pattern. Though neo-classical styles enjoyed the greatest popularity (see Figure 2) with the Churches of England and Scotland,[6] the range of architectural styles, as Douglas Richardson has pointed out, was "astonishingly varied."[7] Some groups did not consider the style of their churches very important and simply adapted domestic buildings and vernacular forms to religious purposes. Others thought a good deal about religious architecture. For example, David Willson, the leader of the Children of Peace, saw himself as a contemporary Solomon relying upon the Bible and divine inspiration to reconstruct the temple of Jerusalem in the backwoods of East Gwillimbury township (see Figures 3 and 4). The result was extraordinarily creative[8] and increased the ecclecticism of the religious architecture of old Ontario. In effect, the deeply divided religious structure of the colony in the period before Confederation was reflected in the heterogeneity of the colony's religious architecture.

In the period before 1840 examples of medievalism were rare and very tentative, a few Gothic details added on to what was still essentially a neo-classical church.[9] After this date, however, architectural references to the Middle Ages became more precise, the use of masonry construction increased, and buttresses, window tracery, and arch mouldings became more convincingly medieval. By the mid-Victorian decades the new style had swept through all the major Protestant denominations. Though the revival was led by the Anglicans, the Methodists, Presbyterians, and

Baptists quickly followed with their own stylistic interpretations of the Gothic theme. Some of the architectural idioms employed by the more evangelical groups might have offended the high-church partisans of the movement, but the medieval ethos of their churches was unmistakable. By the end of the century the Gothic and Romanesque had achieved an exalted stature in the hierarchy of architectural forms. These were not simply two styles that an architect might choose from among many others; they were now the only styles an architect could employ to build a church. By the time of Confederation medievalism was triumphant and had imparted an unusually non-sectarian character to the ecclesiastical architecture of Ontario.[10] Religious architecture confirmed visually the growing unity of Ontario Protestantism itself.

A short architectural history of four important Toronto congregations illustrates the dramatic changes that were taking place in the architecture of Protestant worship. The churches of these four congregations, which were from different denominations, each displayed distinctive traits that reflected the particular needs of that congregation; but all of them tell basically the same story, a story that was repeated time and again, not only in Toronto but throughout the province.

The arrival of the Gothic revival in Toronto was announced by the great fire of 1849 that consumed a large part of the Georgian town (see Figure 5). Early on Saturday morning, the day before Easter, the conflagration threw a burning shingle against the wooden spire of St James' Cathedral. The spire conducted the flames into the building itself, where they spread throughout the structure. In the morning only part of the walls of what had been a handsome Georgian structure remained standing.[11]

The rebuilding of the cathedral began about a year after the fire, and the architecture of the new building was never in doubt. Rejecting the classical forms of their old church, the Anglicans demanded that all the submissions for the new building be in the Gothic style.[12] The successful architect, F. W. Cumberland, created a church that incorporated many of the most advanced principles of ecclesiological design,[13] and where wilderness had stood only a few decades before, a church arose that became a general model for new Anglican churches in the Diocese of Toronto and a living expression of the new Anglicanism now flourishing in Ontario. When the church opened in 1853 it was little more than a Gothic shell, financial constraints having prevented the construction of more than the bare bones of the design. Over the next twenty-five years, however, the church became more "correct"[14] both internally and externally as it received side porches, a tower, and a tall spire (see Figure 6).

While the Anglicans were completing their cathedral, the other important Protestant congregations in the city were also abandoning their classical churches (or plain meeting houses) for clearly medieval structures. Just to the north of St James' Cathedral, the congregation of St Andrew's Presbyterian Church found that its old building, a flat-roofed classical box with a spire, no longer satisfied their requirements (see Figure 7). Although most members agreed that they must build a new church, the location of the new building divided the congregation. In 1875 the majority moved south and west along King Street to a new "Norman" edifice built by William G. Storm (see Figure 8), while the dissenting minority followed Presbyterian custom by moving in the opposite direction. They built their church to the east and north, on Jarvis Street at Carleton. It was a large Gothic structure designed by Langley, Langley & Burke (see Figure 9). These two churches became, somewhat confusingly, the new St Andrew's and the new Old St Andrew's respectively.[15]

In 1870 the congregation at the Adelaide Street Wesleyan Methodist Chapel moved to what was obviously intended to be the most ambitious religious structure in the new Dominion of Canada. Once again the Gothic style was set down as one of the rules of the architectural competition.[16] The winner, Henry Langley, built the new church in what his contemporaries called the "French Gothic style."[17] The change in the name of the church as it made this short journey is revealing; the church now became the Metropolitan Methodist Church. A truly massive pile, it was indeed a cathedral of Methodism (see Figure 10).

The same pattern recurs with the leading Baptist congregation in the city. In the early 1870s, the members of the Bond Street Baptist Church decided to leave their old neo-classical conventicle for a church that participated fully in the medieval revival. The new Jarvis Street Baptist Church was a substantial Gothic building with a tall spire rising up at the southwest corner of the site (see Figure 11). The interior was arranged in a way that became a model for many Methodist, Presbyterian, and Congregational churches. The pews were arranged in an arc facing the pulpit platform, and the floor of the sanctuary inclined towards this central point. In this way the whole congregation could see the entire religious service. Behind the pulpit platform was a baptistery set in polished marble.[18]

The story of these four congregations was repeated all across the city. In 1875 the Primitive Methodists moved from two older churches, the plain frame Bay Street Church and the more classical Alice Street Church, to the new "Norman Gothic" church on Carleton Street, built by William G. Storm.[19] In 1853 some of the members of Bay Street United Presbyterian Church established themselves as a new congregation at Gould and Victoria Streets, where they asked William Hay, another young and talented architect, to build "a Gothic church with a spire."[20] By 1878 this beautiful Gothic structure had become too small for the congregation, which sold it to the Irvingites (whose views of architecture were quite sound) and moved to a larger Gothic structure built by the firm of Smith and Gemmell on the north side of Gerrard Street at St James Square. Zion Congregational Church had a similar architectural history. The old classical building at Bay and Adelaide was destroyed by fire in 1855, and on the same site was built a new church that had some medieval features but was rather awkward and tentative in appearance. When the congregation, however, built again in 1882, it hired Smith and Gemmell to construct an impressive example of revival architecture on College Street.[21]

The revival was so extensive and inter-denominational that as the city grew, almost every new Protestant congregation built its church on the same scale, using the same basic variations on the Gothic theme. On three of the corners of Allan Gardens for example, there were large and imposing Gothic churches belonging to three different denominations. Around the edge of the city stood a number of smaller Anglican, Presbyterian, Methodist, Baptist, and Congregational churches that evoked a more "rural" parish ethos.[22] Though each denomination modified this style, only a practised eye could identify the affiliation of each church from its external appearance.[23]

In the mid-Victorian period, when the revival was beginning, a new congregation often built either a small Gothic church with a spire (or bell cote) or, if the congregation was larger a more substantial high-Victorian church along the lines of the new Old St Andrew's. A few decades later the small rural church had given way to a more substantial stone and brick building often referred to as "modern Gothic"[24] (such as the Bathurst Street Methodist Church), while the larger-scale church had become a new romanesque "tabernacle." Although the Romanesque style predated the Gothic historically, the medieval associations of the Romanesque (and Norman) allowed this style to become part of the medieval revival. All the main denominations, including the Anglicans, built in both the Gothic and Romanesque variations of the revival during the Victorian period.[25]

The revival came at a crucial point in the development of the architectural profession in Ontario. The aesthetic principles of the new style as well as the technical skill it demanded separated a young group of architects from an older generation of architects and builders, while the high demand for new churches gave their talents a wide field on which to play. Men like William Hay, Thomas Fuller, and Henry Langley benefited enormously from this conjunction of a new religious aesthetic and the high demand for churches.[26] As a consequence, their practices ranged well beyond Toronto, with Langley especially serving a geographically widespread audience. One of the truly great Canadian architects, he built churches for all Protestant denominations in almost every part of the province.[27]

Although some neo-classical churches survived the medieval revolution, church architecture in Ontario had changed dramatically. As the Gothic spread through the villages and towns and as the rate of church construction increased, the revived medieval form came to dominate the landscapes and the streetscapes of Victorian Ontario. Medievalism and church building had become inseparable.

It might be tempting to attribute this change simply to a shift in fashion and the vagaries of international taste, as something analogous to change in the width of a gentleman's lapels. And, in fact, the currents of fashion that played upon the religious architecture of Great Britain, Europe, and the United States in this period also muddied the gentle backwaters of Ontario, leaving behind some interesting imitations of British and European archetypes. But the manner of building churches, like the manner of writing books, changes for substantial and important reasons, and certainly those who witnessed this transformation in architecture treated the change in style very seriously. As they sought to explain the significance of the new church, they specifically rejected the proposition that style was merely a matter of taste. For example, when one of Canada's leading architects, William Hay, analysed what he called "the present revival of Christian architecture," he argued that the new style must be seen as a part of a general social and religious movement. The style of a church reflected religious belief, and for this reason the shift from the neoclassical to the Gothic marked a basic change in the religious character of society.

Like all good critics, Hay understood that real criticism began by telling people how they should look at art and the world: "Christian architecture," he explained in 1853, "is the name given to that peculiar style of building, commonly called Gothic, which predominated in western Europe in the Middle Ages. It derived its origin from the efforts of Christians ... to embody the principles and characteristics of their faith in the structures which they reared for the services of their religion. The name is used to distinguish it from Pagan Architecture [which continues to be] the favourite style for civil and monumental Architecture and until the late revival of Christian Art, most of our ecclesiastical edifices came under this category."[28] Hay was not only challenging the predominance of neo-classical styles but also redefining the meaning of style itself. The form of a building actually embodied and expressed certain social and cultural ideals. The Gothic, he asserted, embodied Christian beliefs and was therefore a Christian style of architecture. Consequently, the choice between neo-classical and Gothic was a question, not of personal preference or social fashion, but of moral and spiritual significance. The difference between these "styles" marked the difference between paganism and Christianity; to choose Gothic was to choose Christianity. In his eyes, and the eyes of many others, the revival of medieval forms signified the determination of religion to proclaim anew a world of spiritual values at the very time when these values were in danger of being lost. In his aesthetic, architectural style and religious belief were inseparable. By building Gothic churches, Hay argued, architects were promulgating the doctrines of the faith and advancing the cause of Christ's kingdom on earth.

In making such an association between Gothic architecture and Christianity William Hay broke one of the great commandments of twentieth-century architectural criticism, committing what later commentators on the revival have termed "the ethical fallacy"[29] – one of the "old and ghostly dogmatisms which effectively darken the counsel of critics."[30] Hay confused architecture and ethics by asserting that a building embodied moral principles that had a direct impact on those who worshipped there and even on those who happened to look at the building. He argued that the quality of a building must not be judged on its own terms and dismissed "value-free" standards that had no ethical component. Since a building embodied and expressed religious values, architecture was a moral system and it was the duty of critics to evaluate the ability of a work of art to embody and convey moral values.

The frequency with which Gothic theorists and builders committed this fallacy is a sign of the popularity and importance of this aesthetic principle. Augustus Welby Pugin, who established many of the basic ideas of the revival, summarized his doctrine in one short sentence. In Gothic architecture "we find *the faith of Christianity embodied, and its practices illustrated.*"[31] Pugin was a convert to Roman Catholicism, and his advocacy of the Gothic style was embellished by the enthusiasm of those who suddenly find a new faith. Somewhat ironically, however, his ideas tended to influence Anglicans and Protestants more than Catholics. The leaders of the Cambridge Camden Society, for example, whose ever vigilant journal, *The Ecclesiologist*, had an enormous influence on both Anglican and non-conformist church architecture, made precisely the same link between architectural form and religious belief. In a Gothic church "the material fabric symbolizes, embodies, figures, represents, expresses, answers to some abstract meaning ... something inward and spiritual."[32] The same theme, the consubstantiality of the Gothic and Christianity, ran through John Ruskin's great work, *The Stones of Venice*.[33] This series of books was perhaps the most popular study of architectural criticism ever written in the English language and undoubtedly carried this moral aesthetic to a wide and broadly Protestant audience.

The conviction that a building embodied and expressed a body of religious and moral values defined the other aesthetic and architectural principles of the revival. Since architecture was a religious lexicon, the best architecture was the one that expresses the finest religion most clearly and truthfully. Since the architecture of the Middle Ages was the finest expression of Christian belief, it was the duty of architects to revive medieval forms. Nineteenth-century architects, therefore, must re-create an old manner of building rather than invent something new. Re-creation became one of the principles of the revival. The *Ecclesiologist* set this down in its first number: "Instead of new designs, ... real ancient designs, of acknowledged symmetry of proportions or beauty of detail should be selected for exact imitation in all their parts, arrangements and decorations."[34] The revival of ancient forms became the *avant garde* of Victorian art; the old was made new.

The same doctrine of moral association helps to explain the architectural principles of "truthfulness" and "purposefulness." Since the sacred dwelt in the actual structure of the church, the construction materials, decoration, and overall design of the church must testify to this "sacramentality." Architects must reject all sham and disguise and avoid the common practice in early Toronto churches of covering brick with plaster to make it look like stone.[35] The church must be "truthful"; brick and stone and wood were acceptable if used honestly; indeed Canadian architects demonstrated very well how wood could enhance the Gothic design.[36]

The decorative effect of the church must also rely on the inherent (or truthful) properties of the construction materials. The variation of brick and stone – the one smooth and regular, the other rough and uneven – or the popular Canadian practice of using bricks of different colours used the "real" character of the material to achieve a strong visual effect. Truthfulness was also achieved by clustering decoration around the essential features of the building, for example, at the arch of a window or at the foot of a vault. Long expanses of wall where decoration had to be "applied" remained relatively unadorned.

The architectural composition of the church as a whole also had to maintain the same principles. Here the external form of the building should express clearly the specific purpose of each part. In Anglican churches the reform of religious architecture stipulated that the outline of the building should differentiate the three most important elements of a church – the porch, the nave, and the chancel. Consequently Gothic architects altered the height of the roof line to correspond with a change in function. In the Cemetery Chapel of St James the Less in Toronto, F.W. Cumberland handled this technique with extraordinary care and sensitivity (see Figure 12). At the west end a low roof covers a porch that extends far enough to shelter both pallbearers and coffin as they wait to enter the church. Above the nave the roof is quite high, while over the chancel the roof continues at a height approximately midway between the low roof of the porch and the high roof of the nave. In this particular church the ground level falls off at the chancel end, so that a door could be placed below the chancel to allow the coffin to be carried out of the church for burial.[37] This new desire for a clearly distinguished chancel led a number of congregations to alter their buildings in order to display this important part of the church more forcefully. Holy Trinity and Little Trinity churches in Toronto, for example, had a general medieval character but predated the full flowering of the Gothic revival. In order to catch up with proper architectural and liturgical practice, the former reorganized the interior of the church to increase the length of the chancel in relation to the nave, and the latter drew up plans to tear out the east end of the church in order to throw out a full chancel extension.[38]

Taken together these aesthetic and architectural principles made a bold cultural statement. By declaring the church to be a house of God, they gave the sacred a distinctive place in the secular world. From this perspective the architecture of the revival was not florid or lavish. What we might now regard as excessive and opulent was seen at that time as purposeful, severe, and chaste. In a very real sense form followed function; every part of a Gothic church expressed the purpose it served. The revival, however, defined purpose and function in religious terms: all of its principles were intended to proclaim the reality and power of the sacred as a force in a secular world.

The Gothic church had yet a higher purpose. The truthful use of materials, the honesty of decoration, and the external expression of internal function not only declared the reality of the sacred, but did so in a way that advanced the cause of Christ. "Do not consider the restoration of ancient art as a mere matter of taste," demanded Augustus Welby Pugin, "but remember that it is most closely connected with the revival of the faith itself."[39] The Gothic was a missionary style of architecture that sought to inspire Christendom by impressing its meaning directly on the heart of the observer. The variation of materials and colours, the alternation of plainness and decoration, the asymmetrical massing of different volumes and forms tried to arrest the eye of the beholder and call up a sense of majesty and awe before the real presence of God. "The men who fabricated those ancient fanes," declared the *Anglo-American Magazine* "could give an expression to the mere exterior outline of their buildings capable of striking awe and wonder into the minds of the rude and unlettered."[40] *The Canadian Architect and Builder* expanded on the same theme: "The form and every part of a church should speak to mortal man of God and immortality." How can a person be inspired with a sense of the sacred if everything in a church "speaks in the coarse and vulgar tongue of his weekly surroundings" A church, "should speak through every stone in its walls of refinement and culture, meekness and courage, and obedience and reverence to the Almighty."[41] The church had a creaturely character, the stones clothed a living presence. Thus the revived forms had a very real calling: architecture could help to win the world for Christ.

When the Gothic revival is understood in this way, it becomes clear that the transformation of the religious architecture of Ontario was one part of a more general cultural transformation that strongly influenced the attitudes and beliefs of English Canada. The new aesthetics of architecture had their counterpart in the nature poetry of the Confederation poets, in the landscape painting of Horatio Walker and Lucius O'Brien, and in the new melodic structure of popular songs and hymns.[42] In all these one can discern the basic elements of the romantic form, a common set of assumptions about the relationship between art, audience, and social and cultural change.

In the Gothic architecture that recalled the religious ideals of the Middle Ages, in the stories set in a lost and more heroic age, in the landscape paintings that tried to portray a fast disappearing rural life, indeed, in the primitive and spiritual qualities that artists and historians conferred upon the rivers and rocks of the Canadian landscape, there was the same passion for recreating a world which stood in marked contrast to the one that was coming to dominate the life of the Victorian age. If the real world was materialistic, the imaginative world was spiritual; if the real world was regular and predictable, the other world was spontaneous and magical; if the real world required the individual to conform to the new routines of life and work, the other world glorified the individual and invested in each person the possibility of living a heroic life. But this attempt to recreate another world was not simply a nostalgic longing for a golden age. For the counterworld of romantic ideals, although set in the past, served as the model for what the real world might become. The ideals of a heroic past were the goals towards which the present must strive. In the romantic form, the past and the future, history and idealism, went hand in hand. Moreover, romanticism offered a way to realize this ideal. The ability of romantic art to inspire and in time to transform the beholder became the very engine of social and moral change. Inspired by the holy values embedded in the great building or noble ruin, the individual experienced a moral awakening and, like the hero of old, set off on a quest to redeem the world.

During the Victorian period the romantic form provided the means of explaining the nature of the new Dominion to English Canadians. The Canada First Movement drew heavily upon Gothic aesthetics and romantic associations. John Ruskin described the Gothic as a northern and savage style of architecture, an architecture of the cold forests that expressed the strivings of a Christian people to overcome the adversities of both human and non-human nature. The imperialists of the Canada First Movement easily transposed these values onto the Canadian north. What had once been an obstacle to economic progress now became a symbol of a new nationality. The savage wilderness moulded and purified this northern nation and made Canadians into a heroic and moral race.[43]

Nationality, architecture, and the romantic form were drawn together by the Canadian poet and historian, Wilfred Campbell when he described the Parliament Buildings in Ottawa:

The ideal of our Western European races was to aspire, to achieve; hence we have evolved our wonderful Gothic architecture, of which the cathedrals of Britain, France, and Germany are the greatest examples.

And herein lies, perhaps, the greatest lesson which our majestic buildings can teach us. For while we speak of them as Canadian, every tower and arch, every buttress and carving, every groin and bastion, every window and doorway is an evidence of the spirit and ideal of our Celtic, Saxon, and Norman forefathers. In these buildings we have as a people, both French and British ... epics in stone, revealing to us not only universal beauty and inspiration, but emblematic of our common ideal, our common artistic sense, our common ancestry, and our common Christianity.[44]

The buildings were "epics in stone" whose moral lessons were embedded in the structures themselves. The Parliament Buildings embodied the social and religious ideals that transcended differences of language and race to bind Canada together as one nation and one people. Romanticism provided the artistic form for a national style, which became so firmly fixed in the Canadian imagination that it continues to inform English Canadian art, literature, and history. Gargoyled images of icebergs, ghosts, and vampires still populate our imaginative wilderness – the natural environment and life are still explained in romantic terms.[45]

II

Why did romanticism have such an impact on Protestant culture in Ontario? After all the movement was not a Canadian creation. It began elsewhere and, as in so many other things, Canadians simply imitated what others had already done: architects in Ontario, for example, often drew heavily upon buildings in Britain, France, Italy, and even the United States. And yet the romantic movement in general and the revival of medieval architecture in particular prospered in Ontario in a way they did not prosper in other places. American architects built many Gothic churches, but the Gothic never rivalled the classical style of the New England conventicle in defining for Americans how a church should appear. Why was the Gothic embraced so passionately by so many groups in Ontario? Why did it become in effect a national style?

Romantic architecture prospered in Ontario because the ideas and beliefs it embodied addressed directly the very real problems that religious institutions faced as they went through the jarring process of administrative, financial, and cultural reorganization. The breakdown of older patterns of culture raised questions that the romantic language of re-creation, inspiration, and moral reform were able to answer. Romanticism also offered the new Protestant alliance a way of speaking to the world that was opening before it.

The romantic form met the needs of both ends of the old religious spectrum. As Methodism moved away from the otherworldly and sectarian extreme and tempered the old-style revivalism with more moderate forms of worship, it needed a culture that maintained a sense of continuity with the past and at the same time did not threaten the expanding structure of Methodist institutions. The beliefs and assumptions of the romantic revival performed these tasks very well. Though the spirit of the Lord was still all-powerful and all-seeing, it no longer moved throughout creation with such abandon, tearing religious bodies apart with its searing emotion. The new Gothic church proclaimed the power of God, but it tied the sacred to the institutions of Methodism and reinforced the authority of the church itself. At the same time, the inspiration and moral regeneration so highly valued by romanticism linked the new culture to the old. God still spoke to a fallen world through the feelings rather than the intellect, through the heart rather than the mind. In this respect the Gothic church was a cultural descendant of the old revivalist camp meeting. But the "religious experience" it tried to evoke had shed a good deal of the emotionalism of the earlier age. The beauty of the church inspired the heart with great thoughts and the mind with noble deeds; rather than striking down without warning and leaving the sinner writhing in agony.

Many Methodists at this time spoke of the close tie between cultural change and the new styles of ecclesiastical architecture. It was in the mid-1840s and the 1850s that church architecture became important for the Wesleyan Methodists. Up to this point their other-worldliness had encouraged them to treat architecture as a purely practical matter, because if God was omnipresent and the Kingdom of God was not of this world, it made little sense to invest much thought or capital in such matters: any building could serve as a Methodist church. Many Methodists also shared a traditional Protestant antipathy to "decorated churches," seeing them as Popish inventions that broke the second commandment. All this, however, began to change. At the annual conference of 1845 the Methodists called for the adoption of standard plans for new churches to "avoid a continuance of the present diversity and sometimes deformity in our buildings."[46] "Some places of worship," the resolution observed, "are specimens rather of domestic than ecclesiastical architecture, and more suitable for dwelling-houses or barns than temples of the living God."[47]

Figure 2 The neo-classical church. Elevation for a church by John G. Howard. Howard borrowed the elevation from Peter Nicholson's *The New Practical Builder, and Workman's Companion*, vol. 2, plate 17. (Courtesy Metropolitan Toronto Library, Baldwin Room, Howard Collection, drawing 309)

Figure 3 The temple of the Children of Peace, Sharon (1825–31). (Photo courtesy Archives of the Newmarket Historical Society)

Figure 4 The meeting house of the Children of Peace, Sharon (1834–42). (Courtesy Archives of the Newmarket Histori- cal Society)

Figure 5 "View in King Street Looking Eastward" by Thomas Young. The neo-classical townscape, York (Toronto), in 1835. Left to right: jail (1824–7), courthouse (1824), St James' Church (1831–3) with the upper part of the tower added by the artist. (Courtesy Metropolitan Toronto Library, Baldwin Room, John Ross Robertson Collection, T 10248)

Figure 6 The Gothic cathedral: St James' Cathedral, Toronto. Cumberland & Ridout, architects (1850–2). (Courtesy Archives of Ontario, Horwood Collection, (750) 1)

Figure 7 Presbyterian neo-classicism: St Andrew's Presbyterian Church, Church Street, Toronto. John Ewart, architect and builder (1830'4), spire by John G. Howard added in 1841. (Courtesy Metropolitan Toronto Library, Baldwin Room, John Ross Robertson Collection, T 10706)

Figure 8 Presbyterian medievalism: St Andrew's Presbyterian Church, King Street, Toronto. William Storm, architect (1874–5). (Courtesy Archives of Ontario, Horwood Collection, (670) 10)

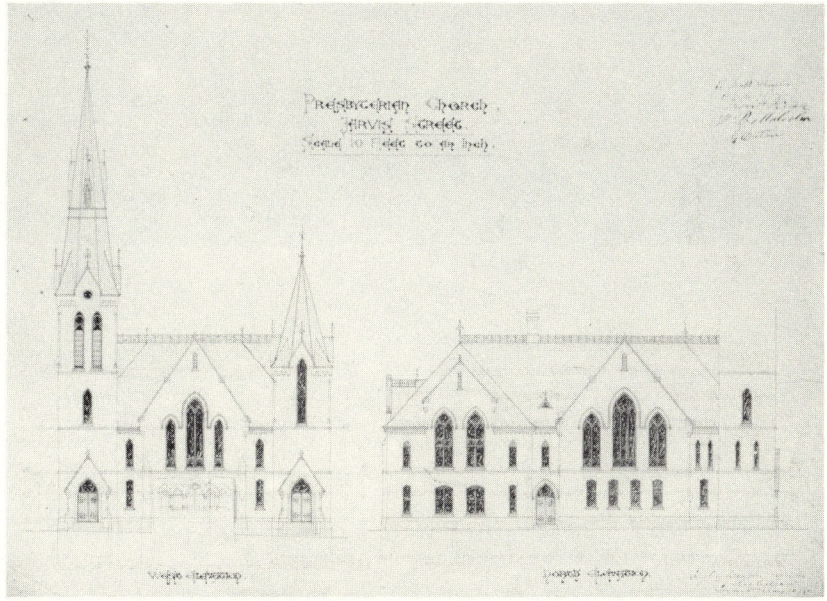

Figure 9 Presbyterian medievalism: the new Old St Andrew's Presbyterian Church, Jarvis Street, Toronto. Langley, Langley & Burke, architects (1877). (Courtesy Metropolitan Toronto Library, Baldwin Room, Langley Collection, drawing 86)

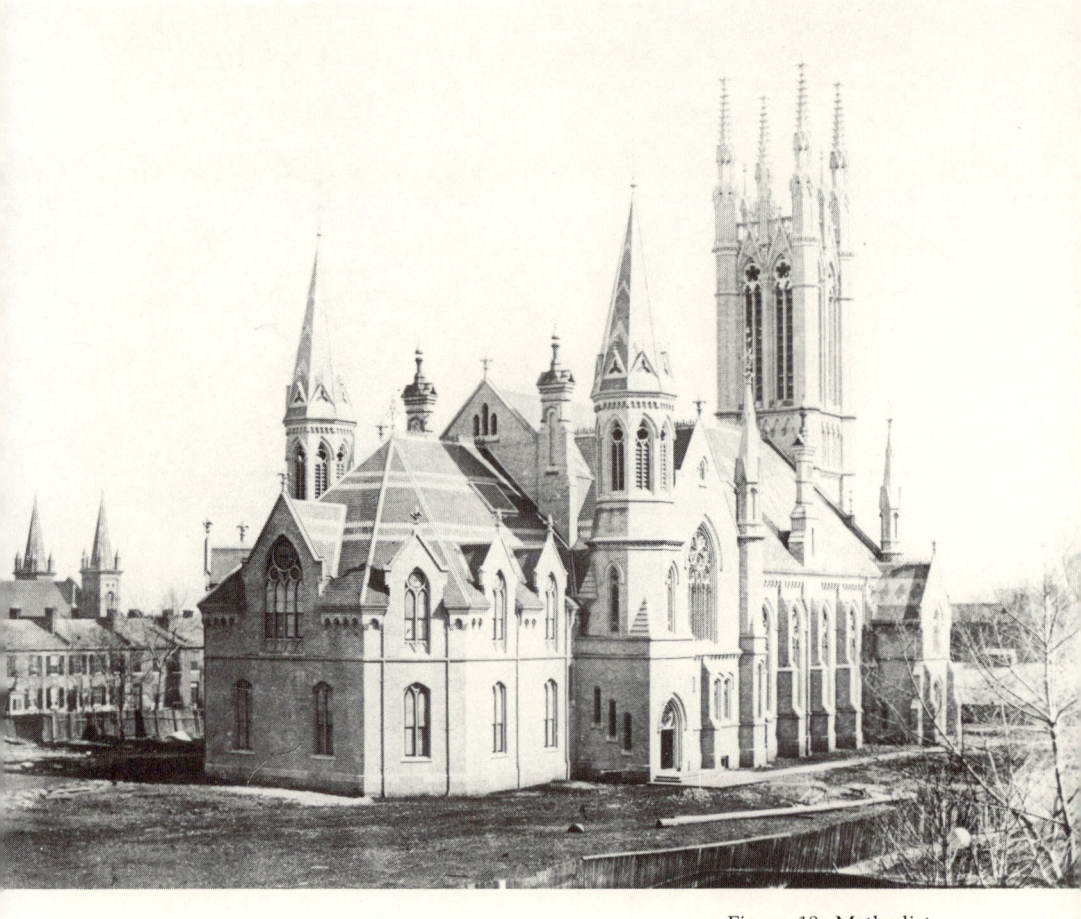

Figure 10 Methodist
Gothic: Metropolitan
Methodist Church,
Toronto. Henry Langley,
architect (1870–2).
(Courtesy Metropolitan
Toronto Library, Baldwin
Room, T 10655)

Figure 11 Baptist Gothic: Jarvis Street Baptist Church, Toronto. Langley, Langley & Burke, architects (1874). Note the neo-classical Bond Street Baptist Church at the bottom of the photograph. (Courtesy Archives of Ontario, Horwood Collection, (599) 1)

Figure 12 The Cemetery Chapel of St James the Less, Toronto. Cumberland & Storm, architects (1860–1). (Courtesy Archives of Ontario, Horwood Collection, (132) 39)

Figure 13 Adelaide Street Wesleyan Methodist Chapel (1832). The chapel is the building in the foreground at the southeast corner of Adelaide and Toronto streets. The spire of St Andrew's Presbyterian Church is visible in the background. (Courtesy Metropolitan Toronto Library, Baldwin Room, T 12418)

Figure 14 The great transformation: the Cathedral of Methodism, Metropolitan Methodist Church, McGill Square, Toronto. (Courtesy Metropolitan Toronto Library, Baldwin Room, T 10653)

Figure 15 The medieval model: St Michael's Long Stanton, Cambridgeshire, England. (Photograph courtesy Professor Malcolm Thurlby)

Figure 16 Following the model: St Stephen's-in-the-Fields, College Street, Toronto. Thomas Fuller architect (1858). (Courtesy Metropolitan Toronto Library, Baldwin Room, 972-1-1)

Figure 17 Adapting the model: "New Baptist Church, Port Hope, CW." Attributed to Henry Langley, bearing signature Langley & Burke, architects (1867). (Courtesy Archives of Ontario, Horwood Collection, (566) 5)

Figure 18 Adapting the model: "Proposed New West Presbyterian Church, Toronto." David Dick, architect (1889). (Courtesy Archives of Ontario, Horwood Collection, (164) 4)

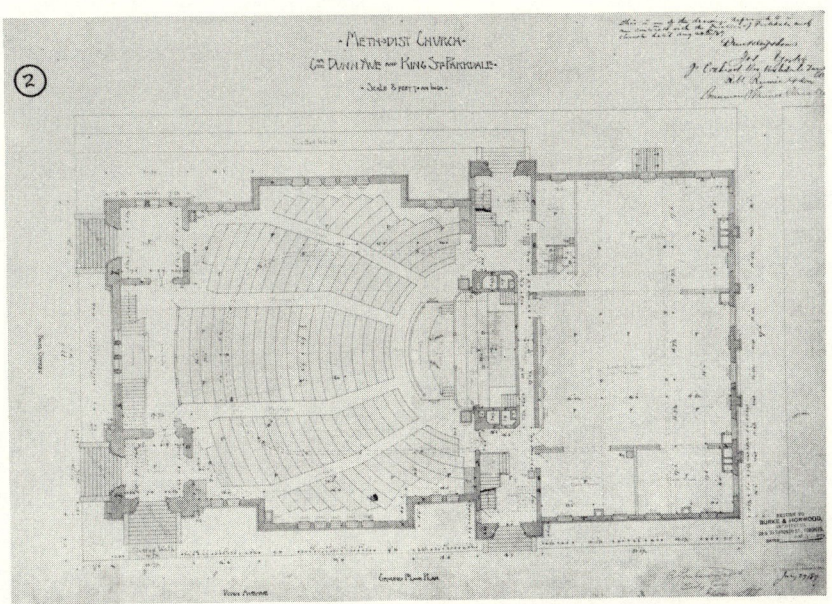

Figure 19 Adapting the model: Parkdale Methodist Church, Toronto. Langley & Burke, architects (1889). (Courtesy Archives of Ontario, Horwood Collection, (532) 23)

Figure 20 "To domineer by its elevation." Bloor Street Presbyterian Church, Toronto. William Gregg, architect (1888–9). (Courtesy Archives of Ontario, Picture Collection, 58111)

Figure 21 The new setting for worship. The interior of Trinity Methodist Church, Robert Street, Toronto. (Courtesy Metropolitan Toronto Library, Baldwin Room, T 10827)

Figure 22 The new setting for worship. The interior of All Saints' Anglican Church, Sherbourne Street, Toronto. (Courtesy Archives of Ontario, Horwood Collection, (972 a) 1)

The same note was struck in the Methodist press. "I confess," wrote an observer of architecture to the *Christian Guardian*, "that I do not like to have a traveller ask, when passing the place where I worship, 'is that a *mill*, or a *barn*, or a *factory*, or what is it?'"[48] The writer went on to emphasize the new importance of religious architecture in words that paraphrased a number of the aesthetic principles of the Gothic revival. "There should be something in the general appearance and impression of the edifice which tells the passer-by, *it is a house of God*."[49] Associationism, inspiration, honesty, and purposefulness all contributed to this new appreciation of the architecture of Methodist churches. "There is more in *association* than most persons are aware of, especially with the young ... The house of worship should be correct in its proportions, neat and tasteful in the manner of its execution; and the interior should be fitted up in a way suited to the purposes for which it is designed."[50] It was also at this time that the official Methodist press began to question the long-standing Protestant practice of equating of decorated churches with the superstitions of Rome. Decoration, the *Christian Guardian* now argued, enhanced worship, for just as the ancient Hebrews kept the Ark of the Covenant in the finest and most elaborately decorated tent, so should congregations now give up their plain meeting houses and build more fitting and beautiful churches.[51]

These architectural and cultural themes were woven together in the dedication services marking the opening of the new Metropolitan Methodist Church in 1872. By this time Gothic was rapidly becoming the dominant style for new Methodist churches, and the dedication of this building – by far the largest and most important Methodist church in the new Dominion – provided a suitable occasion on which to remind a grand audience of the importance of architecture in general and of the new church in particular. Romantic aesthetics informed the hymns, the passages of scripture, and the sermons that filled the series of religious services that dedicated this "Cathedral of Methodism."

An architectural metaphor graced almost every part of the dedication, which began with "Before Jehovah's Awful Throne,"[52] a singularly appropriate hymn for this occasion. A paraphrase of the Hundredth Psalm, it described an awe-inspiring God and concluded with a vision of the future when all would share in the power and glory of God's kingdom. This hope was reinforced by the American Methodist preacher, Dr Otis T. Tiffany, who preached on the first epistle of St John, "for whatsoever is born of God overcometh the world, even our faith."[53] The Rev. John Potts from Montreal made the same association between the new church and the Kingdom of God, taking his text from St Paul's letter to Timothy (a text often used for dedication services) "laying up in store for themselves a good foundation against the time to come, that they may lay hold on eternal life."[54] The same theme was developed by the Rev. William Stephenson from Ottawa, who preached on the second and third verses of the fourteenth chapter of St John. The first of these verses brought together the new church on earth and the kingdom of heaven. "In my Father's house are many mansions: if it were not so, I would have told you. I go to prepare a place for you." The second intensified this association by alluding to the millennial return of Christ the king. "And if I go and prepare a place for you, I will come again, and receive you unto myself; that where I am, there ye may be also."[55]

The most important dedication service in this extended program took place on the morning of 7 April. The lesson was taken from the Eighty-fourth Psalm: "how amiable are thy tabernacles, O Lord of hosts! My soul longeth, yea, even fainteth for the courts of the Lord: my heart and my flesh crieth out for the living God."[56] The sermon was preached by the Rev. William Morley Punshon, president of the Wesleyan Methodist Conference in Canada and one of the great preachers of the Victorian age.[57] Punshon had come out from England in 1868 at the urging of Egerton Ryerson, and his presence at the head of the church contributed greatly to the growing respectability of Canadian Methodism. During his presidency Punshon dedicated many new Gothic churches; indeed men like Punshon and the Rev. Anson Green, a former president of the Conference, led the campaign for the new style.[58] In their eyes the Gothic was the most fitting architecture for Methodism in Canada because here Methodists did not have to live in the shadow of an Anglican establishment. Indeed, as the most numerous and influential denomination in the Dominion, they had become the leaders of an informal Protestant establishment, and the Gothic style testified to this exalted status.

Punshon's sermon was itself an expression of the new romantic sensibilities that were coming to dominate Canadian sermon literature. He took his text from the Hundred and Thirty-second Psalm: "We will go into his tabernacles: we will worship at his footstool. Arise, O Lord, into thy rest: thou and the ark of thy strength."[59] His sermon used a three-part structure: it began with the past by recounting the Old Testament story, then explained the relevance of the story for the present day, and concluded by drawing out the lessons that the text held for the future.[60]

In this psalm, David proclaimed that he would build a temple to honour "the mighty God of Jacob." Such testimony, declared Punshon, "has a special appropriateness to such occasions as that which has gathered us to-day."[61] He realized that many Methodists who still accepted "a kind of domestic Pantheism" felt that there was no need to build special places to worship the Lord, especially "houses made with hands." Consequently, Punshon wanted to use this Old Testament story to explain how architectural beauty could glorify God. If one looks to history, he explained, one sees that David and the Jews believed that God had given "special honours for places which are set aside for his worship." Nowhere does the Bible accept "the idea that all places are equally sacred, or that God has ceased to find his 'rest' in Zion, and to honour its services with his tokens of peculiar regard."[62] Just as the Jews believed that the Ark of the Covenant must have a special place, so in the present day, "the sacred symbol ought to have a sacred home." Therefore, it was most seemly and becoming that these Methodists "have combined to build this house for God. It is costly, it is beautiful. Taste has conceived the design, and skill has wrought the execution; the ideal thought has grown into the stately pile."[63] Although the church was expensive and beautiful, it was not a monument to the wealth and social position of the congregation. The spirit that built it was distinct from the attitudes and values of everyday life, because here wealth and beauty honoured God. With "unfeigned hearts and motives free from guile we have contributed to the setting apart of this divine pavillion."[64]

In the final part of his sermon, Punshon argued that God's presence in the church was an important part of a grand and awe-inspiring design for the future of the world. As he came to a close his words rose to an oratorical climax. The presence of God in the church was a sign that Christians (and Methodists in particular) could create a new world. The sacredness of the church offered a remarkable glimpse of the new moral order that might dwell upon the earth; it proclaimed the ability of God to redeem the world. God was power: "power to bear down the vast and varied hindrances which interfere with the growth of the soul – power to make the wretched happy, and the selfish bountiful, and the whole man a nobler man, rising higher and still higher in divine civilization until he reach the crown of Christian manhood, even the fulness of the stature of the perfect man in Christ. With a firm hold of this strength, how can our zeal be languid and our services fruitless?"[65] The church nobly enrobed the spirit of

God and captured the progressive vision of romantic Christianity: it was a sign of the future kingdom, a part of a new heaven that might transform the old earth.

This new church in itself made a bold statement about the transformation taking place in Methodist culture. Before moving to the new church, the congregation had met in the old Adelaide Street Chapel. Undistinguished by any distinctive religious features, it sat unobtrusively in the Georgian streetscape of the small provincial town and could easily be mistaken for any of the offices and shops on the street. The new church that was built in 1870 just to the north in McGill Square presented a powerful contrast to the old. Its pointed arches and irregular massing of volumes and shapes set it apart from its immediate surroundings, while the high roof of the nave and the soaring tower at the west end raised the Metropolitan Methodist Church dramatically above the buildings that encircled it. A massive presence, the Gothic church looked down majestically and perhaps with a certain foreboding over the secular city below. The Methodists had found a style that captured their own sense of themselves and proclaimed a new image of the church and God to the world[66] (see Figures 13 and 14).

At the same time the establishment side of the old religious spectrum was also being drawn to romanticism and the medieval revival because they helped to solve serious cultural problems. Above all, they helped to give the Anglicans a new identity that did not appeal to the corrupted alliance of church and state. In this case the concurrence of architectural and cultural change can be precisely documented because the transformation of architecture and worship was so radical and the leaders of the church explained the significance of this architectural and cultural revolution in considerable detail.

Unlike the Methodists, who had no style, the establishment churches had begun the nineteenth century with a clear and well-established architectural tradition. The Anglicans and Presbyterians preferred to build their churches in the neo-classical style, which expressed perfectly the ideology and character of these institutions. Both the internal organization and the external features of these churches spoke volumes about that essential cornerstone of the religion of order, the close relationship between church and state. The interior of the church acknowledged the importance of the state by setting aside seats for the mighty – the crown, the senior government officials, and the military. Anglican churches led worthy guests to the chancel from whence they had a good view of the pulpit, which was often directly between the chancel and the nave. In a number of Presbyterian and Anglican churches high box pews, sometimes with tables, were owned (and sometimes occupied) by the well-to-do, while precarious galleries and benches were left for those of lower estate.[67] Externally, the classical lines of St Andrew's Presbyterian Church in Toronto and the early Anglican cathedral harmonized with other institutions of order. The symmetrical proportions of these churches were repeated in the classical forms of the Court House, Osgoode Hall, the Don Jail, and the new lunatic asylum. The architecture of these churches expressed a set of social and religious beliefs that integrated religion and society in a hierarchical social system.

The collapse of the old order forced the establishment churches to change their religious architecture completely. Unlike the Methodists, for whom the Gothic was the first denominational style, the Anglicans and Presbyterians had to reject a well-established architectural and cultural tradition and take up a new one; but in spite of the magnitude of this shift they took up the new style with enthusiasm. Although some neo-classical churches remained – St George's Kingston and St Andrew's Niagara-on-the-Lake are notable examples – the new style transformed the architecture of their worship, and once again the ability of the Gothic to address the problems of the old establishment helps to explain the success and the extent of the revival.

As we have seen, the breakdown of the alliance of church and state caused fundamental problems in the administration, authority and mission of the church. As the colonial and imperial states failed to live up to their part of the old alliance, the church began to search for a way of acquiring and exercising the powers that the state had enjoyed over the church. At the same time the church had to find a culture that did not rely on the rational and utilitarian arguments that had traditionally justified its special place in society. The Church Society and the diocesan synod constituted the church's response to the first set of problems; a judicious selection of ideas from the Oxford Movement helped to solve the second. Both gave the church a new independence that separated it from the state and the type of society the state was creating.

The Gothic revival translated these changes into a powerful set of cultural symbols. In the new romantic art the physical forms of the church actually embodied the sacred and gave the church the power to act as an independent sacred force in a secular world. The historical associations of the Gothic with a distant and more Christian past also affirmed the distinctively religious nature of the church; it no longer had to defend itself in terms of the social benefits it gave to the state. In this sense the Gothic was the architecture of apostolic succession.

Romanticism and architecture went hand in hand: romantic sensibilities provided a fertile ground for the new architectural style while the flowering and propagation of the style sustained and enhanced the authority of the new cultural form. The changing language in the church illustrates this reciprocal relationship. Language is an important measure of how a culture organizes the world, and in this case the new language of Anglicanism indicates both the power of romanticism and the way architecture expressed the values of this culture. In the early nineteenth century Anglican discourse was rational and deductive. Strachan's early sermons, for example, almost invariably followed the same pattern. He set out a general issue, then defined the broad principles that governed the issue, and finally drew from these principles the conclusions that applied to the matter under consideration. The whole form appealed to reason and logic; it was the proper formal equivalent to the principles of the religion of order that the sermons themselves espoused. The form told the story. By the mid-1840s Strachan's language began to reveal a growing attachment to romantic forms as his sentences became longer and more periodic and medieval allusions and historical metaphors appeared more frequently.

The same changes were even more pronounced among the younger generation of Anglican clergy, who immersed themselves in the new ways of speaking and writing. About this time the Society for the Propagation of the Gospel asked the colonial church for articles about Canadian religious life that could help the Society appeal to the public for financial support.[68] Though Strachan was reluctant to write such stories, younger missionaries unhesitatingly offered their services. The Rev. T.B. Fuller (who became Bishop of Niagara) sent the Society a description of a "new stone church of the Gothic order of architecture" that had just opened for worship and that expressed both the new romantic style and the new architectural associations that went hand in hand with the new way of speaking. He organized his account as a narrative of events rather than as a series of premises and deductions; he told a story instead of constructing a syllogism. His words were rich and evocative and drew large, detailed pictures of the setting and the people. He also introduced the type of dualism that was central to romantic art by constructing two parallel series of events, the first secular, the second sacred. The people who acted out the specific events in this new church were also rehearsing another religious drama that imparted a higher moral significance to the scene. There was a story behind the story: while the eyes and mind read the first, the soul and heart read the second. It was the church, both as a building and a metaphor, that drew the two stories together.[69]

The setting of the new church was especially romantic, part way up the side of the escarpment, at the point that divided the civilized world from the primitive world of nature. "Before [the church] you behold the well-cultivated lands of the industrious farmers, and above it the noble trees of our primeval forest." Even though this church had not opened its doors for worship, it nonetheless evoked strong historical associations and inspired religious feelings in all those who looked upon it. The church "boasts not indeed the marks of a thousand years upon its walls; but it looks as if those marks might yet be there."[70] It was set apart "from all profane and common uses, [it was] a place of worship ... a temple blessed ... by the highest officer of Christ's church for the holiest and best purposes."[71] This sacredness elevated the heart of each worshipper. "And when its beautiful tower [was] pointed in its uprightness towards heaven, and it was fitted for Divine worship, the feeling of his heart was similar to that of old Simeon, 'Lord now lettest thou thy servant depart in peace, for mine eyes have seen thy salvation.'"[72] The song of Simeon provided, of course, the very associations that Fuller wished to convey by linking the scene before him to the primitive age of Christianity and placing the opening of the new church within the unfolding of God's plan for the world. As the sight of the infant Jesus fulfilled the promise made by the Holy Ghost to this just and devout man, so too the physical presence of the new Gothic church was a living testimony of Christ's promise to redeem the world.

The association of the new church with the future kingdom drew this remarkable scene to a close. In a long invocation, Fuller again brought the two strands of events together, the present scene foretelling a future one. "I would pray the Giver of all good to grant that all who worship there may worship in spirit and in truth; that all who proclaim the glad tidings of salvation there may be attended with a blessing from on high; that all who enter those courts may enter the courts of God's house in heaven; and that all, who on that joyous day rejoice together, may rejoice forever in the paradise of God."[73] What was taking place here was a preparation for what was to come; the people who worshipped God in this new church might look forward to life eternal. Was this not a glorious benediction?

To incorporate these romantic sensibilities into the physical form of new churches became a major preoccupation of the Anglican Church. As early as 1845 Bishop Strachan had requested the secretary of the SPG to ask the Oxford Architectural Society to provide him "with drawings and elevations of economical churches."[74] Strachan had already received drawings and descriptions of church furnishings and ornaments from the Cambridge Camden Society and read "with pleasure and profit" J.H. Markland's book on churches and sepulchral monuments.[75] *The Church* also began to publish frequent articles on church building that conformed to the aesthetics of the romantic movement. "A Gothic church, in its perfection," one of these articles explained, "is an exposition of the distinctive doctrines of Christianity clothed up in a material form."[76] The Rev. Henry Scadding took up the same theme: "Christianity is being represented to the eye of the world by the visible, constantly-teaching, though silent symbols, of noble and durable buildings ... Let us therefore foster that sacred style of architecture which has been so well introduced among us."[77]

The Church Society of the Diocese of Toronto joined the campaign to medievalize colonial church architecture. The building of new churches had been one of the original mandates of the Society, and as early as 1843 the Society addressed the form these churches should take by establishing a special committee to publish detailed architectural guidelines for new churches. Following the advice of "those persons who [had] bestowed much study on the subject, and [had] a practical acquaintance with it,"[78] the Society published a long list of rules for almost every conceivable architectural consideration – site, churchyard, building materials, external features, internal arrangements, and furniture. In every case the committee's recommendations adhered strictly to the principles of the Gothic revival. A vaguely medieval appearance was not enough, "merely having the arches of the windows and doors pointed,"; churches must be built in an ecclesiologically correct manner.[79]

The rebuilding of St James' Cathedral brought architecture and cultural change together. The old cathedral was scarcely ten years old when it burned down in 1849. Although praised for its beauty at the time of its construction, it had now become in the eyes of the Bishop a "plain" building "destitute of architectural beauty"[80] and thoroughly unsuited as a model for the new church. The new cathedral must be Gothic; it must make a bold romantic statement and serve as a model for church building in the diocese as a whole. These demands were well satisfied by the church that opened for worship in 1853. Although the building did not realize its full effect until it was completed in 1874, the Gothic character of the church and its architectural qualities were readily apparent even in this partially finished state. The height of the nave made the building immediately imposing, and the addition of side porches, tower, and spire gave the church a monumental quality – for many years it was the tallest structure in the city. The cathedral made an architectural statement that was thoroughly fitting for "the metropolitan church of Canada West."[81] The building in fact earned a place in the history of the Gothic revival by contributing to the solution of two architectural problems that puzzled the leaders of the revival in England. The architect, F.W. Cumberland, designed a church that served as both a parish church and a cathedral (a recurrent problem in colonial churches), and also transformed what was in essence a model for a rural church into a large urban structure. In doing so he anticipated many of the ideas of the famous English architect George Edmund Street.[82] The Diocese of Toronto received an imposing church that was at the very forefront of the Gothic revival.

The dedication of the cathedral confirmed the series of changes that had taken place in the Anglican Church. Using a trowell, level, and mallet of Gothic design, the Bishop placed in the foundation stone a copy of the constitution of the Church Society of the Diocese of Toronto, the society that had helped initiate the administrative and financial reforms that had led the colonial church to its hard-won independence and had done much to advance the cause of Gothic architecture in the diocese.[83] It was also fitting that the diocesan synod and Trinity College should receive a memorial inside the new cathedral. The rebuilding of the cathedral, the establishment of Trinity College, and the meeting of the first synod were part of the same transformation. Trinity and the synod constituted an institutional response to the breakdown of the old alliance of church and state. Expelled from the provincial university and the colonial state, the church now had to create its own university and control its own affairs if it hoped to advance the cause of Christ in the world. The new cathedral expressed this new spiritual independence and proclaimed it to the world.

The synod, the college, and the cathedral were brought together in the stained glass windows that were added to the nave of the church towards the close of the Victorian era. Each window depicts a station in the history of the church. The story begins near the lectern with a representation of the Pentecost and continues in the second window with the appearance of the Lord to St Paul on the road to Damascus. The next three windows on each side of the nave depict the beginnings of Christianity among the English people, and the last two carry the story to British North America. The first of these depicts the consecration of the Loyalist Bishop of Nova Scotia, Charles Inglis. The other (the window nearest to the pulpit) carries the story down to the modern age by presenting three events that were of special importance to the Diocese of Toronto and the Anglican Church as a whole. In the centre of this window Bishop Strachan presides over the clergy and laity assembled for the first diocesan synod. Above him are two angels, one holding a likeness of Trinity College (it was also built in the Gothic style), the other holding the ground plan for the new Cathedral Church of St James.[84]

This window imparts a peculiar and distinctive sense of place and time to the building. The walls rise high above, and the mysterious darkness of the church is pierced by the rich light filtering through these scenes. As one stands in the same cathedral being offered by the angel, history seems to have fulfilled the promises that God made to the world: the ideal has become real. The church is triumphant, a living presence, enclosing and protecting a part of the Kingdom of God, a sacred refuge in the midst of a secular world.

III

The belief that the Gothic church actually embodied an ideal faith and could help recreate a golden age gave the Protestant denominations a strong identity and sustained their position as sacred institutions in a secular world. The ability of the Gothic to proclaim the power of the sacred by dominating its surroundings also reinforced the moral authority of these churches. Like a sermon in stone, the Gothic church preached in a language of moral symbols to the society surrounding it. To be effective, however, symbols must be integrated with the life of a culture. However boldly the Gothic made its moral pronouncements, it would quickly lose its power once it became detached from the day-to-day activities of the people who were supposed to be inspired by its presence. Monuments speak in a symbolic language, but not all monuments speak with the same authority. Although Gothic churches were monumental, their enormous power lay in their ability to satisfy the practical needs of the people who worshipped inside them. Since the church was a living institution, the Gothic had to be a living form.

Unfortunately the Gothic was not an especially practical style. Although the aesthetic principles of re-creation and inspiration helped Ontario Protestantism to respond to a cultural crisis, the same principles created problems for the architects and builders who had to translate them into churches that could satisfy specific congregations. In solving these problems, architects adapted the Gothic form in a number of ways; they joined together a romantic sense of place and the religious life of a culture, and by so doing helped to create what became an Ontario architectural style.

The leaders of the revival admonished aspiring architects to follow "real and ancient designs" in every detail. This command to recreate the old defined the basic architectural form of a Gothic revival church. As a specific model for colonial church buildings, the *Ecclesiologist* recommended the parish church of St Michael's Long Stanton, a small church in a village just north of Cambridge (see Figure 15). This building had all the qualities that the leaders of the revival held in high esteem: low-walled and roofy, its exterior displayed clearly the porch, nave and chancel, and in this old village the church as a whole was picturesque and inspiring.

This "real and ancient design," however, did not readily satisfy the religious needs of the Protestant denominations in Ontario. The architectural division of the church into porch, nave, and chancel corresponded to the liturgical traditions of medieval worship in which the chancel was especially important. While the liturgical reforms in the Anglican Church that accompanied the Gothic revival made this architectural arrangement especially functional for this denomination (which in effect rediscovered the religious significance of the chancel), Methodists, Presbyterians, and Baptists found this arrangement of ecclesiastical space neither ideologically appropriate nor especially useful. Chancels, after all, had Romish associations and served no clear liturgical function. These groups asserted that the word of God – in scripture and sermon – must be the focus of worship, and that chancels were not necessary. But if the chancel was simply cut off, the external shape of the building would change and reduce the romantic effect of the church as a whole.

The principle of inspiration created another problem. The aesthetics of the romantic revival demanded that the church make a bold architectural statement by standing out from and in a visual sense controlling its environment. The church at Long Stanton was able to do this because it was not overpowered by the surrounding structures. But Ontario was not Cambridgeshire; medieval sites did not exist in British North America. Here churches had to achieve their romantic effect in a landscape that was being continually altered by rapid economic and social change. Once again, architects had to modify and develop the medieval form in order to harmonize the Gothic revival and the Ontario environment.

All these problems were most apparent in towns and cities. Although a small rural congregation could worship comfortably in a church that followed the rules of the Cambridge Camden Society, and many examples of this simple Gothic form recur throughout rural (and what once was rural) Ontario[85] (see Figure 16), larger congregations in towns and cities found that their own liturgical needs and the cost of urban building placed severe strains upon such "ancient designs." Congregations in Ontario wanted to build for the future by maximizing the seating capacity of new churches while keeping construction costs to a minimum. To reconcile these two competing goals, architects and builders in Ontario often added galleries to the design for a smaller Gothic church. Even Anglican churches adopted this technique in spite of objections from the leading ecclesiological authorities.[86] This innovation tended to make the nave wider and side walls taller, giving the small Gothic church in Ontario an appearance that was decidedly different from its British counterpart.

The Gothic was further modified by the introduction of amphitheatrical seating arrangements in a number of Protestant churches as Methodists, Presbyterians, and Baptists tried to adapt the Gothic form to their own liturgical needs by arranging their pews in a series of arcs that faced a raised pulpit platform. [87] This new arrangement, however, could only achieve very limited success if architects tried to fit it into the long rectangular design of the traditional Gothic church, because the narrowness of the nave restricted the circumference of each row, defeating the purpose of this change. Again the practical needs of congregations forced architects to widen the nave, and the "real and ancient design" began to assume proportions that were more square.[88]

The new seating arrangements forced architects to reconsider the function of the chancel in Protestant churches. Once the seats were arranged around a central pulpit platform, the old chancel in the medieval design became a non-conforming architectural member. But the architectural options were limited: simply to abandon the chancel would remove an essential element of the medieval structure. The answer was to give the chancel a new purpose. Victorian Protestants had a number of administrative needs that the design of medieval churches could not address. During the mid-nineteenth century many congregations required space for Sunday schools, administrative offices, libraries, auditoriums, and kitchens to serve the growing list of church-related activities. Anglicans often built parish halls beside the church, and when these were grouped with the church and the rectory they could form a cluster of ecclesiastical buildings that evoked a pleasant monastic and collegiate ethos.[89] Other Protestant groups approached the problem differently, sometimes putting the Sunday school and offices in the basement of the church, a solution that again increased the height of the building (see Figure 17). The most popular solution, however, was to put all these new rooms in what had been the chancel in the older medieval archetype. The architects reworked Gothic and Romanesque designs so that the part of the church immediately behind the sanctuary wall housed the Sunday schools, the offices, and the auditorium. This at once made the church more functional and maintained (although in altered form) the basic rhythm of distinct architectural volumes so important to romantic aesthetics.[90] In this way the Gothic form became wedded to the religious practice of denominations for whom such a union might first have appeared unsuitable (see Figures 18 and 19).

The religious architecture of Ontario was also shaped by the impact of the external environment on the medieval design. According to romantic aesthetics the church building must make a powerful social and cultural statement. By its size and appearance it must stand out from and control its surroundings: in the words of one of the leaders of the revival in England the church should have the power "to domineer by its elevation."[91] To a certain extent the way architects had solved internal problems helped the exterior of the church to make such a bold romantic statement. As galleries, new seating arrangements, and schoolrooms increased the mass of the building, the large Gothic and especially the Romanesque church acquired a more monumental appearance.

But the power of the church to inspire was also determined by the buildings that surrounded it; for example, a small church in a village might achieve a romantic presence whereas the same church in a large town or city might not.[92] Medieval churches were most effective in medieval settings, but Ontario forced these churches to achieve their romantic effect in a setting that was decidedly unmedieval in its spatial organization. Ontario towns and cities, at least in their early stages of growth, conformed to Georgian principles of town planning, in which building lots, squares, and markets were part of a symmetrical pattern of straight streets giving prominence to such public buildings as town halls and courthouses. Like so many other aspects of classical taste, this urban plan emphasized harmony, order, and balance and affirmed visually the confidence of the age that reason could impose form and order on the world. The classical lines of the first Anglican and Presbyterian churches in Upper Canada were part of the classical aesthetics that had shaped urban space.[93]

The revived medieval style rejected both the aesthetic and social principles of classical design. The Gothic church set out to separate itself from the secular world and dominate its surroundings. In one respect it could use the Georgian character of urban space to its own advantage, because the grid pattern could provide a prominent site for the new church while the low height of the Georgian streetscape could act as a counterpoint to the substantial massing of revived medieval forms. The large Gothic or Romanesque church built on the corner of the old town square (or, like the Metropolitan Methodist Church, on top of the square) illustrates the romantic interplay that could result from the juxtaposition of the Gothic church and the neo-classical town.[94]

But urban space was continually changing, and the townscapes of Ontario did not continue to abide by the principles of Georgian design. Towns and cities grew beyond the limits of their old town plans and incorporated new areas that developed haphazardly, monitored only by the financial interests of real estate promoters and the general habit of setting building lots in a right-angled pattern of intersecting streets. It was this type of urban space that was the setting for countless churches throughout Ontario in the mid-Victorian period. In such towns a street of shops and houses, often of irregular height, could easily obscure the romantic elements of a revival church. Occasionally this problem could be prevented by setting the church apart on a large parcel of land or by building it on a hill or elevation. Such sites, however, were expensive and rare. Consequently, architects in Ontario tried to give more presence to their churches by adapting the towers and spires that were part of the medieval design to this type of urban site.

In the vocabulary of ecclesiology, the spire was a symbol of the resurrection, its soaring height reaffirming the promise of eternal life and proclaiming it to the world.[95] In Ontario the pattern of intersecting streets led architects to use the tower and spire boldly, moving them all around the building to mark a change in function and especially to enhance the visual impact of the church as a whole. The placement of the tower and spire was almost always determined by the sight lines of the streets; the tallest spire, and many of these were very tall indeed, rose up at the principal corner of the site so that the church could stand out boldly when seen from all directions (see Figure 20).

Henry Langley, perhaps the finest church architect in the history of Canada, was a master at reworking the Gothic form for urban sites. The architectural drawings of the front elevations of a number of his churches reveal some of the techniques he employed with such effect to achieve an imposing presence in urban settings. Beginning with a basic Gothic or Romanesque model, Langley arranged and rearranged towers and spires within the general design. When each plan is examined in relation to its site, the reason for a particular composition of towers and spires becomes clear. In every case these features respond to the character of the streetscape.[96] Two specific examples of Langley's treatment of spires (both of which survive) are especially noteworthy. When he designed Jarvis Street Baptist Church in Toronto, he placed a massive tower and spire at the southwest corner of the site and then turned the tower at an angle to the lines formed by the intersection of two prominent streets. In this way the church opened to both the south and the west, and the spire was clearly visible from all four directions, rising above and dominating the streetscape of shops and homes.[97] In Guelph, he achieved a dramatic effect in a different way. Here the site of the new Anglican church terminated the vista of a short but important street running from the centre of the town (where the previous church had stood) to the river. Langley placed the tower and spire of the new church at the precise point where this street could frame the new building and the spire could dominate the street and this part of the town. This architectural statement remains powerful and striking.

As church builders in Ontario modified the archeologically correct medieval forms that they had inherited from abroad to meet the demands of Ontario congregations and the Ontario environment, they created a "Protestantized" medievalism that may have strained the limits of high-church ecclesiological orthodoxy but did not violate the social and cultural principles of the romantic revival. The interior of Protestant churches altered the traditional arrangement, but it was nonetheless "purposeful" and "truthful." The spires may not have conformed exactly to medieval models, but they soared above Ontario towns and gave the church a majesty and presence. And the church as a whole still had the massing of shapes that arrested the eye of the beholder.

The architecture of Protestant worship also expressed a new set of attitudes about religion and society. In pre-revival churches in Ontario, the inside of the church expressed the social and class divisions of that society. In many Methodist churches, for example, men and women sat on opposite sides of the centre aisle; in Anglican and Presbyterian churches the well-to-do owned their own pews, while the poor had to make do with benches or sit in the gallery. Now the organization of worship expressed different religious and social attitudes. In revival churches the principal division was not between rich and poor but between the secular and the sacred. In the amphitheatrical churches, the pulpit platform, which often contained a reading desk, pulpit, and table, received special architectural treatment. Slightly raised above the level of the floor, this most sacred part of the church was given visual power by adding seats for a gowned choir and then setting the whole against a background of highly decorated organ pipes (see Figure 21).[98] The new arrangement of Anglican worship created a similar romantic effect. The chancel and the nave were cleansed of box pews and free benches,[99] and the church divided into two main parts: the nave, which was relatively unadorned, was reserved for the people, whose long pews were undistinguished, at least in theory, by wealth and class, while the chancel was reserved for the clergy and choir. The nave was relatively plain and undecorated, whereas the chancel, introduced by the chancel arch and completed by the altar, was finely appointed. The vestments of the clergy and the gowns of the choir added further adornment to this most sacred part of the church.

The cultural needs of Protestant Ontario provided a fertile soil for the introduction of romantic architecture, but it was the skill of architects and builders in reconciling the medieval design with the demands of the congregations and environment of Ontario that explains the longevity of medieval styles in the religious life of the province. Architects created churches that integrated a rich aesthetic and everyday use, and in the process they defined what was in effect an Ontario architectural style.

This way of proclaiming the place of the sacred in the world gained so much authority that the Gothic was able to transcend the very concept of an architectural style. Style is a plural concept, for if there is one way of organizing art, there must be many others. The Gothic, however, became synonymous with religion.

By clothing the way this society defined sacred space and then placing itself in the midst of the day-to-day life of the people, the Gothic assumed the attributes of the sacred itself. It became the only way to give form to the sacred.

Historians (and many others) who search for things distinctively Canadian lament that they often search in vain. Perhaps the fact that the Gothic was not born in Canada has caused them to overlook what might be quintessentially Canadian. Though the Gothic came to Ontario from abroad, it developed here in a way that it did not develop elsewhere. The cultural crises it had to address and the practical needs it had to satisfy shaped the revival in a distinctive way, refashioning the Gothic into an Ontario style. If historians lament anything, perhaps they should lament their failure to appreciate either the process of cultural formation or the structures that best express the true character of the Canadian culture they seek.

CHAPTER SIX

Progress and Millennium: The Structure of Time

Thus, as the view we take of the Millenium must influence immediately our present action, and the direction of our prayers, it is of the utmost consequence that we hold right views as to its character.

The Rev. James S. Douglas, *The Reign of Peace, Commonly Called the Millenium: An Exposition of the Nineteenth and Twentieth Chapters of the Book of Revelation*

Although the Victorian sense of place encompassed the secular and the sacred, these two "spheres" were not totally separate. The secular and the sacred dwelt together in institutions and indeed in individuals so that the line between them was often blurred.[1] Secular and sacred institutions also attempted to change the environment in which they co-existed. Many Victorians, for example, believed that the course of history would eventually alter the relationship between the two categories, that it might break down the dualism itself.

As we have seen, both secular and sacred institutions were preoccupied with the future. When Lord Durham, for example, described the Canadian landscape in his *Report*, he was obsessed with change and progress:

An almost boundless range of the richest soil still remains unsettled, and may be rendered available for the purposes of agriculture. The wealth of inexhaustible forests of the best timber in America, and of extensive regions of the most valuable minerals, have as yet been scarcely touched. Along the whole line of sea-coast, around each island and every river, are to be found the greatest and richest fisheries in the world ... Unbounded materials of agricultural, commercial and manufacturing industry are there: it depends upon the present decision of the Imperial Legislature to determine for whose benefit they are to be rendered available.[2]

History has proved Durham to have been a keen judge of the ability of simple greed to sustain Canadian life, for economic and social change did indeed become the dominant themes in the secular world of Victorian Canada.[3]

Religion also turned its eyes to the future. Romantic Protestantism believed that human nature and the physical environment must both be changed. It was determined not only to present God to the world but also to prepare humanity to receive the blessings of the Kingdom. This hope for the future was expressed in the architecture of the Gothic revival, which tried to convey a sense of movement from the secular to the sacred and to display in visual terms the means given by God to elevate humanity from one level of existence to the next. "Some Christian people," said *The Ecclesiologist*, "are now in heaven with God, but some are in the world here. Therefore do some parts of the church denote the glory of the heavenly kingdom, while some parts mark Christendom on earth. The *Choir* marketh saints in heaven; but the *Nave* Christian men on earth. The *Altar* marketh CHRIST ... the *Crosswall* which is between nave and choir, marketh the HOLY GHOST; for, like as we do enter into Christendom through faith in CHRIST, so do we enter into the glory of heaven by the door of grace and of the *HOLY GHOST*."[4] In somewhat less exalted language[5] the new styles of worship that were gaining popularity at this time made a similar statement about time.[6] The church as well as the rituals of worship were signposts along the course of sacred time.[7]

The concept of time is a crucial part of all cultures, for every individual, group, and society must have a sense of time that can organize and explain every moment of existence in relation to what has gone before and what is yet to come. The very ability to act in the world demands a structure that can encompass the goals that an act sets out to achieve, and the more distant the goal, the more complex the structure of time becomes.[8] Within a culture the sense of time is not uniform and consistent. Religion and culture attribute special significance to particular moments in existence: at that moment God entered the world, at that moment I was saved. The culture builds on these moments and ennobles them in the myths and stories that give meaning to every individual and group in society.

The answers that the older cultures had given to questions of time again provide an important context in which to analyse the process of cultural formation. The religion of experience had interpreted time with the same sense of immediacy that coloured its understanding of place, bringing the vision of future glory directly before the sinner in the most awful apocalyptic terms: "Repent and be saved for the Kingdom of God is at hand." Every moment in time was at once secular and sacred, and contained the possibility of both timelessness and the end of time itself; the millennium and the end of the world were clear and immediate prospects. The religion of order presented a different vision of the future. It too saw time moving towards a state of blessedness on earth, but its garden of the Lord was not the revivalists' millennium. Upper Canada would not be transformed into the Kingdom of God in a sudden rapture of divine brilliance. Time moved gradually according to fixed principles, and only careful and patient cultivation would transform the secular into the sacred. The sacred future also had many attributes of the present: it was a world of reason, order, and balance that represented the perfection of the gifts already enjoyed by mankind.

The conception of time reveals a good deal about the assumptions and beliefs of the culture as a whole: the way a society explains time also illuminates the character of its culture. For this reason the study of time penetrates to the very heart of the culture. Moreover, time raises the question of the role of culture in the social system. Since social action and social stability demand a coherent explanation of time, a study of time can help to analyse how a society achieves a sense of order and coherence.[9] To put the matter in a slightly different way, if the failure of society to achieve a sense of time leads to individual disorientation and social chaos, then the sense of time that society accepts can reveal the values and assumptions that hold society together.

And yet, however essential a sense of time may be, every conception of time is a cultural creation. Time has no meaning or structure on its own; it only becomes real and coherent in relation to the humanity that gives it form and meaning. Like all elements in a culture, conceptions of time are moulded by the forces that shape and reshape society as a whole. In effect, time is relative. Each particular conception of time, however, must appear to be objective and independent. To organize and explain the world it must enjoy the authority of an iron law of nature, for without this authority it cannot maintain the allegiance of those who use it. Time must appear to provide a standard that is immune to the forces of both time and place. Here again is one of those delicious ironies of cultural history: the very ability of time to change – its ability to reshape itself in relation to the demands of society – allows time to perform a crucial role in a culture and gives tremendous social and cultural power to a particular sense of time. The ability to change explains why time has an aura of timelessness.

In the middle decades of the nineteenth century the structure of time in Ontario was changing very rapidly. Although the Victorian era might appear in retrospect to be one in which there was widespread confidence and optimism about the future, in the years between the rebellions and Confederation there was in fact no consensus about the structure and meaning of time. People disagreed vehemently about what the future might bring, and these disagreements presented a serious cultural problem. The same cultural crisis that we have seen so many times appears in a slightly different form. As society began to shape itself in new ways, the systems of time that had enjoyed a wide measure of support were no longer able to explain either the course of events or the new society that was being created. The world seemed to be moving at a pace that few could calculate and in a direction that fewer still could understand. Many people believed they were living in an era of unparallelled disruption and change.

At such points in history the relationship between religion and time assumes a special significance. Religions play a major role in creating and sustaining a sense of time because they help to answer the questions that people inevitably ask about the meaning of time.[10] What will happen in the future? What is the relationship between what we do now and how we will live in the world to come? Not only do religions answer these questions, but they answer them in a special way. Since religions are a bridge between society and the sacred, the structure of time that a religion sets out acquires an authority no others can enjoy.

Protestant Christianity, especially the type of Protestantism that flourished in mid-nineteenth-century Ontario, seemed particularly well-suited to this task. After all, it was a religion that emphasized the importance of history, interpreting the Bible as if it were a history book with a beginning, a middle, and an end that explained how God both created and saved the world. For this reason it should come as no surprise that when society faced a crisis of time it should turn to the doctrines of Protestantism and the biblical account of time.

It is a mark of the depth of this crisis that the Bible and the Protestant religion had great difficulty in answering the questions of time. People were so unnerved by the events of the 1840s that they interpreted the biblical stories in very different ways: some tried to find in the chaos of rapid change a divine thread of optimism and hope, while others read their Bibles in apocalyptic terms, seeking, as thousands of Christians had done before them, counsel and comfort in the frustratingly precise description of the end of the world in the Revelation of St John the Divine. Looking upon a rapidly changing society they concluded that the world was moving quickly to its awful conclusion. Time, in other words, was about to stop.

Social change and the breakdown of older cultures sparked an intense debate over the character and meaning of time. Eschatololgical questions became important cultural issues. How would the world end? When would Christ return to the earth? In what form would He (or She) appear? In this environment the belief that Christ was about to return to earth was especially significant. When people raised the midnight cry – behold the bridegroom cometh – they also raised the cultural question of time in the most dramatic manner and forced society to explain the meaning of time. The crisis of time generated a debate between those who argued that contemporary events were a sign that the world was about to end, and those who argued that change itself was part of a divine scheme to build up gradually the Kingdom of God on earth. In effect the debate brought what had been unspoken assumptions about the meaning of time to the surface, where they could be seen not only by those who debated these issues but also by those who now seek to understand their historical significance.

I

"Progress," Professor Carl Berger has observed, "was the major certitude of Victorian culture and the extent of progress was invariably measured in material terms."[11] People believed that everything was improving, and they sustained this belief by counting the increase in population, the growing mileage of railway track, and the rising acreage of agricultural production. What began as a description of the recent past was transformed into the first law of history: progress became a principle of social development. The present would inevitably lead on to a boundless and abundant future. Not only the twentieth century, but all the centuries to come belonged to Canada. Looking back on a golden and optimistic age, Professor Berger's statement seems to capture the very essence of the Victorian attitude towards time.

The idea of progress and its place in Victorian culture, however, is more complex than this generalization might suggest. Far from being an exclusively materialistic and secular ideology, the belief in progress encompassed a series of religious ideas that deeply coloured the way Victorians described their world. Two examples illustrate this religious dimension of progress: "In view of what has been achieved in the century of Methodism in Canada, now closing," wrote the Rev. George H. Cornish, "and the foremost position occupied by Methodism in the growing Dominion, may we not expect that by the blessing of God this great Church, with her multiplied and ever-increasing agencies will go forward in the work of winning souls to Christ, and so haste on the millennial glory by His Kingdom?"[12] With these words Cornish concluded his "Statistical Record of the Progress of Methodism," an essay that overflows with a mass of data on almost every conceivable aspect of Methodist life in Canada. And yet the ideas behind his words differ quite markedly from the materialism that often defines the idea of progress. Although Cornish's examples of progress can be measured statistically, they illustrate the handiwork of spiritual rather than secular forces. The building of new churches and the growth of religious institutions were not the same as the expansion of branch banking or the increase in the yield per acre of a new strain of wheat. In his eyes, the "multiplied and ever-increasing agencies" of Methodism were part of the unfolding on earth of a transcendent religious scheme. This sacred progress – the ability to "go forward in the work of winning souls to Christ" – was carrying the world to a glorious conclusion. Time led to "the millennial glory of His Kingdom," a future that was not quite synonymous with unending lines of railway track and an ever-rising material prosperity. Like so many other historians since the beginning of time itself, Cornish was trying to integrate a specific series of events, in this case the first hundred years of Methodism in Canada, with what he and his society understood to be the general structure of religious time. He was trying to incorporate what he saw before him into God's plan for the history of the world.

The popular Victorian hymn, "All Hail the Power of Jesu's Name,"[13] reveals the character of this divine plan for recounting in abbreviated form the stages that lead humanity from sin to salvation. Like so much of Victorian life, the language of the hymn is decidedly romantic. After proclaiming the power of the sacred – "All Hail the Power of Jesu's Name" – the hymn tells the story of creation and the Old Testament covenant between God and the chosen people. The next verse sets out the Christian dispensation of grace: "ye seed of Israel's chosen race/ye ransomed from the fall/Hail Him who saves you by His grace," and the fourth and fifth verses describe the glory of this promise by contrasting the wages of sin and the rewards that await the saved. Both these verses refer directly to the Revelation of St John the Divine. The last verse sings of the glorious return of Christ the King: "O that with yonder sacred throng/We at His feet may fall;/Join in the everlasting song/And crown Him Lord of all."

In this hymn and in Cornish's account of Canadian Methodism, history advanced by clear and distinct stages (or dispensations). It began with creation and the fall when God expelled our first ancestors from paradise. Although the fall separated God and creation, the Lord did not abandon the world completely. In the Old Testament God offered protection to the people and in the New God offered through Christ's sacrifice the promise of divine reconciliation. In the future, mankind might return to the paradise it once enjoyed. From this perspective it is clear that the idea of progress went far beyond the rampant materialism that seemed to dominate nineteenth-century life. Progress was also a religious doctrine that attempted to integrate the events of this world and the promise of happiness and peace given by God to a people who in retrospect scarcely deserved such a gift.

A second aspect of Professor Berger's description also merits closer consideration. Progress might indeed have become a "major certitude" of Victorian culture, but in the early decades of the reign of the young Queen, many people seemed decidedly uncertain about the immediate future. In the early 1840s, for example, the Rev. John Roaf, the leading Congregational minister in English Canada, had no doubt that many people did not accept a progressive interpretation of the course of contemporary events: "Both the Old Testament and the New," he maintained, "point to a state of blessedness on earth. In this respect revelation differs from human systems, which put the golden age at the commencement of our race, whereas it is to be the result of the remedial system of Christ, and to come at the end."[14] Roaf described two different concepts of time, one religious, the other "human," and then argued that in his own day these two systems were opposed to each other. The sacred conception of time was progressive – "the last best state is still future," but the human or secular system was not – the golden age was in the past and history was leading the world away from the glorious state it had once enjoyed.

Roaf wrote these words as he was trying to respond to a major outbreak of millennial expectancy. He raised the question of time because many people in Toronto believed that time as they knew it was about to stop: Christ was returning to earth and the world was about to end. Nor were these people alone in their hopes and fears, for in the middle decades of the nineteenth century millennialism was a powerful and widespread force. According to one historian, "probably well over fifty thousand people in the northern United States became convinced that time would run out in 1844, while a million or more of their fellows were sceptically expectant."[15] The fervour in English Canada matched the excitement on the other side of the line. All along the lower lakes and the upper St Lawrence Valley, millennialists preached their vision of the end of the world to a receptive audience. "Lecturers from the states have flocked into the Province, like swarms of locusts from the desert," wrote the British Wesleyan missionary the Rev. John Tompkins, "and by this combined agency multitudes have been carried away from their respective churches."[16] The Bishop of Montreal was unnerved by "the impetuous flood of fanaticism"[17] that rolled over many villages and towns. Bands of believers wandered through Canada West calling on people to prepare for the end. One of the leading millennialists of the era, William Miller, brought his message to Toronto only a few months before the end was to take place. A large and enthusiastic throng greeted his arrival and responded to his message by rioting in the streets.[18]

In these circumstances Roaf's analysis of the popular conception of time was accurate. Far from believing their age to be one of unrelenting improvement, many people in the Canadas interpreted contemporary events in apocalyptic terms, readily accepting the interpretation of scripture preached by the millennial groups. Devolution and destruction rather than progress and glory marked the course of human history. Recent events were a sign that the prophecies of the Old Testament and the New were about to be fulfilled, as every disaster and plague, every shipwreck and storm, found a place in this prophetic structure.[19] Evil was so widespread that only the sudden return of Christ in a physical form could lead the forces of good and save the world. Only the second advent could arrest the downward spiral of time and usher in the millennium, the reign of Christ on earth for a thousand years (see Figure 23).

Millennialism forms a persistent (and largely neglected) theme in the religious history of Ontario. During the early Victorian period, there were many active millennial groups, a number of which had a strong influence on the religious structure of the province. The Mormons arrived in Upper Canada shortly after their founding, and Joseph Smith himself carried the Mormon message to the province at least twice. Many Upper Canadians left the colony for Nauvoo and the Great Salt Lake, where they helped to establish the Mormon vision of a divinely ordered society. Some of these converts occupied important positions in the church during its formative years; indeed, a former Toronto Methodist, John Taylor, became president of the Mormon Church.[20]

The religious life of the colony was also disrupted by the Catholic Apostolic Church (popularly known as the Irvingites), a movement that began in England under the leadership of a group of very respectable gentlemen, including some bankers and politicians, who became entranced with the spiritual gifts that manifested themselves in the congregation of the Rev. Edward Irving. Irving was one of the most famous preachers of his day and until his apostasy was an ordained Presbyterian minister who occupied the very fashionable pulpit of the Scottish church in London. The Irvingites believed that Christ was about to return to the earth and judge the nations, and by the early 1830s they had brought this adventist message to Canada, where they enjoyed considerable success. They won over a number of prominent Anglicans and Methodists, including William P. Patrick, the same Upper Canadian Methodist who had welcomed the Mormons when they first came to the town of York a few years earlier.[21]

Perhaps the most famous (and disruptive) millennial movement in the early Victorian period were the Millerites. This group took their name from William Miller, an American deist who had become a Baptist after a harrowing experience in the War of 1812. Miller's long and detailed calculations based on certain prophetic passages of scripture convinced him that the world would end in either 1843 or 1844. Although a number of people immediately came to the Millerite standard, the group did not become a powerful force until the Boston religious leader, Joshua Himes, took up the cause. Under his skilful leadership the Millerites prospered and expanded at an amazing rate. The first Millerite camp meeting in North America was held at Hatley in Canada East on 21 June 1842, and soon Millerite preachers were spreading their message throughout the Canadas, establishing adventist newspapers in Montreal and Toronto. Methodism was especially vulnerable to the Millerite message, and a Wesleyan missionary to Canada, the Rev. Richard Hutchinson, became one of the leading figures in the movement.[22]

In the 1860s the millennial crusade was renewed and extended by the Plymouth Brethren. Established in England, they quickly developed an extensive program of missionary work that included large summer meetings in western Ontario near Guelph, which the founder of the movement, John Nelson Darby (a former Anglican), often attended.[23] They were especially successful among Presbyterians in Canada, who found their mixture of revivalism and a modified doctrine of the elect very appealing.[24] This distinctive theology was developed and popularized in the 1880s through a series of Prophetic Conferences, most of which were held in Canada near Niagara Falls and drew large audiences that included many respectable Protestant ministers. At these conferences millennialism was transformed into a conservative theology that defended the literal interpretation of the Bible and attacked almost the entire range of reforms that tried to reconcile the Bible and modern thought.[25] These positions became in turn the cornerstone of a Protestant fundamentalism which gained enormous strength in both Canada and the United States during the early twentieth century.[26]

These groups were only the most visible part of a general religious and cultural movement that included many other "heretical" movements with strong millennial associations. Hornerites, Campbellites, and Perfectionists were active in the province, while groups like the Children of Peace tried to establish utopian communities.[27] Prophecy, visions, and personal encounters with God were an integral part of the religious life of Protestant Ontario. A Mr Russell, for example, who lived near Port Hope, began in the 1830s to receive a series of messages from the Lord. These came to him during such diverse activities as driving a wagon, ploughing his fields, reading at home, or attending Methodist camp meetings. He was told that Christ was about to return to the earth in physical form and that Russell himself was the herald of this joyful event. When he asked when the millennium would commence, the Lord said unto him, "IT SHALL BY NO MEANS PASS THE YEAR 1877; BUT IF THE RIGHTEOUS PRAY EARNESTLY FOR ITS ARRIVAL IT WILL COME SOONER."[28] Russell gathered a large enough following to have his account of these visions published in a small pamphlet for a posterity that, he believed, would not be present long enough to speculate at length upon the meaning of these slender remnants of his beliefs. Given the religious culture of the period, stories such as his must have been common.

Although millennialism is an important part of the religious history of Ontario, it is exceedingly difficult to reconstruct it in detail. Little has been written about the groups in Canada who uttered the midnight cry, and what has been written too often treats them with scorn and amusement. Historians seem to enjoy repeating stories that have little basis in fact and tend to distort the true character of these groups. We are told of people wearing ascension robes waiting on roof tops for the return of Christ.[29] Even the fine work of S.D. Clark has reinforced the outlandish and ridiculous image of these groups. Although he is one of the few scholars to analyse the relationship between sectarian activity and social and economic development, his church-sect typology separates the millennial sects from the more established religious bodies and quarantines the church side of the relationship from this sectarian contagion.[30] The millennium remains outside the mainstream of Canadian religious life.

The evidence that the historian must use to reconstruct the millennial story presents another problem. Since many groups existed for only a short time, they left very few records. Furthermore, as one might expect, those who believed that the world was about to end did not place much value on a proper system of archival management: as these groups passed out of existence, so too did the documentation of their histories. Without a large body of material written by the millennial groups themselves, it is extraordinarily difficult to know who the millennialists were, why they came to be caught up in these movements, how they compared to other members of society, and what became of them when Christ did not return.

The absence of such documentation forces the historian to piece the millennial story together from a different body of primary sources. If few of the records of the groups themselves survive, those of their opponents have withstood the rigours of time quite well. The Anglicans, Methodists, Presbyterians, Baptists, and Congregationalists who suffered under the onslaught of the millennial crusades were assiduous in preserving their past, and their archives are filled with material on the outbreaks of what they regarded as a persistent and threatening heresy. Such documents, of course, must be treated with great care; but beneath their hatred and invective are insights that help us to see millennialism in a more balanced and reasonable manner.

Millennialism must first be set in its proper religious environment: where did this "outlandish and ridiculous" movement fit into the world of Protestant Ontario? If we look closely at the beliefs and practices of these groups, it soon becomes clear that the gap between orthodoxy and heresy was not nearly as wide as the major Protestant denominations would like us to believe. Far from being an outlandish phenomenon, millennialism touched the core of Protestant life at a number of important points. This proximity helps to account for the real success that millennialism enjoyed – millennial groups prospered because they struck a sympathetic chord in many people. This fact also confirms one of the major doctrines of cultural analysis, that heresy gains power and authority because it is so close to what it tries to oppose.

One obvious point of contact is the second coming, which is a very orthodox doctrine. The expectation that at some future time the Lord will come again to judge all nations and transform the relationship between heaven and earth rests upon the authority of scripture and forms an important part of the eschatological doctrines of Christianity.[31] This joyful hope was held by the primitive church and is expressed in the creeds, rehearsed in divine service, and celebrated in one of the seasons of the Christian year.[32] Nor is the fact that the millennial groups tried to predict the exact moment of Christ's return sufficient grounds for branding them all as raving heretics. In the early nineteenth century, interpreting prophecy was a popular Protestant practice. The Rev. William Paley, for example, argued that prophecy was one of the most important evidences of Christianity because the fact that all prophecies were always and completely fulfilled proved beyond doubt the reality of God and the truth of scripture.[33] People often read the meaning of everyday events in prophetic terms. "There is a moral meaning," said *The Church*, "in the day's minutest event."[34] Even that pillar of Anglican orthodoxy, Bishop John Strachan, tried his hand at interpreting the adventist prophecies and occasionally espoused a decidedly apocalyptic view of the future.[35] Adventism did not create the second advent, nor did it invent the interpretation of prophecy. The midnight cry simply imparted a sense of urgency to what were already well established and popular customs.

Millennial expectancy was also fuelled by the attitudes and practices that had made the religion of experience such a popular force. In fact many people at the time pointed out the close ties between millennialism and revivalistic religion. The Rev. Mark Young Stark, a Presbyterian minister in Dundas, who watched in horror as the Millerites broke up a number of congregations around the head of Lake Ontario, attributed their success to the ability of millennial preachers to feed upon a popular religious culture that demanded excessive emotion and extreme doctrines. "Where there is no check upon opinions and preaching is too often a mere tirade, he who can propound the newest and strangest doctrines has the greatest chance of hearers and consequently the best hope of recompense."[36]

Stark's comments suggest a number of other links between revivalism and millennialism. Revivalistic techniques played directly into the hands of adventist preachers. Methodists, for example, subjected the prospective penitent to a veritable onslaught of emotion, telling preachers to "preach for a verdict," to cast everything into the categories of good and evil and to sustain a high level of emotion by cataloguing the pains and punishments that awaited the unrepentant at the latter day.[37] Repent and be saved, for the Kingdom of God is at hand. Even the Rev. Stark, who was scarcely a revivalist, employed these rhetorical techniques.[38] Millennial preachers simply built on these foundations, using emotion and repentance to their own advantage. The technique of dividing the world into good and evil and commanding true believers to come out of a fallen world was extraordinarily well-suited to the millennial cause. How easy it was to increase the emotion of the call to repent before it was too late by confidently predicting the very moment at which the end would come.

Millennialism and revivalism also saw the universe in the same way. As Jerald C. Brauer has shown, millennialism was revivalism writ large. It used the conception of God and creation that underlay the revivalistic interpretation of individual salvation and applied it to the structure of society and the world at large. The personal struggle with evil became the cosmic battle between the forces of Christ and the forces of darkness; sudden redemption became the sudden return of Christ; individual perfection became the millennial garden that encompassed the whole earth.[39]

An account of the conversion of a Canadian Methodist to a millennial sect demonstrates the close ties between millennialism and popular religious culture at a more personal level. In 1832 the Rev. George Ryerson, Egerton's elder brother, was in England on official Methodist business when he heard the preaching of Edward Irving and soon converted to the Catholic Apostolic Church. It is easy to speculate about the forces that turned this prominent member of the first family of Canadian Methodism against his former faith, but Ryerson's own account of his conversion makes it quite clear that he did not believe he had forsaken Methodism. Rather, he emphasized the links between his new faith and his old religious loyalties. The preaching of Edward Irving had given him the type of religious experience that a good Methodist always sought. His eyes were now opened to the true meaning of the world: "I have never in my life," he wrote to Egerton, "been shut up to walk in all things by simple faith than I have for some months past, yet I was never kept in greater steadfastness of power of mind nor had such openings of the spirit of the life of Jesus in my soul."[40] The Biblical passages that had been so mysterious were now perfectly clear; a new light had chased away the darkness. The Irvingites, in effect, fulfilled the religious expectations that Methodism had implanted in his soul, but now the experience of conversion told him to leave the Methodist Church, and he called on Egerton to follow his example, to give up politics, Methodism, and his attacks on the Irvingites "lest you be found fighting against God."[41] Egerton chose not to follow that advice, but he did attend an Irvingite service when he visited London in June of 1833. He was not especially impressed by the service, although he found Irving a fascinating and charming person.[42]

And finally, there was the matter of the Antichrist. Millennial rhetoric portrayed the last days as a great and bloody battle between the forces of good and the legions of the Antichrist, a battle in which the armies of the Lord would be arrayed against the great beasts and the infamous whore of Babylon. In the millennial lexicon these figures had a very specific meaning, representing most often the Roman Catholic Church and the Pope. Though all this might now seem ridiculous in the extreme, anti-Catholicism was one of the great staples of popular Protestant thought, and such associations would have been accepted by many Ontario Protestants as the gospel truth. The *Christian Guardian*, for example, after ridiculing many aspects of Millerism, praised the movement for attacking the Pope and trying to stem what it saw as the rising tide of Catholicism in Ontario: Miller's strictures on Popery were "not mere declamation, but the alarming truth."[43]

The close ties between the millennialism and Protestantism help to explain the success of so many of these groups. Methodist ministers offered their pulpits to Millerite preachers because they did not find anything heretical in Millerite doctrine.[44] Methodists who left their church continued to see themselves as good Methodists even after they had been cast out for heresy,[45] while those who had expelled them were not especially confident about the actions they had taken. In 1834, for example, the York Station Chapel expelled four Methodist class leaders for teaching Irvingite doctrine. The local Methodists, however, took great pains to acknowledge the "blamelessness of their lives" and prayed for their speedy return.[46] Nor could the Anglicans quite bring themselves to abandon one of their clergymen, the Rev. Adam Hood Burwell, who left the priesthood of the Church of England to become an Angel in the Church of God. Burwell was a member of a very prominent Loyalist family from the western part of the province. A well-

educated man and a gifted poet, he advanced quickly in the colonial church and became the protégé of the Bishop of Quebec.[47]
But about 1836 he became "irregular in his doctrines"[48] and joined
the Irvingites, and his name was struck from the list of SPG
missionaries. Yet Burwell believed he was still an orthodox Anglican and continued to describe himself as an Anglican missionary,[49] while *The Church* continued to publish his letters,[50] and even
Bishop Strachan spoke of him more with regret than condemna-
tion.[51]

If the millennial "heresy" was so orthodox, why were the millennial groups such a threat to the more established religious
groups? The answer to this question can be found in the way
millennial groups reworked and rearranged the ideas and practices that they borrowed from the general Protestant culture. Although they shared a good deal, the millennial groups put the
material together in new ways. Millennialism was like a mirror
to the dominant religious culture; the image it captured reversed
the elements it reflected. Thus millennialism functioned as a
counterculture to the religious world that the major religious groups
were creating.[52]

The way millennialism interpreted human action is a good
example of this countercultural quality. When the Methodist leader,
Anson Green, confronted the Irvingite Adam Hood Burwell at a
missionary meeting in Bytown, their argument centred on what
role Christians can play in God's plan for the world. Green interpreted social change and human action optimistically; Burwell
did not. "He told us," Green recounted, "all our efforts to convert the heathen were in vain. The world was growing worse and
worse, and would continue in its downward course until Christ
came and dashed his enemies to pieces as a potter's vessel."[53]
The resignation expressed by Burwell is a vivid contrast to the
heroic individualism that was coming to dominate Protestant attitudes towards the world. Methodists, Anglicans, and even Presbyterians championed the ability of individuals to alter the course
of history, indeed to redeem the entire world. Millennialism took
the same materials and created the opposite doctrine, greatly re-
ducing the field of human action. Individuals could prepare for
the end of the world, but they could not control the course of
history; they could try to put their own house in order and tell
others to do likewise, but time itself was in the hands of God.
People gave up their jobs and farmers let their crops rot in the
fields as they awaited the coming of the Lord.[54] The beliefs and
practices that millennialism shared with most Protestant groups

made it easy for many people to join the various millennial groups, while the fact that these groups could rearrange many of these beliefs and practices allowed them to offer a coherent alternative to the dominant culture for those who sought refuge from the new world.

All this leads one to speculate upon why so many people left the Protestant churches and moved into the counterculture of millennialism. Without detailed biographies of the people who were caught up in these movements,, it is difficult to know why millennial groups, which had always existed, became so strong in the 1840s and 1850s. Nonetheless, those who had first-hand contact with these groups offered a long list of social, economic, and religious reasons for their growth. They singled out the absence of well-established religious institutions, especially in the newly settled areas of the colony, the economic dislocation and financial panic that gripped the colony in the late 1830s and early 1840s, and poor harvests, bad weather, and even the poor state of the roads that added to the distemper of society. They also spoke of the unsettled state of Canadian politics and religion, especially the battles over responsible government and the disruption of the Church of Scotland.[55] All the reasons have a common theme: in each case the growth of millennialism is linked to social and religious change. In fact, the millennialists and their opponents agreed that the disorientation created by social change was at the root of millennial success. "Are not the nations being stirred up against true religion by infidelity, popery, and puseyism?" asked the Rev. John Roaf. "There is a strange delirium of society arising from the disturbance of vital principles."[56] The Canadian sociologist, S.D. Clark, has also emphasized the relationship between social change and the growth of millennial sectarianism, arguing that the shift from church to sect marks both the character and pace of social change. In the 1840s and 1850s Canada was expanding so rapidly that the dominant religious and social institutions were not able to control the social dislocation created by this growth. The rush of social and economic development left a vacuum in which sectarianism grew and flourished.[57]

The cultural changes taking place at the same time undoubtedly contributed to the inability of religious institutions to respond to social change. Traditionally, religions serve as a beacon that guides society through the storms of uncertainty and change; in times of crisis people turn to religious institutions in order to understand the problems they face. But in the 1840s and 1850s these religious institutions were themselves changing very rapidly. People looked to their churches for the "vital principles" that they so desperately needed only to find that the churches had abandoned many of their old principles as they redefined their culture. The guiding light of religion did not shine very brightly.

This sense of social and religious disorientation was preyed upon by millennial groups. The Catholic Apostolic Church, for example, appealed directly to those who did not accept the changes taking place in the old establishment churches. Adam Hood Burwell attacked the growth of democracy and the voluntary principle and argued that disestablishment and the proliferation of new religious groups were clear signs that the end of the world was near.[58] He asserted that his own ideas were consistent and orthodox; it was his own former church, in trying to accommodate itself to the new society, that was flirting with heresy. Given the way the old establishment had seen itself and the world in the early 1830s, Burwell may well have been correct.

At the other end of the religious spectrum the Millerites appealed directly to those who still accepted the old-style religion of experience. As the Methodists moved towards the centre, they left behind many people who were not prepared to give up their religious traditions and who fought hard to stop the trend towards moderation and respectability. The close ties between revivalism and millennialism[59] made this group especially receptive to the midnight cry. How easy it was to follow the Millerite call when this group seemed to embody the traditions that Methodism had abandoned.

The changes taking place in the Presbyterian Church also help to account for the success of the Plymouth Brethren. As evangelicalism became a dominant force in the church, Presbyterianism modified the old doctrines of primitive election and justification by faith alone. It now emphasized the religious value of good works and held out the hope that a sustained program of missionary endeavour could win the whole world for Christ. The Brethren successfully appealed to those who still accepted the old orthodoxy.[60] The elect, justified by their faith alone, were most likely more comfortable in the new sect than in the old church.

All these examples show how millennialism was fuelled by the process of religious change. The ground was shifting. People did not necessarily abandon their old faith and take up the millennial cause; many simply stood still while the religious structure moved around them. What some regarded as new and outlandish, others regarded as orthodox and thoroughly acceptable. New heresies were, in effect, old orthodoxies.

The impact of millennialism, however, only increased the sense of crisis that had given it birth. Although the millennialists themselves may have taken solace in the prospect of the Lord's sudden return, millennialism as a social movement was an extraordinarily disruptive force. The prediction that the world was about to end was in itself rather unsettling, especially for those not fully assured of their place in the Kingdom to come. More provocative still were the specific instructions that accompanied this powerful prophetic message. If the millennial groups had simply preached the end of the world, they would not have threatened the social and religious order so seriously, but when they attacked the existing religious institutions, they became an enormous problem.

When millennialism sounded the midnight cry, schism and disruption inevitably followed. At first millennial groups often tried to work within the existing religious system,[61] but as the hour of Christ's return drew near, they increased the intensity of their preaching, dividing the world into the saved and the damned and calling on the saved to come out of the fallen world. At this point the millennialists turned their message against the churches that had often helped them. In their eyes the fallen world now included not only the unrepentant (and of course the Catholics), but also the Methodists, Anglicans, Presbyterians, and Baptists. Even the most fervent and evangelical members of the Protestant churches were numbered among the forces of darkness, flourishing within the ample recesses of the whore of Babylon.

All the major religious groups in English Canada suffered from the devastating impact of the millennial call. The expulsion of four prominent Methodists from the York Chapel in 1834 – William P. Patrick, Thomas Vaux, William Warren, and Joseph Easton – threw the local Methodist meeting into confusion.[62] The apostates quickly established an Irvingite congregation to which they welcomed George Ryerson when he returned from England. Egerton was extremely worried about the influence of "the Bay Street folks."[63] Certainly they were persistent and successful; George was elevated to the rank of Angel and led a large and respectable congregation for many years. The Anglicans also had to contend with the Irvingite disruption. The parish of Hull, where Adam Hood Burwell was a missionary, was deeply divided by Burwell's decision to become an Irvingite, and Kingston, where Burwell next turned his energies, suffered a similar fate.[64]

The Millerite "madness" was even more intense and widespread. "Thousands in our own country are deceived by this sophistry," wrote the *Christian Guardian.* "Many members of our church ... are carried away by these delusions."[65] Wesleyan, New Connexion, and Methodist Episcopals were all shaken by the Millerite prediction, the Episcopals suffering an especially serious loss when several "local preachers fell in with Miller's views of the Second Advent."[66] Wherever the Millerites set foot they received an enthusiastic welcome. Whole congregations were caught up in the movement. On Good Friday 1843, the day on which many believed the world would end, the large throng that filled the Methodist church in Beverly, Canada West, were "all in commotion." The Rev. George Ferguson described the events in his journal: "The house was crowded and as soon as liberty was given they would rush to the altar from all quarters. I never saw so much disorder and confusion in any meeting."[67] Similar scenes took place when the Millerites appeared in Picton, Brighton, Oshawa, Bytown, and Toronto. Looking back on the period, the Rev. John Carroll singled out Millerism as one of the most disruptive forces in the history of Methodism in Canada.

Millennialism created two problems. First it threatened religious institutions. The call to come out of Babylon tore individual congregations apart, carried ministers out of their churches, and reduced the strength of missionary and charitable institutions. Millennialism had a devastating effect on the institutional structure of the Protestant churches, which bore the brunt of the onslaught. The second problem was more intellectual and cultural. The expectation of Christ's immediate return raised the question of time. When would the world end? What could be done to prepare for this awful event? According to contemporary accounts the prospect of the end of the world caused many people to abandon the routines of their daily existence and adopt a watchful inactivity in secular and sacred affairs.[68] The two problems were closely related – the millennial groups were able to disrupt religious institutions because they presented an interpretation of time that appealed to many people. By the same token the Protestant churches had to provide their own interpretation of time in order to stop the destruction caused by millennialism.

II

The Protestant churches responded to the millennial threat in a number of different ways that at times went well beyond the bounds of Victorian propriety. The churches ridiculed the predictions of the millennialists, expelled those who had gone over to the enemy, and bitterly attacked the leaders of the movement, often accusing them of immorality. But to meet the challenge they also had to develop an alternative explanation of the events that were at the root of the outbreaks of millennial enthusiasm. When the Rev. George Ferguson saw the "disorder and confusion" the Millerite predictions had created, he wrote in his diary, "I saw it necessary to state our views and feelings."[69] The Protestant churches as a whole had to do the same thing. Individuals and congregations, societies and nations had to be able to understand the meaning of time. Organized religion had to answer the important cultural questions that the millennial movements asked so forcefully.

Many of the charges against the millennial sects were so distorted, unsubstantiated, and misleading that one doubts seriously if they discredited the millennial cause in the minds of the general population, although some historians have unfortunately accepted these charges at face value. Any testimony that undermined the respectability and moral authority of the millennial leaders and their followers received wide circulation: the books of Mormon were nothing more than a fraud;[70] millennial leaders were corrupt and dishonest;[71] the people who became millennialists were simple-minded and gullible fanatics[72] – witness the disappointed watchmen with their ascension robes untested by flight returning home by the light of a dawn they had expected never to see.[73] The churches also dwelt on the morality of the relationship between converter and converted on the night preceding the latter day. Thinly veiling its innuendo behind the parable of the wise and foolish virgins, the *Christian Guardian* speculated on the pleasures that accompanied the wedding feast. "Christian churches were broken up in the excitement. Christian ministers left their flocks and ecclesiastical associations to trumpet the doctrine in the ears of slumbering virgins."[74]

It is likely that these attacks had little effect on those who had already left the churches because many of these people believed it was the old churches, not the new sects, which had lost their doctrinal purity and moral authority. One would also expect the millennial groups to have high and rigid moral standards, especially in view of the immediacy and the terror of the judgement they so vociferously predicted. Presumably they would have been much more concerned with moral probity than those who believed that the time for repentance was considerably more generous. Indeed, if one reads the evidence carefully, the same people who attacked millennialism also acknowledged that millennialism raised, at least initially, the moral and religious character of the con-verted.[75] It should also be pointed out that although there is no clear evidence that millennialism went hand in hand with dishon-esty and licentiousness, it is very easy to document the recurrence of these vices among the clergy of the Protestant groups who cast the first stones.[76]

A more substantial problem for the millennial movement was caused by the course of time itself. The failure of the affairs of the world to be wound up at the appointed hour did not help the groups that had staked so much on their ability to predict the moment of truth. The Millerites in fact had to face this prob-lem a number of times. When their prediction of April 1843 proved unsatisfactory, they went back to their sources and calculated a new date, 22 October 1844. Once again as the hour approached, the excitement reached extraordinary heights, but once again the end failed to adhere to their timetable. Undaunted, they tried again – one account gives a new date of 12 October 1861[77] – but the fact that the world remained twice unburnt seriously weak-ened the group as a popular force.[78]

The religious press, of course, turned the failure of time to its own advantage. "Figures are stubborn things," commented the *Christian Guardian*. "Christian time would not yield, Jewish time will not. What then? Doubtless Chinese time will be tried for true chronology!"[79] Time had baited the trap for all the millennial groups preaching the immediate return of Christ. The ultimate test of all millennial predictions was whether or not they came to pass. When God was not seen at the appointed hour and time continued its normal course, the entire millennial movement began to collapse. The strong empirical and experimental qualities of Protestantism that had helped millennialism to flourish also prevented millennialism from achieving permanent success.

The failure of these predictions offered another line of attack to the movement's enemies. The Protestant press was quick to claim (needless to say, *after* the end had *not* come) that millennialism did not increase evangelical spirituality but rather caused people to reject religion altogether. Some people had committed themselves so thoroughly to the adventist message that when Christ failed to appear they gave up not only millennialism but all forms of reli-gion. "When the End did not come [many people] threw away their Bible, saying they would believe it no more."[80] What began as a religious awakening concluded in irreligion and insanity.[81]

But the success of these counterattacks was limited. The Rev. Anson Green unwittingly demonstrated one of the primary weaknesses in this position. After attacking the Millerites and describing with horror the disruption they had caused, he admitted, "Some of the arguments of Miller, Himes, and Letch were very plausible, if they could only have proved that they had the correct beginning, or starting point."[82] To ridicule inaccurate predictions while still accepting the practice of calculating the hour of Christ's return most likely strengthened millennialism, since any reasonable person would conclude that the problem did not lie in the practice of predicting the end of the world but in the difficulty of predicting the end accurately. One should keep at it until one got it right.

The close ties between millennialism and the major Protestant denominations presented similar difficulties to the attackers. It was hard to ridicule millennial sects when one agreed with them on so many points. The Methodists for example, attacked the Irvingites for stressing so strongly "the workings of the spirit," and pointed out how a faith rooted in such highly charged religious experiences could lead easily to antinomianism. Adam Hood Burwell made a simple but effective reply. Did not Methodism believe in religious pluralism, did not Methodism believe that anyone could set up a religious organization? Since the Methodists had established the principle of religious free trade, could not the Irvingites enjoy its benefits? Moreover, how could Methodism possibly attack the workings of the spirit?[83] Was this not the doctrine that defined Methodism? Burwell was cutting very close to the bone.

Methodism must have felt the same discomfort on several other occasions. In September 1843 the *Christian Guardian* made one of its frequent attacks on the Millerites. After criticizing the "Second Advent Men" in a variety of ways, the writer gave what he must have felt was a damning critique of this religious enthusiasm. Millerite preachers were "uneducated," preaching "with more zeal than knowledge or discretion."[84] What a choice of words! Certainly they must have stuck in the craw of many Methodists as they mouthed them silently in disbelief. Here was Methodism playing the part of Strachan, while the Millerites took the part once played by the young Egerton Ryerson. In attacking millennialism, the Methodists found themselves attacking a reincarnation of their former being.

As long as Protestantism provided a fertile ground for the growth of millennialism, disruption and the threat of disruption continued. The ties between the mainstream and the sectarian edge were so strong that many Canadian Protestants must have awaited 22 October 1844 with trepidation. The persistence of this threat demanded that Protestantism distance itself from these millennial groups, but to do so it had to attack the root of the plant by offering the wavering Canadian Christian a coherent and positive alternative to the adventist interpretation of scripture and the millennial organization of time.

At the centre of the millennial message was a common set of beliefs that form a consistent pattern and on which all the groups tended to agree, in spite of other differences on minor points. The world was in the last days, the prophecies that foretold the conclusion to this phase of history were now being fulfilled, and the millennium was about to begin. In the words of a Canadian millennial newspaper, *The Voice of Elijah*, the earth would soon be "restored to its Eden state as it came from the hand of its Maker before the fall."[85] The millennialists also believed this new era would be introduced by the sudden return of Christ, who would reign with the saints over the new kingdom. At the end of this thousand-year reign the final judgment would take place.

Since the leaders of the Protestant churches readily acknowledged that contemporary events could be interpreted in prophetic terms and that in time the Kingdom of God would be established on earth, none of them was prepared to attack the idea of the second advent and the millennium. When the Rev. John Roaf began his long and detailed analysis of the millennium, he proclaimed unequivocally his faith in Christ's return to earth: "I am a believer in the Second Advent as much as any of my neighbours."[86] Even though the Millerites threatened his own congregation, Roaf and his fellow Protestant clergy realized they could not attack the millennium itself. Instead they concentrated on the nature of the millennium and the forces that would bring about this glorious state. Most millennial groups were "pre-millennialists"; that is, they believed that the second advent would precede the millennium and that it would begin as Christ returned to the earth in a physical form. He would reign upon the earth for a thousand years and then judge the nations for the last time. Here the pre-millennial exegesis ran into some rather sticky theological problems. As many Protestant leaders quickly pointed out, this interpretation was truly adventist in that Christ seemed to be leaving and returning to earth several times. He had come in the past to save the world and would come again to usher in the millennium. Then He would come a third time at the final judgement. This interpretation also seemed to reject the basic Christian belief in the sufficiency of Christ's sacrifice. Christ had come into the world to save sinners and his death was the propitiation for the original sins of our ancestors. To argue that another physical coming was necessary to bring about the millennium was to argue that the crucifixion was not enough, that grace had its limits since Christ had to come again to finish what he had failed to accomplish on the first attempt. Millennialism, a Methodist writer argued, was wrong because it denied "the gospel its own prerogatives and power; it [overthrew] the economy of grace."[87]

What then was the correct interpretation of the Biblical passages that provided the scriptural foundation of the entire millennial movement? The Book of Revelation described an earthly millennium in no uncertain terms and stated clearly that Christ will reign on earth for a thousand years:

> And I saw an angel come down from heaven, having the key of the bottomless pit and a great chain in his hand.
> And he laid hold on the dragon, that old serpent, which is the Devil, and Satan, and bound him a thousand years,
> And cast him into the bottomless pit, and shut him up, and set a seal upon him, that he should deceive the nations no more, till the thousand years should be fulfilled: and after that he must be loosed a little season.
> And I saw thrones, and they sat upon them, and judgment was given unto them: and I saw the souls of them that were beheaded for the witness of Jesus, and for the word of God, and which had not worshipped the beast, neither his image, neither had received his mark upon their foreheads, or in their hands; and they lived and reigned with Christ a thousand years.[88]

Since all agreed that the Bible was the word of God and must be interpreted literally, these verses had to be explained, they could not be simply dismissed out of hand or treated as so fanciful and symbolic that the specific words and phrases were unimportant.

It was, however, quite possible to believe in the millennium and still reject the pre-millennial interpretation of time. Since Christians already had the power to convert the world, there was no need for Christ to return to the earth before the millennium. The second advent therefore must refer to the final judgement and must take place after the millennium, not before. In short, the leaders of Ontario Protestantism formulated what has become known as the "post-millennial" interpretation of the second advent, arguing that the millennium is the logical conclusion to the dispensation of grace and that Christ in a physical form will return only at its conclusion.

In keeping with this approach, Protestantism then made a crucial distinction between a *physical* and *spiritual* reign on earth. Since Christ would not return to earth in a *physical* form until the end of the millennium, the passages that described Christ's reign on earth must refer to the *spiritual* presence of Christ. They described a thousand-year period in the future when the principles of Christianity would be supreme; the risen Christ, in a physical form, would not be present. Roaf underlined this important word. "If his *principles* be general on earth," he explained, "if his laws be paramount in governments, and churches, and families, and individuals, will he not reign here?"[89] The *Christian Guardian* drew precisely the same conclusion when it attacked the Irvingite interpretation of the same Biblical texts: "We therefore conclude that the Kingdom of Christ is a spiritual kingdom on earth, which is to be carried on through the instrumentality of God's holy spirit ... and also by man's own free will. This is the plan laid down by Christ, and to be duly attended to by his church to enlarge and spread our Messiah's kingdom through the world."[90]

If the second advent of Christ was put at the end of the millennium and if the millennium was defined in spiritual rather than physical terms, then the social and cultural implications of the millennium were entirely different. The immediate effect was to temper the apocalyptic nature of Christ's immediate return. Time was not going to stop; Christ would not appear in a sudden flash. The millennium was no longer a radical departure from the basic Christian scheme of human history, but the logical and inevitable result of Christ's own sacrifice. If Christ had given the world the possibility of saving itself from sin, then the millennium was the triumph and fulfilment of this promise.[91]

The post-millennial interpretation also emphasized the value of human action in helping to bring this era of peace and joy to earth. The millennial sects, on the other hand, believed that the course of time was beyond human control since God had ordered human history. Indeed, the Millerites assumed that the exact moment of Christ's return had been set down in scripture by the Old Testament prophets. Consequently, the scope for human action was severely limited: one could prepare for the end, but one could not influence the time of its arrival. Deeply embedded in this attitude, which the *Christian Guardian* termed "passive obedience,"[92] was a pervasive scepticism about the world and the possibility of social reform. The world was evil and getting worse, and only the immediate return of Christ could arrest the decline and usher in a new and different age. There was no point trying to improve the world. An individual could do nothing to change the course of cosmic events, and whatever one might do in this world had no value because this world was about to come to an end.

It was precisely this resignation and pessimism that so unnerved the Rev. James S. Douglas, a Presbyterian missionary who tried to combat the threat of millennial sectarianism: "It is not the future, then, in itself, we must consider, but the influence the future ought to have over our present conduct." The millennialists argued that "Christians should keep quiet, and sit still, till Christ should come for the destruction of all his enemies, and the salvation of his saints."[93] But the millennium was a time when Christian *principles* would extend over the earth, and every Christian and every Christian institution had a vital part to play in the unfolding of this divine scheme. Scripture, said Douglas, "calls us to be up and doing, while it is called to-day."[94] If people devoted themselves to working towards Christian goals, they could help to bring about the spiritual reign of Christ on earth.

The post-millennial interpretation also redefined the arrival of the millennium itself. According to the millennial sects, God would appear suddenly and the present world would immediately end. But now the millennium became a more gradual and measured event that would occur in stages as human beings completed certain tasks. Immediate change and divine intervention, although possible, were neither necessary nor likely. The millennium would grow gradually as Christians converted the world to Christ. "It is requisite to bear in mind that the Millennium is a moral event, and however rapidly it come on must be brought about gradually."[95]

The specific "moral means"[96] that these people believed could transform the earth into the garden of the Lord were the "preaching the Gospel, ... the efforts of private individuals, ... the pious attention of parents and the heads of families to the salvation of their households, ... the zeal of the teachers of youth, [and] the improved demeanor of civil rulers towards the cause of Christ."[97] In the millennial debate we see the moral and social issues that were coming to dominate Ontario Protestantism. Here in a new setting was essentially the same list of moral and social issues that John Strachan had proposed as the basis of a new Protestant alliance that would combat both modern infidelity and the dangerous advances of the Church of Rome.[98] In fact, the vision of an earthly spiritual kingdom added a new urgency to this alliance. By linking these "moral means" to the fulfilment of God's plan for the world, what began as a common set of social and moral attitudes became an all-encompassing messianic mission. If the Protestant religion informed the minds and hearts of individuals and society, not only Upper Canada, but in time the whole earth, might become the dominion of the Lord.

III

The Protestant critique of the pre-millennial interpretation of the second advent was not especially original. In general, orthodox groups have always responded to millennial enthusiasm by arguing that the millennium will take place in the distant future and will be more spiritual than physical. The leaders of Ontario Protestantism used words and ideas that had been used before. But as we have already seen, old phrases and ideas can assume new meaning when placed in new contexts or combined in new ways.

The millennial excitement focused upon the question of change, a fact readily acknowledged both by the sects and by their opponents. It was social and religious change that gave such power to millennial expectancy, and it was the same changes that the millennialists and their opponents tried so hard to explain. The former saw change as a sign that the world was lost, the rapid succession of riots, plagues, earthquakes, and other disasters foretold the destruction of the existing order and the immediate return of Christ. The latter made social change an integral part of God's plan for the world.

In one sense, change has always been a staple of the Christian economy of salvation. Christianity calls on sinners to accept God's saving grace, throw off their sinful inheritance, and receive the blessings of everlasting salvation: God makes all things new. The post-millennial conception of time, however, gave this command an added meaning by transforming an account of individual change into a doctrine of social development. The changes that took place on a personal level provided an analogy for explaining the more general phenomena of change in society as a whole. In the same way that individual change was a sign of the workings of God's grace, so too were changes in the world a sign that time was moving towards its spiritual destiny. If monitored and controlled properly, change could help to establish the Kingdom of God on earth. The post-millennial arguments did not reject change, nor did they call upon the people to turn their eyes away from the world and focus upon purely spiritual kingdoms; instead they incorporated change and the world directly into their conception of history and their vision of a future earthly paradise.

Nowhere is this optimistic view of social change more evident than in its interpretation of the significance of modern technology. The forward march of time and history were confirmed by new inventions, especially new forms of transportation which, ranked alongside the building of schools and churches, seemed to offer irrefutable proof that the world was improving – the more rapid the pace, the stronger the evidence. Who could have imagined, wrote one clergyman, that "so much could have been accomplished in so short a space of time? Churches, schools, governments, sciences, arts, commerce, conveyance and communication have advanced so rapidly in Britain, America and other countries, that we almost fancy ourselves to have been transported to a new world."[99]

Technology and change also fulfilled religious hopes and expectations in a more profound manner. Protestants took these forces as a sign that God was returning to humanity the attributes of the divine that it had lost at the fall. In paradise Adam and Eve had lived in harmony with God and the natural world, but God punished Adam and his descendants by taking away their ability to control the natural world, forcing them as the wages of sin to struggle continually against human and non-human nature. But if the goal of this struggle was to overcome the fallen nature of humanity through the grace of God, could not the growing ability to control and master the natural world be seen as a sign that society as a whole was realizing this sacred goal? If God had taken away the mastery of nature at the fall, the fact that He was returning this mastery might prove that He looked with favour on the current course of the world. Technological change was then a divine reward for moral improvement. As society continued to improve, God would continue to reward society by returning even more power to the people. "By this means," wrote the Rev. James Douglas, "the human mind will delight to understand God's works and ways; and God will teach him to know how to regain that dominion over all creatures, of which satan deprived him, by seducing him to sin into bondage to himself. We see that much has already been regained by man in this way; of which his power over water, air, steam, electricity and light may be specified as examples. And who can tell how far this newly acquired power may ultimately be carried?"[100] The answer of course was implicit in the question. If technological change was a sign of secular and sacred improvement, social change must be leading the world towards the creation of the millennial kingdom on earth.

It was to be a millennium of a very special kind, for the kingdom would be distinguished, not by the physical presence of Christ, but by the reign of Christian principles on earth. It would come about not in a single, sudden and cataclysmic event, but in a slow, gradual evolution. This process would occur not through a divine power acting alone, but with the active participation of ever increasing numbers of Christians, whose moral lives would shape the course of human history and help fulfil God's plan for the world.

This conception of time makes an important statement about Protestant thought in the mid-Victorian period. It eroded even further the radical other-worldliness that had been a mainstay of Protestant sectarianism in the early nineteenth century. Groups like the Methodists who had called upon the saved to come out of an evil world now dwelt on the positive characteristics of the world they had once rejected. In this sense post-millennialism marks another phase in the process by which Methodism moved from one extreme of the religious spectrum to the middle ground it occupied so firmly by the mid-Victorian period.

This conception of time also helped to redefine the way Protestantism interpreted salvation. By tradition Protestants understood salvation as an intensely individual process; after all they had rebelled against Rome because the Pope had tried to place himself and his priesthood between the individual and God. Even camp meetings were essentially individualistic affairs. Though God might come to many people at the same time, salvation still entered each person separately. Now, however, though Protestant churches continued to emphasize the individual, they also began to address more directly the place of Christianity in society. Since the character of a society was one measure of progress towards the millennium, the ability to improve the moral character of society went hand in hand with the ability to attain this religious destiny. The redeemed now saw many social problems that were crying out for immediate religious attention, and their determination to reform the world sustained the participation of both the individual and the churches in the secular world. A strong and highly institutionalized form of religion took strength from the belief that such an organization was helping to fulfil the course of history; the vision of a moral millennium ran through the vast array of missionary societies, temperance organizations, and in time the social gospel.[101] Though the churches were not social agencies in the modern sense, they were no longer the type of religious bodies they had been at the start of the century. The moral millennium was an important link between the old religious preoccupation with the sins of the individual and the later Victorian interest in the moral and social reform of society.

This conception of time also helped to answer the important cultural questions being asked by Protestant Ontario. For the battle between the sects and the churches was in essence a battle over the meaning of time itself and in arguing about the end of the world, each side was expressing a different view of the relationship between how one acted in the world and the course God had set down for history to follow. The belief that triumphed – that moral action in a secular world could lead to a glorious future state – reveals a number of important features in the emerging patterns of Victorian culture.

In the early Victorian period, the Rev. John Roaf argued that in the minds of many Canadians sacred and secular time opposed each other. Whereas religious time was progressive, secular time was not. According to the Bible the best state was yet to come, but in the popular view the golden age was in the past. Undoubtedly the fact that the pre-millennial sects could draw on this popular attitude explains a good deal of their success: the course of human affairs was so bad that only the physical return of Christ could break this pattern and return the world to the harmony and peace it had once enjoyed in a garden long ago. Although the popularity of these attitudes cannot be measured statistically and Roaf's generalization remains a generalization, the basic structure of the pre-millennial argument forms a long and persistent theme in Canadian intellectual life. From that day to this, many groups have argued that the present is evil and time is carrying us away from a golden age in the past.[102]

The response to these black prophecies offered a different interpretation of the relationship between secular and sacred time. Post-millennialism integrated the secular and the sacred within a progressive and evolutionary framework. Though the secular and the sacred were still two distinct categories, they came together in the idea of progress, with the secular now seen as a stage through which society advanced on its way to the sacred. "The affairs of the world," wrote John Roaf in 1844, "are only a scaffolding by which the building of God's church is reared."[103] Later in the Victorian period, the Rev. Alexander Miller, a Presbyterian minister in Huron County, made exactly the same point: "The material is an introduction and a help to the spiritual ... Heaven, as the coming age, is reflected here even as the new dispensation was embedded in the old."[104] Material events – the affairs of the world, the lives of the people, and the host of events that were shaping and reshaping Canadian life – became integral parts of the progress of secular and sacred time. Well before the publication of Darwin's famous works (let alone their arrival in Canada), the belief that time was progressive and that the character and evolution of the material world were signs of progress had become important features of the Protestant interpretation of time.

Even change and disruption, the very events that sparked the outbreaks of millennialism and confirmed in so many minds that human history was not progressive, acquired a progressive meaning. New inventions, new discoveries, and the rapid pace of change were carrying the world towards Christ and His Kingdom. "Jesus Christ is being travelled to in this forward movement; and when this will come to be more realised, then the prayer for his second advent will come to have more significance in it, and will come to be more articulate, united, sincere, and heart felt ... Common humanity is becoming common Christianity."[105] Technology and change were carrying society towards the millennium. In Canada railways not only drew the country together, but also carried the nation to a higher level of existence.

In this way time brought together the two categories through which Victorian culture tried to understand and interpret existence. By the mid-nineteenth century the duality of the secular and the sacred was coming to dominate the way Victorians defined people, society, and the environment. If the railway symbolized the secular world, the Gothic church testified to the presence and power of the world of the sacred. It was the concept of time that joined these two elements. The secular introduced the sacred; if properly monitored and controlled, secular progress led directly to sacred conclusions, and for both the golden age lay in the future; indeed the secular and the sacred would eventually come together at the same time and at the same place - during the millennial reign of Christ here on earth.

With this progressive framework firmly in place, the forces of organized Protestantism worked diligently to alter the popular conceptions of time. The more Protestant ministers preached upon the new Kingdom, explained the rewards awaiting those who followed God's will in their daily lives, and explained in detail the specific ways to advance God's plan for the world, the more this progressive view of time became embedded in the mind of society. Progress, to quote Professor Berger once again, did indeed become "the major certitude of Victorian culture."[106]

But however pervasive the belief in progress may have become, millennial sectarianism did not disappear from the cultural landscape of Protestant Ontario. Though progress held out the prospect that secular time led on to sacred goals, when some people looked at their world it was by no means clear to them that history had chosen to follow the course laid down for its guidance by the ideology of progress. The disjunction between ideas and events continued to create many cultural problems as individuals and groups continued to search for other ways of interpreting time and place.

Both post- and pre-millennialism were systems of ideas for organizing and explaining the past, present and future. Time after all has no structure, and history and prophecy have no meaning when detached from the humanity that has created them. Both systems of ideas were cut from the same cloth and both set out to answer the same eschatological questions. But one of them interpreted time in a gradualist and progressive manner, while the other believed that time was about to end in a sudden cataclysmic event.

In the light of this paired but antithetical relationship, the tensions that arose between explanation and what needed to be explained led to a predictable result. Many people found in the progressive organization of time an interpretation that described to their satisfaction the world that surrounded them. Others, finding that optimism and progress did not explain the course of time or the meaning of existence, embraced the pre-millennial account of time, as so many had done before them. They rejected the dominant cultural form, entered the counterculture of Victorian Protestantism, and sought solace and refuge among the dark shadows that the very brightness of progress had cast across the face of the nineteenth century.

CHAPTER SEVEN

With Confident but Questioning Hope

Boundless are the possibilities of the future upon which the eyes of Canada are now fixed with confident but questioning hope.

Charles G.D. Roberts, *A History of Canada*

There is a basic human need to give order and meaning to life. In all times and places people have woven ideas and beliefs together and told and retold stories, to help them understand themselves and their world. Though the process of creating a culture is a universal human endeavour, every culture is unique because it is shaped by the diverse social forces that have influenced the course of history in so many different ways. Culture is universal, but the language of cultures speaks with a special resonance for a particular group at a particular place and time.

In the middle of the nineteenth century a variety of materials were reforged in the fire of new circumstances and problems into a new culture that provided a young colonial society with a way of interpreting a rapidly changing world. As we have seen, it defined a sense of place and time that helped to organize and give meaning to existence and in doing so the culture itself became an important element of the social system and in this capacity served a number of vital social functions. Culture not only gives society a way of perceiving the world, it also shapes society in many important ways. What then was the place of Protestant culture in mid-nineteenth-century Ontario society? How did it shape the character of Protestant Ontario?

To analyse the social function of this culture, we must return briefly to the process of cultural formation, identify the specific functions that culture was called upon to perform, and then examine how the culture tried to address these tasks. These issues invariably carry the conclusion of the study into the realm of prophecy. As cultures explain the world, they attempt to define the future; by their nature they link the past and the present to goals and ideals that have not yet come to pass. Culture (and history) are in this sense open-ended and have no conclusion. This fact also raises a number of tensions because culture offers society an interpretation of the future it cannot fully understand. The imperfection of humanity necessitates our search for understanding, but it also prevents us, at least in this dispensation, from finding it.

I

At the beginning of the nineteenth century, Upper Canadian society disagreed on a number of important religious and cultural issues, with each of several different religious groups espousing its own interpretation of the nature of God, the world, and salvation. The difference between the religion of order and the religion of experience indicates the deep divisions in the religious structure of the colony, and without a common set of religious beliefs Upper Canada was not able to establish a unifying culture.

As the religious and cultural structure of the colony began to change under the pressure of internal and external forces, the religion of experience realized its central tenet was a source of weakness as well as strength. Though a direct and overwhelming religious experience might be a powerful weapon against sin (and competing religious groups), it also made this religion less able to grow and prosper. Experience might win countless souls to the cause of a truly living God, but it could not keep the saved in a permanent religious structure.

The religion of order also faced a crisis. This religion was built on a close alliance of church and state in which both institutions were supposed to work together to advance the cause of Christ and the King by restraining human passions and reshaping society in keeping with a common social and religious ideal, and in which both tried to create a harmonious, hierarchical, and well-ordered social and religious system. It was this world of reason, harmony, and reciprocal obligation that began to collapse in the 1830s, leaving the old establishments in a religious and cultural crisis of enormous proportions. These internal problems were closely tied to larger social and economic changes. The new state, in its determination to reorder Canadian society along capitalist lines, broke the old alliance of church and state, thereby creating a host of new problems that religion had to confront. Materialism and development drove religion into a separate sphere, where it stood on its own and tried to address the social issues of urbanization, immigration, and class tensions created by the new state. The same social forces led the other end of the old religious spectrum to abandon the other-worldliness that had dominated its attitudes towards society and politics. In the early nineteenth century, the religion of experience had radically divided the existing world from the world of God, in large part because the existing world favoured a system of religion that seemed intent on attacking the followers of the true God. Sectarianism, however, declined as the state stripped away the exalted status and the temporalities it had bestowed on the establishment. Now Methodists could enter the arena of society and politics and work to change the world they had once rejected.

As the Methodists entered the world and abandoned their excessive emotionalism, they became a much more tolerable group in the eyes of their former adversaries, who in turn were able to appeal to the Methodists because they no longer claimed the privileges that had contributed so largely to their exclusiveness in the past. These internal and external forces broke down the walls of religious division and opened the way for a long period of Protestant co-operation. The new era of denominational harmony sustained a common body of religious and cultural beliefs as the old and conflicting cultures were slowly transformed into a common Protestantism. The extreme emotionalism of the old-style camp meeting began to give way to more moderate forms of worship, and Methodist thought and practice came to be dominated by a rather moderate form of romanticism that allowed the church to incorporate feelings and inspiration into its theological and institutional structure. If romanticism gave the Methodists a way to moderate and control the intense emotionalism of the old-style religion of experience, it also gave the old establishmentarians a way to break out of the ordered, reasonable, and rational world of their eighteenth-century inheritance. It imparted a strong emotional appeal to what had been a rather dry religious style and offered the church a new historical definition at the very time it was rejecting the doctrines of utilitarianism and expediency. The romanticism of the sacred, now embodied in the doctrine of apostolic succession and in the trappings of the Middle Ages, gave the church exactly what it was seeking. This cultural change carried the Anglican Church towards the common meeting ground of Ontario Protestantism. It was becoming a self-governing and self-sufficient Victorian denomination, much like the other religious groups which had journeyed a considerable distance to reach the same place but from a different direction.

The new culture of Protestant Ontario shaped the materials it had found into a distinctive and consistent form. Three aspects of this form are of particular importance, especially for what they reveal about the functions this culture served in mid-Victorian society. First, the new culture interpreted the world through an almost limitless series of paired categories, all of which turned on the distinction between the secular and the sacred.

The division between the secular and the sacred is of course as old as humanity itself and can be found in almost every religion and culture including both the older cultures of the colony. The religion of experience had made a rigid distinction between these two categories; indeed, the suddenness and emotionalism of the conversion indicates the stark contrast that sectarians made between these two concepts. The religion of order had also used this duality, but here the two worlds often came together, the very structure of the world reflecting the mind of a rational and divine intelligence, even though the sinfulness of human nature might obscure this fact.

The romantic culture that succeeded these older cultures rejected the distant and other-worldly associations of the sacred that were so much a part of the religion of experience, but maintained the two distinct categories that the old religion had so forcefully proclaimed. It also rejected the sense of harmony and integration that was such an important aspect of the religion of order, though it retained the belief that the sacred was an important component of the social world surrounding the individual. In effect, the new culture introduced the dualism of the secular and the sacred into the immediate environment. It was given simultaneously a distinct and separate character and a presence in the world. This presence ennobled the institutions of Protestant Christianity and was embodied in the religious practices and architecture of Protestantism. Protestant culture in Ontario proclaimed the power and reality of the sacred in a secular world.

A second characteristic of the new Protestant culture was its attempt, during the middle decades of the nineteenth century, to draw the sacred and the secular together through a distinctive interpretation of time. Christianity, especially Protestant Christianity, has always attempted to resolve the dualism that defines its very nature. The old revivalism believed that a sudden and dramatic transformation would usher in a new heaven on earth, whereas establishments built their ideal worlds more slowly and were careful to keep heaven at a greater (and much safer) distance. The social and religious order that the earth should imitate had divine attributes, but heaven itself was not part of this world. Now Protestant culture became caught up in the vision that the secular could be transformed gradually into the sacred and heaven brought within the grasp of those on earth who worked diligently for its coming. The dream of revivalism was tempered by the more deliberate pace of organization and development. Time, if properly marshalled, could resolve the dualism and lead the secular world towards sacred conclusions. Christianity has always proclaimed the power of grace to change evil into good; now Ontario Protestantism applied this concept to the categories that organized reality. It divided everything into two worlds, which it then brought together; Ontario and indeed the whole earth would become the garden of the Lord.

A third element of the new culture was its belief that strongly motivated individuals could convert the world to Christ, thereby reconciling the sacred and the secular. A number of millennial groups argued that the world was about to end in a sudden and cataclysmic event as God intervened directly to bring the secular order to its awful conclusion. Since time and history were in God's hands, humanity could do little to influence this divine drama. The intellectual and institutional crisis created by this interpretation of time forced Ontario Protestantism to emphasize not only the gradualness of change but also the power of Christian men and women to carry history to its appointed destiny. By working actively through the institutions of the Protestant churches, these people could save society. Since the task of redeeming the world fell almost entirely upon these Protestant crusaders, everyone could be a romantic hero.

But how could people be persuaded to take up this great moral crusade? How could religion not only save the individual but also motivate the newly redeemed to go out and save the world? The romantic form answers these questions. The new culture relied heavily upon the power of inspiration to speak directly to the heart of a people; it tried to capture and present the sacred in a way that would inspire the individual to put on the armour of God. The power of the eloquent sermon, the majesty of the noble cathedral, the poignancy of the great event could transform human nature by inspiring people to put aside self-interest and dedicate themselves to the higher goals of a sacred calling. Protestant culture, in effect, tried to institutionalize romantic individualism, believing that art and religion could transcend reason and self-interest. It relied upon a highly romantic appeal to impress a grand system of moral ideals directly upon the heart of a society.

The institutions of Ontario Protestantism, which carried this culture to a wide and receptive audience, influenced many parts of Ontario life. The division of the world into the sacred and the secular sustained the popular custom of dividing up people, institutions, and life itself into distinct and contrasting spheres. The conception of time as a series of gradual and progressive dispensations enabled Canadian historians to organize Canada's past, present, and future into a series of stages through which the nation was supposed to pass on its way towards an earthly millennium of national greatness. The inspirational qualities of romantic religion helped to nurture the first flowerings of Canadian literature and painting. The culture that was born amid the pains of religious and social change came to dominate the way Protestant Ontario saw the world.

This cultural transformation helped to destroy the last vestiges of the curiously eighteenth-century world that had prospered in Upper Canada before the rebellions of 1837. During that period the distinction between church and dissent was largely the distinction between the Tory universe of compacts, hierarchy, and loyalty on the one hand, and the radical universe of yeomanry, reform, and independence on the other. Now those old divisions were subsumed in a new political, social, and cultural formation, in which religion as a whole secured one part of the dualism of Victorian culture. The distinction between church and dissent had been overwhelmed by the Protestant consensus, but the strength of this consensus helped to place Protestantism as a whole in a sphere of its own. By proclaiming the power of the sacred in a secular world, religion helped to divide the culture into secular and sacred elements. Religion as a category was set against the secular forces that were reordering contemporary society. From this exalted position it then set out to nurture and sustain a counterworld of moral values that could temper the materialistic excesses of the modern world and in time remake the secular world in its own image.

II

To this point the new culture has been analysed in relation to the creation of a new political economy. It was the nascent capitalist system that destroyed the old religious structure and led to the problems the new religious structure had to address. At the same time the new culture became a part of the new society, for in responding to what it saw as a social and moral crisis, it inevitably influenced and defined the character of that new society. To understand how the new culture and the new society came together, we must first understand the place of religion and culture in the social system: what is a religion and what functions do religions in general perform in society?

Unfortunately, the historians who have examined religion and society in Canada have passed over such theoretical questions in favour of more specific empirical issues. They have analysed, for example, the way the Protestant denominations and various individuals responded to a number of social and economic problems in the late nineteenth and early twentieth centuries.[1] They have examined how movements like the social gospel tried to solve the problems of large-scale immigration, widespread poverty, desperate living and working conditions, and the wide divisions between social classes. Although these studies have identified the important place of religion (in either orthodox or unorthodox form) in the social and political thought of English Canadian reformers, they have not analysed the more basic theoretical issues that such studies inevitably raise; for example, how religion was to reform society or how such reform movements influenced the social system itself. To a large extent the study of reform has become the study of religion, but few actually study religion itself, either as a cultural system or in its specific social relations.

The failure to consider these deeper issues has had an especially unfortunate effect upon how historians have interpreted society and religion in the mid-nineteenth century. Since this period was not marked by the flurry of social reforms that characterized the late Victorian and Edwardian eras, the study of religion has retreated to the margins of historical interest. The Protestantism of this era was like a somnambulant, walking through society without direction or a clear idea of the social role it might perform. This impression is reinforced by the type of comments made by social reformers in the early twentieth century about their own religious inheritance. Many of those who preached the social gospel were highly critical of the social outlook of the mainstream Protestant churches. They believed that the individualism and the narrow ethical concerns of traditional Protestantism could not address the crisis of the new social system; consequently they tried to forge a new Christianity.[2] The proliferation of new religious nostrums was in itself a similar critique, because it was the failure of existing religion that caused so many people to experiment with a host of religious surrogates.

All this seems to suggest that Ontario Protestants only became aware of social questions at the end of the Victorian period and that when they made this discovery they realized the existing religious system could not solve the new social problems. But as happens so often, the preoccupations of one age distort the historical reality of an earlier period. A considerably different picture of the mid-Victorian society emerges as one looks at this era on its own terms and asks some of the questions that Canadian historians have largely ignored.

What function does religion perform in society? A rich and well-established tradition of sociological analysis has focused upon the ability of religion to impart coherence and order to the social system.[3] It has argued that every society, from the most primitive to the most modern, creates a body of common values that rest largely upon religious beliefs. This common value system serves a number of important social functions: it explains the past, the present, and the future; it provides a framework for social action; it helps to explain and justify the existing structure of society and limits the conflicts that arise over the allocation of wealth and power; and it helps to reduce the disruptive social effect of events such as death and other disasters. Sociologists like Durkheim, Weber, Marx, and Parsons agree that a society achieves order and coherence from the ability of religion to provide and sustain a body of common values and beliefs. Some applaud this ability; some fear that religion may not be able to continue to serve this function; some decry the power of religion and offer more scientific opiates for the masses, but all acknowledge the close link between religious belief and social stability.

In the early nineteenth century Canadian religious leaders were also preoccupied with the relationship between religion and social order, and their writings are an interesting commentary on this tradition of sociological analysis. On 4 July 1821 the Rev. John Strachan preached a sermon on St Paul's second letter to the Corinthians in which he expounded the importance of religion in society in his clear and deductive manner:[4] "A love of order is not only essential to the tranquility but to the very being of any State." Without a love of order society will quickly degenerate into "anarchy and tyranny," as every individual follows "the dictates of his own corrupt will" and every "desire of change [produces] ferment and threaten[s] the public peace."[5] He then went on to explain how society can create and sustain this "love of order." There were two cornerstones of social stability, a love of order and a love of religion. Then in a telling phrase he joined the two together: "A love of order may with great propriety be included in a love of religion and then one principle only is necessary."[6] Religion, in effect, was the barrier to Hobbesian anarchy; if people were religious, society would be protected from chaos and enjoy peace and stability.

In other sermons Strachan expanded on this theme. Neither "the laws" nor "the natural consequences of vice and virtue" in themselves guaranteed peace and tranquillity.[7] Though the law undoubtedly helped to promote virtue and order, so many crimes went undetected and unpunished that the law could not be an effective deterrent. Nor did the ultimate consequences of vice and virtue sustain public order because the pleasures of virtue were too distant and the gratification of vice too immediate to dissuade people from yielding to a life of sin and crime. Religion, however, acted in a continual and immediate manner to restrain evil and promote good. It provided specific ethical norms and ideals that guided people in their daily lives, and it sustained this code by holding before the people the rewards and punishments that awaited those who followed – or did not follow – God's law. If people accepted God, as a matter of course they would lead an ordered life. Religion, therefore, was "the only firm and lasting foundation upon which the tranquility and security of a people can be strengthened and established."[8] Almost exactly the same words were used by John Beverley Robinson in his charge to the grand jury in Kingston in 1841: "Order, stability, peace, security the great blessings of social existence ... can be reaped only as the rewards of a religious adherence to what is right and true."[9]

This argument was of course one of the mainstays of the religion of order: order was essential to the very existence of society, and religion provided the only way of securing that order; people who believed in a God of order and reason would lead ordered and reasonable lives. Religion reinforced the work of other institutions (such as the law) and in concert with the state helped to create a hierarchical and ordered social system. This ideology, however, did not accept and defend the world as it was. While proclaiming the value of order, it also recognized the need for social change; but social change must advance the conservative ideals of this social ideology by reforming human nature and society to make them conform more closely to those ideals. Only after society had reached such a state of perfection would the need for restraint and law disappear. Freedom came later.[10]

The religion of experience also emphasized the close ties between religion and order, but it drew the two together in a very different way. Salvation began by rejecting the existing structure of social relations and the very ideals that the religion of order held so dear. The revivalists of the early nineteenth century asserted that the world of reason and hierarchy was a false world and only by breaking the shackles of this world could sinners find the true and Godly order of salvation. The saved were set apart from the world as a divine community of true peace and joy. In this religion there were, in effect, two types of order, the false order of the present world and the true order of God's Kingdom, and the bridge from the one to the other was a deep religious experience.

This brief comparison reveals three important elements of the relationship between religion, order, and social change in the early nineteenth century. First, in spite of the enormous differences between these two religious cultures, both agreed that religion, order, and change were intimately connected. Both agreed that religion was necessary for order and that religion must work to change human nature and society in order to achieve the proper social order. No one argued that there should be a world without change or without order. Secondly, the two religions could not agree on the specific terms of this relationship. Although both tied religion and order together, they interpreted this relationship in quite different ways: the social order that the first one glorified the second tried to overthrow, and the radical change that the second demanded the first regarded as part of the chaos that it was the duty of religion to suppress. Thirdly, these fundamental differences on such important issues raised serious doubts that religion in general could satisfy the social function so many people asked it to perform. Although society agreed that religion held the key to true peace and order, it could not agree upon what change and order really meant, and without a general cultural consensus on these matters, society could not establish a value system acceptable to most groups in society. Undoubtedly, these religious and cultural divisions contributed to the social instability so vehemently decried by all religious leaders, and it should come as no surprise to find religious issues at the centre of the tensions of that era. Far from promoting order, religion was the wellspring of intense social, political, and class conflict.

The relationship between religion and social order was redefined by social and political change. As the mid-Victorian state reorganized society and politics, it reshaped the structure of Ontario religion and cast aside the old establishments: the separation of church and state and the secularization of the reserves and the university were among the first triumphs of liberal-nationalism.[11] These changes however went a long way towards removing the obstacles that had stood in the way of a broadly based Protestant alliance. Once the reserves and the university questions were settled, what Anglicans, Presbyterians, and Methodists held in common became more important than what kept them apart. Now they could present a single vision of the world and a single set of social and moral values. What the early nineteenth century had failed to do the mid-Victorian years were able to accomplish. Ontario had found a culture.

The new developmental state also redefined the problem of social order that this new Protestant alliance had to confront. For centuries religion had been trying to overcome chaos and promote stability, but when the old religion of order confronted the social ramifications of a fallen human nature, it had a number of allies at its side. The law and the state were supposed to help the church restrain the greed and disruption that were the inheritance of Adam's transgressions. But by the middle of the nineteenth century this supporting cast had left the stage; indeed the state was now working against religion. No longer an institution of hierarchy and order, it was encouraging the greed and self-interest that religion was supposed to restrain. With responsible government came railways and progress; materialism was the cornerstone of colonial capitalism.

By institutionalizing the unfettered pursuit of economic self-interest, the state raised the question of social order to a new level. No longer were anarchy and disruption problems that could be explained in individual terms, for capitalism had made them inherent in the structure of society itself. As more and more groups fought to control the means of advancing their own interests, society became an arena of conflict between those who controlled the instruments of production and those who did not. As some groups won and others lost, new class divisions became part of the social structure of Victorian Canada.

How then did this alliance of independent religious bodies attempt to deal with the crises that grew out of a capitalist political economy? The answers to this question can be found in the character of the Protestant culture that began to dominate Ontario life during the same period – once again it is the form that tells the real story. In proclaiming the power and reality of the sacred in a secular world, in predicting that time would transform the secular into the sacred, and in calling upon morally attuned individuals to work unceasingly to bring about such a transformation, the Protestant alliance was attempting to integrate a new type of religion into the new society.

It was a common theme in the religious discourse of the mid-Victorian period that a strong moral code firmly grounded in the Protestant religion was the only basis for social stability in a period of rapid economic change. The Rev. A.N. Bethune, the second Bishop of Toronto, made this point when he contemplated with horror a society in which such a code did not exist. He immediately demanded that the government tie religious instruction to secular education so that society would not suffer from the anarchy that the unrestrained pursuit of economic self-interest inevitably produced: "The child taught and trained for this world's vocations only, without a deep inculcation of the love and fear of God, and the penalty hereafter of an irreligious and wicked life, will have but one leading idea – self-aggrandizement and self-indulgence, and will be checked by no restraint of conscience in the ways and means of securing them. Gigantic frauds will be perpetrated ... atrocious murders will be committed."[12] Bethune's interpretation of morality, education, and crime was by no means unique. Egerton Ryerson made precisely the same associations (in less gruesome detail) when he argued that Christianity must be one of the three guiding principles of public education. While the school system should be universal and train people in the practical subjects that would help them to work in the new economic order, it must also teach the youth of the province to act morally throughout their lives: "The cold calculations of unchristianized selfishness will never sustain a school system."[13]

Both men acknowledged the power of materialism and economic self-interest in society; indeed the system of education that they described helped to develop the skills and attitudes that the modern age demanded. At the same time they stressed the social importance of a set of religious and moral beliefs that challenged the materialistic ethos of their society. In opposition to the world of materialism they set out a counterworld of spiritual values, which they called upon to moderate the drive for economic accumulation and by so doing secure a degree of order and stability. As the ethical norms that this counterworld proclaimed became part of the value systems of Ontario Protestants, society would acquire an internal moral code that would restrain the antisocial excesses of unchecked greed. Religion would secure social order.

Why did this moral atmosphere achieve such power and authority? Why did mid-Victorian society accept the normative restraints that the Protestant churches tried to propagate? The power of Ontario's celebrated morality rested on the unique position that religion and religious institutions enjoyed in Victorian society and on the character of the message that they presented. Ontario society saw reality through a culture that accepted both the secular and sacred worlds, and by accepting the power and presence of the sacred within the secular it imparted to Protestant morality an unassailable authority and power, one that could rival even the drive for material acquisition. To answer the question most simply, people were moral because society believed in God.

It is important to distinguish between the social function that religion performed and the reasons why religion could perform this function. Ontario Protestantism helped to stabilize an emerging capitalist economy, but people were not religious because they recognized that capitalism must have a modicum of social order that only religion could provide. People were religious because they accepted the reality of the sacred and believed that the sacred both informed and transcended their environment. It was the independence and reality of the sacred – the basic dualism of the cultural form – that allowed religion to give order and stability to the universe. To put the matter in a slightly different way, if the essence of religion had not transcended its social function, it could not have performed this function. People would not have worshipped a God if they had believed that God's only intent was to suppress their dignity by legitimizing their oppressors.

The sacred strengthened Protestant morality in another way. According to the culture, the sacred was not only a living reality but also an image of what the secular world might become. The Protestant sense of time told society that if a proper system of moral values monitored the course of everyday affairs, humanity would advance from a low to a high estate. Time was progressive and could lead society towards an earthly millennium. Like a guiding star, the sacred drew society towards a special earthly destiny. This sense of sacred expectancy imparted an urgency and immediacy to Protestant moral values, for if society could soon grasp its spiritual destiny, the moral code that helped society to reach its goal became all the more important. In much the same way that the sight of the finish can spur exhausted marathon runners to increase their pace, the prospect of future earthly glory sustained those who dedicated themselves to saving the world from sin.

This sense of time also helped to answer one of the most important social questions in the nineteenth century: what is the meaning of change? Here the issue was not simply to solve the social problems caused by change; society had to confront the phenomenon of change itself. For many people social change was destroying the points of reference that had organized their existence by altering the routines of work, their social relations, and their immediate environment. Traditional religious beliefs could not answer this question because they often treated social change as something that was leading society away from an ideal social and religious order.

The culture of Ontario Protestantism tried to transform what was a source of disruption into a positive religious good by interpreting as progress what others saw as chaos. Protestant culture affirmed that time was progressive and placed the present on the threshold of moral, spiritual and national greatness. Gradually Canadian society would undergo a number of improvements as it became more Christian. The frenetic pace of materialism was only a stage through which society had to pass on its way towards a millennium of sustained moral and cultural prosperity. As so many historians asserted, Canada had to develop its economy before it could enter an era of moral and intellectual development; it had to build railways before it could expect to have great literature and art. Social change was a positive good; progress became a religious doctrine.

Such faith in progress gave those who had to cope with social change a way to interpret their experience. It gave all the groups that had to submit to the new disciplines of economic life, both the businessman and the worker, a positive interpretation of the events that were shaping their lives. It is in this sense that the opium of religion could tranquillize both the Masseys and the masses. At the same time, however, the vision of a more just and Christian world was a fulcrum for overturning capitalism itself, for if time held out the hope of a moral and more just world, some Christians would inevitably ask whether or not reality was conforming to the expectations of that culture. In fact, this attempt to realize the promise of sacred time by carving a new heaven out of the old earth became one of the driving forces for social reform in a later age. However strongly social reformers might question their Protestant inheritance, they built their program on some of its most important cultural beliefs.

Ontario Protestantism in the mid-nineteenth century did not reject the new political economy. Rather, by accepting the distinction between the secular and the sacred, it accepted the reality of the forces that were shaping the secular world. Protestantism in this period approached capitalism as a moral rather than a structural question. It tried to build on the distinction between the two worlds a moral atmosphere of religious norms and values that would cover economic life and provide moral precepts capable of guiding individuals through the hazards of a society torn apart by change. This moral code was largely voluntary, for although religious institutions appealed to the state to legislate on moral issues, it relied on social rather than legal discipline; without a legal establishment, Protestantism had to fall back on the strength of its own authority to convince people that they should live moral lives. And the focus of this moral code was the individual Christian. Even though the campaigns for temperance, Sabbath observance, and Sunday schools were carefully organized social movements, they assumed that religion must convert society by first converting the individual. Morally aware Protestants, like the romantic heroes of old, could fight the good fight to reform the world.

III

Was this the only way religion and culture could play their roles in society? Given the circumstances of that day were there other paths that Ontario Protestantism might have followed? To speculate about what might have been is one of the great gifts that Clio has bestowed on the historical profession, and here let us reflect briefly on at least two alternatives. On the one hand the old establishment ideal attempted to integrate religion and the state by incorporating a particular system of religion directly into society; on the other hand, the sectarian ideal called for the creation of a completely new society that rejected the secular values of Ontario life. Ontario Protestantism cast aside both these alternatives, choosing instead to create the moral atmosphere for which Ontario would become justly famous. Indeed, the culture that sustained this atmosphere gained such power that other possibilities became almost unthinkable, and the image of the world created by the culture came to be an accurate representation of the two forces that were shaping Ontario life – the forces of political and economic change and the religious forces that attempted to temper and control those secular drives. History, as usual, conforms to the way culture perceives it.

In some respects Victorian culture in Ontario survived for a long time, and the shadow it cast covered much of the province well into the twentieth century, giving Ontario a moral reputation that unnerved those who might be unmindful of its social benefits. Nonetheless, even in the mid-Victorian era there were many weaknesses in this culture. Formed to address the problems that had undermined previous patterns of cultural interpretation, it would in time have to face its own day of reckoning as it tried to answer the difficult new questions that arose as the world continue to change.

To give the sacred a tangible presence in society, Victorian Protestantism abstracted it from the world, and put it in a separate category: but once the sacred was in its own sphere, it began to lose the immediacy it had had in earlier cultures. The religion of order, for example, had used the rhetoric of the secular and the sacred, but it had kept the two orders together: proper social values were also proper religious values; the order of nature revealed the character and purpose of God. Although the religion of experience made a much more radical distinction between the secular and the sacred, it tempered this dualism by asserting that God was an omnipresent being who intervened directly in the course of day-to-day life. The Victorian accommodation gave the sacred a distinct and powerful presence, but it also moved it away from the secular by placing it in discrete institutions or in specific places. In much the same way that Victorians took education out of life and put it into schools, so they took religion out of the world and put it safely away in churches, temperance societies, and missionary organizations. In this guise the sacred might justify the canons of public morality, but it was much more difficult for it to sustain the spiritual quality of everyday life. Without a sense of integration and immediacy people could be reduced to worshipping a set of external forms, a hollow shell of public respectability.

The Protestant sense of time also suffered from a number of structural weaknesses. The idea of progress had very strong religious roots, but it could easily regress into a popular ideology that violated some of the basic doctrines of the Protestant religion. The belief that the secular would be transformed into the sacred grew out of a particular way of interpreting individual salvation: in the same way that sinners could be saved, the fallen world could be redeemed for Christ. But in the change from the individual to society something was lost. Individual salvation did not just happen; it relied upon a particular type of relationship between people and God. If one had faith and acted in a certain way then God would change sinners into new people. The popular notion of progress easily cast off its religious inheritance by ignoring the need to change the nature of humanity and society. Progress was no longer a gift of God's saving grace; it simply happened as a matter of course. The proposition that railways and economic growth inevitably led to a new moral civilization turned on the incredible hope that materialism and greed would become disinterestedness and selflessness in the natural order of things. The question of the character of the relationship between society and God was simply ignored as a whole nation tried to pass through the eye of a needle. Progress became a comfortable heresy, a law rather than a divine possibility.

The course of history also caused a serious problem for this culture. In trying to control economic life, religion assumed that it could use the social power of moral norms to temper the worst excesses of a capitalist political economy. The moral atmosphere that it sustained was supposed to serve as a brake on the engine of economic development. A brake, however, has a very limited function – it may restrain the speed of the engine for a period of time, but it cannot change the nature of the engine or the direction in which it travels. Self-interest and greed continued to propel the world along the tracks of capitalistic development, and as the engine gathered speed it easily broke through the rather fragile social disciplines of moral propriety. The mid-Victorian accommodation came apart precisely because it was an accommodation that implicitly accepted the world of economic development in the hope that the world of religion could turn secular activity towards sacred goals. If the accommodation held for one phase in the growth of capitalism, it did not hold for another. Art, once again, provides an interesting commentary on this weakness. By the early twentieth century religious architecture had come to symbolize the crisis facing the older Victorian accommodation. The Gothic towers that once looked down with majestic authority over the city lost their prominence as churches joined the retreat to the suburbs and new temples of commerce rose up to dominate the secular environment.[14]

In effect, the belief that time was progress suffered from a weakness inherent in all forms of history and prophecy. In giving structure to events, progress explains not only the past but also the future. The expectation that time would continue to unfold gradually towards the creation of a spiritual kingdom on earth was just as much a prophecy as the prediction that the world would end in a flash one Friday afternoon. It might fail less dramatically, but it would fail all the same. A people might suffer for many generations in the hope that the future would be different and better, but the course of the world, although too often only a small thorn on the brow of faith, could not be ignored completely. History refused steadfastly to fulfil the expectation that the sacred would come to dwell in the cities, towns, and fields of Ontario, that the Canadian nation would take the first step across the threshold of national greatness.

Finally there was the problem of inspiration. The new culture relied heavily upon the power of romanticism to move the world in the proper direction. Romantic art was supposed to inspire individuals to forgo the materialism of their age and dedicate their wealth and talent to the great moral crusades that were advancing the cause of Christ upon the earth. Inspiration became synonymous with salvation and provided the crucial link between the secular and the sacred. But could a romantic style overcome the forces that ruled the very practical world of everyday life? However sublime the sacred, however well-crafted the noble church and the great sermon, could they transform the character of the individual and permanently sustain this transformation? Even if this was possible, could the Christian hero really change a society in which the range of human freedom was becoming more and more limited by the iron maiden of an objectified world?[15] The failure of inspiration to accomplish the changes it set out to achieve further divided the world of Victorian culture and widened the gulf between the real and the ideal by placing thoughts and feelings in one category and action in another. People could dream about the world of the lamb, but they had to live in the world of the tiger.

This culture had a profound influence on many features of Victorian society in Ontario and provided a degree of order and stability to a rapidly changing society. The form of this culture, however, foretold the nature of its own demise. In an earlier period social and cultural change had broken down the old hierarchical world of the early nineteenth century by creating a new world that attempted to combine economic growth with a broad moral consensus. But in time economic growth undermined the moral consensus that had become the hallmark of the society itself.

Economic progress seemed to assure Canadians a bright and prosperous future: "boundless are the possibilities of the future upon which the eyes of Canada are now fixed with confident but questioning hope."[16] And yet even in this climate of optimism there were genuine reasons for questioning such a hope. The belief that railway builders and industrialists were also nation builders and saints still haunts the English Canadian imagination. But faith inevitably raises doubt. When will the millennium come? When will the Dominion of Canada become the dominion of the

Lord? When will the materialism of everyday life become a world of morality and peace? These are questions that many people, some in sorrow and resignation, continue to ask.[17]

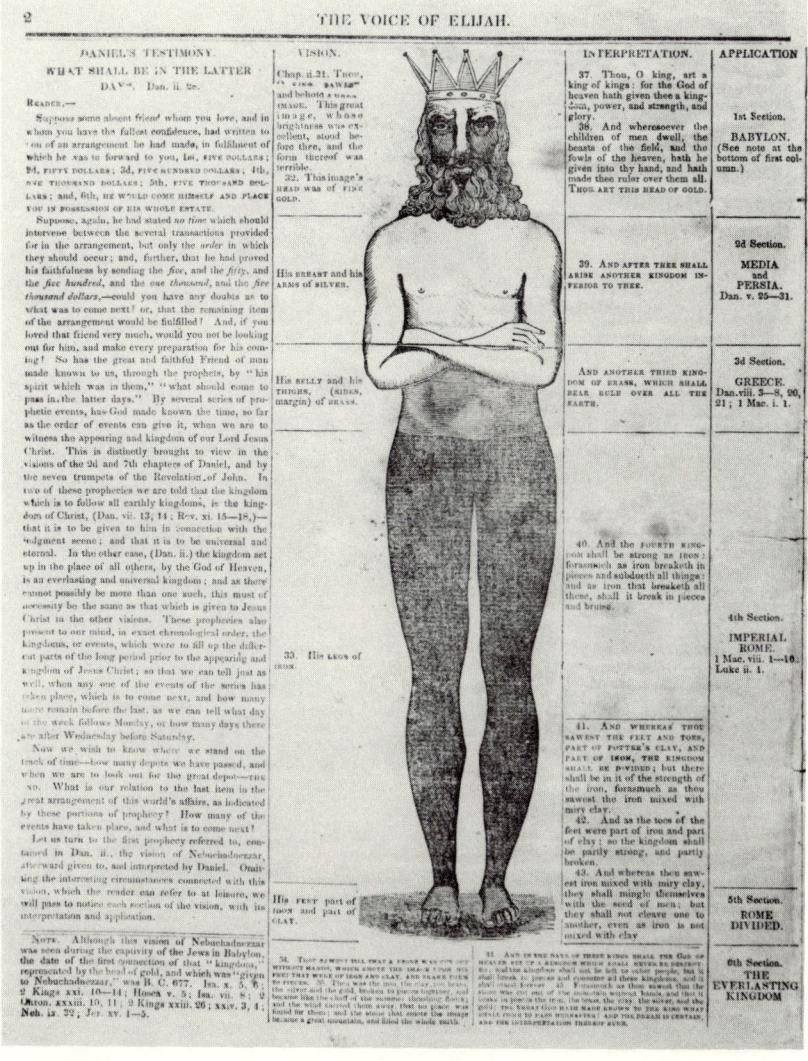

Figure 23 "What shall be in the latter days" from *The Voice of Elijah*, Montreal, CW, 16 Feb. 1844. (Courtesy American Antiquarian Society, Worcester, Mass.)

Notes

CHAPTER ONE

1 Donald Creighton, whose work represents the very apogee of romantic art in Canadian historical literature, remarks upon the appropriateness of the Dominion motto in these territorial and materialistic
   terms. D.G. Creighton, *Road to Confederation* (Toronto: Macmillan
   1964), 423.
2 W.S. Macnutt, *New Brunswick: A History, 1784–1867* (Toronto: Macmillan 1963), 457, 487.
3 Psalm 72:11–14.
4 Zechariah 9:9–10.
5 Roberto Perin, "Nationalism and the Church in French Canada,
   1840–1880," *Bulletin of Canadian Studies* 1 (1975), 27–38; Marta
   Danylewycz, *Taking the Veil: An Alternative to Marriage, Motherhood,
   and Spinsterhood, 1840–1920* (Toronto: McClelland and Stewart 1987),
   esp. chaps 1 and 2; Jacques Monet, "French Canadian Nationalism
   and the Challenge of Ultramontanism," Canadian Historical Association, *Report* (1966); and Nadia Eid, *Le Clergé et le pouvoir politique
   au Québec: une analyse de l'idéologie ultramontaine au milieu du xix^e
   siècle* (Montreal: Hurtubise 1978), 125–59.
6 John Strachan, *An Appeal to the Friends of Religion and Literature, in
   Behalf of the University of Upper Canada* (London: R. Gilbert 1827),
   20–1.
7 Dennis Duffy, *Gardens, Covenants, and Exiles: Loyalism in the Literature
   of Upper Canada/Ontario* (Toronto: Univ. of Toronto Press 1982).
8 Douglas Owram, *The Promise of Eden: The Canadian Expansionist Movement and the Image of the West* (Toronto: Univ. of Toronto Press 1980);

Keith Clifford, "His Dominion: A Vision in Crisis," in Peter Slater, ed., *Religion and Culture in Canada/Religion et Culture au Canada* (Waterloo: Canadian Corporation for Studies in Religion 1977), 23–42.

9 The final chapter of this study examines the character and significance of this moral atmosphere.

10 The narrowness of Protestant morality is one of the staple themes of Canadian literature in English. In the novels of Robertson Davies, Hugh MacLennan, and Margaret Laurence, for example, the central characters must surmount not only the traditional obstacles to self-awareness but also the oppressiveness of their own Protestant environment. It should also be pointed out however that, while religion in one sense is a barrier to self realization, it also provides the means of overcoming the very obstacles that it has placed in its own path. The struggle to triumph over religious oppression invariably ends with an affirmation of religious belief.

11 D.C. Masters, *Protestant Church Colleges in Canada: A History* (Toronto: Univ. of Toronto Press 1966).

12 Religious instruction (in a general sense) took three basic forms in higher education. An institution could offer a full undergraduate program and require that students participate in the religious observances of the college (Trinity). It could offer a full undergraduate program under the general "religious atmosphere" of the denominational college. While it might not demand full participation in the school's religion it could demand that students attend their own church (Victoria). Or an institution might restrict its teaching to divinity courses but attach itself to a non-denominational school so that undergraduates could avail themselves of these courses while living either at the college or with ready access to its religious life (Knox). See Masters, *Protestant Church Colleges.*

13 The works of William Paley, Joseph Butler, and Francis Wayland recur frequently. See A.B. McKillop, *A Disciplined Intelligence: Critical Inquiry and Canadian Thought in the Victorian Era* (Montreal: McGill-Queens Univ. Press 1979).

14 Ryerson to Bethune, Toronto, 13 July 1872, Government of Ontario, Education Department, *Documentary History of Education in Upper Canada, from the passing of the Constitutional Act of 1791 to the close of Rev. Dr. Ryerson's administration of the Education Department in 1876,* ed. John George Hodgins (Toronto: Warrick Brothers and Rutter 1894-1910), 24 (1872), 90. See also *ibid.*, "Report on a System of Public Elementary Instruction for Upper Canada," 6 (1846), 142.

15 Egerton Ryerson, *First Lessons in Christian Morals: For Canadian Families and Schools* (Toronto: Copp, Clark 1871). Earlier religious texts in the public schools were *Scripture Lessons – Old and New Testa-*

ments and *Lessons on the Truth of Christianity.* See "Text Books in the Public Schools, When Sanctioned and When Changed, 1846–1872," *Documentary History of Education* 24 (1872), 106–9.

16 For the most forceful statement of the social control versus reform argument, see Susan Houston, "Politics, Schools, and Social Change in Upper Canada," *Canadian Historical Review* 53 (Sept. 1972), 249–71; and Susan Houston, "Victorian Origins of Juvenile Delinquency: A Canadian Experience," *History of Education Quarterly* 20 (Fall 1972), 254–80. For a much more balanced and credible interpretation see Alison Prentice, *The School Promoters: Education and Social Class in Mid-nineteenth-century Upper Canada* (Toronto: McClelland and Stewart 1977).

17 "Man and Woman," *The Royal Path of Life,* intro. by the Rev. John Potts (Toronto 1879), 17.

18 "Home," *ibid,* 40–5.

19 C.C. Berger, *The Sense of Power: Studies in the Ideas of Canadian Imperialism, 1867–1914* (Toronto: Univ. of Toronto Press 1970), esp. chap. 4, "Progress and Liberty."

20 Rev. Alexander Sutherland, *Methodism in Canada: Its Work and Its Story* (Toronto: Methodist Mission Room 1904), 2. For an account of his efforts on behalf of prohibition see Ruth E. Spence, *Prohibition in Canada: A Memorial to Frances Stephens Spence* (Toronto: Ontario Branch of the Dominion Alliance 1919), 141–7.

21 Rev. Egerton Ryerson, *Canadian Methodism: Its Epochs and Characteristics* (Toronto: William Briggs 1882), 1, 72. For other examples of such a proclamation of the power of the sacred, see Rev. Dr. A. Carman, "The Methodist Church" in *Centennial of Canadian Methodism* (Toronto: William Briggs 1891), 229–51. George F. Playter sets out his interpretation of the relationship between human action and divine agency with great clarity and force: history "may be called the 'Acts of the Methodist preachers' ... The Acts were prompted by the grace of God working in them ... so that the work of spreading the Gospel may be termed God's work, as the first cause, and his ministers' work, as the second." George F. Playter, *The History of Methodism in Canada* (Toronto: Anson Green 1862), 367–8.

22 The statistics for this section are drawn from the following census materials: Province of Canada, *Journal of the Assembly,* 1843, vol. 2, app. FF; *Census of the Canadas,* 1851–2 (Quebec, 1853), esp. vol. 1; xxi, and app. 2; *Census of the Canadas,* 1860-1 (Quebec, 1863), esp. vol. 1; *Census of Canada,* 1870–1 (Ottawa, 1873), esp. vols 1, 4, 5; *Census of Canada,* 1880–1 (Ottawa 1882), esp. vol. 1. For a more detailed digest of these statistics see also William E. de Villiers-West-

fall, "The Sacred and the Secular: Studies in the Cultural History of Protestant Ontario in the Victorian Period," (Ph.D. thesis, Univ. of Toronto 1976), App. 2, "Denominational Growth, Church Building, Union and Disruption," 324–35.

23 S.D. Clark, *Church and Sect in Canada* (Toronto: Univ. of Toronto Press 1948).

24 Roman Catholics accounted for 16.7 per cent of the population of Ontario in 1881. In 1851 their percentage was 17.6.

25 John S. Moir, "The Relations of Church and State in Canada West, 1840–1867," (Ph.D. thesis, Univ. of Toronto 1954), 195.

26 See Barrie Dyster, "Toronto 1840–1860: Making it in a British Protestant Town" (Ph.D. thesis, Univ. of Toronto 1970) and Barrie Dyster, "Captain Bob and the Noble Ward: Neighbourhood and Provincial Politics in Nineteenth-century Toronto," in Victor L. Russell, ed., *Forging a Consensus: Historical Essays on Toronto* (Toronto: Univ. of Toronto Press 1984), 87–115.

27 For a good example of this type of attitude towards the arts and society see George Bourinot, *The Intellectual Development of the Canadian People: An Historical Review* (Toronto: Hunter, Rose 1882).

28 For a more detailed elaboration of this approach see Paul Tillich, *Theology of Culture* (Oxford: Oxford 1959); William J. Bouwsma, "From History of Ideas to History of Meaning," *Journal of Interdisciplinary History* 12 (Autumn 1981), 279–91; and Clifford Geertz, "Religion as a Cultural System," in Michael Banton, ed., *Anthropological Approaches to the Study of Religion* (London: Tavistock 1966), 1–46.

29 See McKillop, *A Disciplined Intelligence*, and Michael Gauvreau, "History and Faith: A Study of the Evangelical Temper in Canada, 1820–1940," (Ph.D. thesis, Univ. of Toronto 1985).

30 See Richard Allen, "Providence to Progress: The Migration of an Idea in English Canadian Thought," in William Westfall, Louis Rousseau, Fernand Harvey, John Simpson, eds, *Religion/Culture: Comparative Canadian Studies* Canadian Issues, 7 (Ottawa: Association for Canadian Studies 1985), 33–46; and Goldwin French, "The Evangelical Creed in Canada," in W.L. Morton, ed., *The Shield of Achilles: Aspects of Canada in the Victorian Age* (Toronto: McClelland and Stewart 1968).

31 Mircea Eliade, *The Sacred and the Profane: The Nature of Religion* (New York: Harcourt, Brace and World 1959), and Paul Tillich, *Theology of Culture*.

32 For a clear general treatment of this question see Raymond Aron, *Main Currents in Sociological Thought* (London: Weidenfeld and Nicolson 1968), esp. the introduction to part 2; and Roger O'Toole, *Religion: Classical Sociological Approaches* (Toronto: McGraw-Hill Ryerson 1984).

33 Talcott Parsons, *The Structure of Social Action: A Study in Social Theory with Special Reference to a Group of Recent European Writers* (Glencoe, Ill.: Free Press 1949), esp. part 4, chap. 18; and Talcott Parsons, "The Theoretical Development of the Sociology of Religion," in Talcott Parsons, *Essays in Sociological Theory* (Glencoe, Ill.: Free Press 1954). The relationship between common value integration and structural-functional analysis is set out clearly in the introduction to the second edition of *The Structure of Social Action* (published in 1949). Here Parsons proposes two possible courses that he might have followed. He could expand the original version of *The Structure of Social Action* by including Freud and certain anthropologists, or he could use the insights of the original work to embark on a new sociological departure. He chose the second. He represented the decision in these terms: "a shift in theoretical level from the analysis of the structure of social action as such to the structural-functional analysis of social systems." He then went on to develop this method in his next great work, *The Social System*. Parsons, *The Structure of Social Action*; Talcott Parsons, *The Social System* (Glencoe, Ill.: Free Press 1951).

34 For a more detailed analysis of Parsons' work see de Villiers-Westfall, "The Sacred and the Secular," esp. chap. 3, "The Sacred, the Secular, and the Social System," 73–126. For other critiques of Parsons' work see C. Wright Mills, *The Sociological Imagination* (New York: Oxford 1959); Alwin Gouldner, *The Coming Crisis in Western Sociology* (New York: Basic Books 1970); and "Talcott Parsons on Religion," *Sociological Analysis* 43 (Winter 1982) [Special Issue]. The relationship between Parsonian sociology and the interpretation of social change provides an important, and largely unexamined, perspective on the work of the pioneering Canadian sociologist, S.D. Clark. Clark was one of the few sociologists who bravely withstood the major shift away from a sociology of social change towards a sociology of order. See S.D. Clark *The Developing Canadian Community* (Toronto: Univ. of Toronto Press 1962), esp. part 4, "Sociology and History," 269–313; and S.D. Clark, "Sociology, History, and the Problem of Social Change," *Canadian Journal of Economics and Political Science* 25 (Nov. 1959), 389–400.

35 In Canada this heresy has had a long and distinguished life. It finds its strongest expression in the environmentalist approach to Canadian literature, history and art, which argues, for example, that the character of prairie literature grows out of the prairie landscape. This argument receives its most brilliant critique in Paul Hiebert's classic *Sarah Binks*. See William Westfall, "On the Concept of Region in Canadian History and Literature," *Journal of Canadian Studies* 15 (Summer 1980), 11.

36 McKillop, *A Disciplined Intelligence*; Masters, *Protestant Church Colleges in Canada: A History*; and Leslie Armour, "Philosophy and Denominationalism in Ontario," *Journal of Canadian Studies* 20 (Spring 1985), 25–38. See also William Westfall and Louis Rousseau, introduction, *Religion/Culture: Comparative Canadian Studies*, 1-7.

37 In the 1960s and 1970s, for example, the study of Canadian religion began to move away from its traditional denominational and biographical framework. Church history became, in effect, religious history. In so doing the study of religion passed from one style of progress (the building of God's dominion) to another (the development of the Canadian nation). In its desire to "come of age" the study of religion attached itself to the models of liberal-nationalism. See N.G. Smith, "Nationalism in the Canadian Churches," *Canadian Journal of Theology* 9 (Apr. 1963), 112–25; John W. Grant, "The Church and Canada's Self-Awareness," *Canadian Journal of Theology* 13 (July 1967), 155–64; and John S. Moir, "The Canadianization of the Protestant Churches," Canadian Historical Association, *Report* (1966), 56–69. For one of the few articles that at least implicitly challenges the process of subordinating religion to other social forces, see Goldwin S. French, "The Impact of Christianity on Canadian Culture and Society before 1867," McMaster Divinity College, *Theological Bulletin* 3 (Jan. 1968), 15–38. The article is very stimulating although, by the author's own admission, tentative.

CHAPTER TWO

1 John Strachan, *A Sermon Preached at York, Upper Canada, Third of July 1825, on the Death of the Late Lord Bishop of Quebec* (Kingston: Macfarlane 1826). Parts of this sermon are reprinted in J.L.H. Henderson, *John Strachan: Documents and Opinions* (Toronto: McClelland and Stewart 1969), 87–94. His text was II Peter 1:15: "Moreover I will endeavour that ye may be able after my decease to have these things always in remembrance."

2 Strachan's private correspondence reveals a picture of Mountain that was much less complimentary. He bridled at the obstacles that Mountain seemed to place in the path of his own plans and ambitions. See Archives of Ontario [hereafter AO], *Strachan Letterbook 1812–34*, Strachan to the Hon. and Rev. Charles Stewart, 11 Jan. 1819.

3 Thomas R. Millman, *Jacob Mountain, First Lord Bishop of Quebec, A Study in Church and State* (Toronto: Univ. of Toronto Press 1947); and "A Sketch of the Life and Work of the Right Rev. Jacob Mountain, D.D., First Lord Bishop of Quebec by the Rev. Thomas R. Millman: A Sermon Preached on Sunday, 31 Oct. 1943 in the Cathedral

of the Holy Trinity on the occasion of the 150th Anniversary of the Arrival of the Bishop" (United Church Archives, Pamphlet Collection).

4 Strachan, *A Sermon Preached at York ... on the Death of the Late Lord Bishop of Quebec.*

5 *Ibid.*, Strachan compared the £700,000 spent on "the Civil and Military Establishments" with the £9,600 paid "for the support and extension of the Religion of the Parent State." For a fuller discussion of church and state see the fourth chapter of this study.

6 See Oliver R. Osmond, "The Churchmanship of John Strachan," *Journal of the Canadian Church Historical Society*, Sept. 1974, 46–59; and the Rev. Mark Charles McDermott, "The Theology of Bishop Strachan: A Study in Anglican Identity" (Ph.D. thesis, Institute of Christian Thought, University of Toronto 1983), esp. chap. 5. For a perceptive treatment of intra-church divisions see Alan L. Hayes, "The Struggle for the Rights of the Laity in the Diocese of Toronto 1850–1879," *Journal of the Canadian Church Historical Society*, Apr. 1984, 5–17.

7 The writings of Strachan are filled with references to the superstitiousness of Roman Catholicism. For two of his more "reasoned" reactions see John Strachan, *A Letter to the Congregation of St. James, occasioned by the Hon. John Elmsley's Publication of the Bishop of Strasbourg's Observations on the Sixth Chapter of St. John's Gospel* (Toronto: R. Stanton, 1834), and *A Letter to the Right Hon. Lord John Russell, on the Present State of the Church in Canada* (London: George Bell 1851).

8 Strachan, *A Sermon Preached at York ... on the Death of the Late Lord Bishop of Quebec.*

9 *Ibid.* This particular image of the garden of the Lord recurs frequently in Strachan's writings. See for example, *An Appeal to the Friends of Religion and Literature, on Behalf of the University of Upper Canada* (London: R. Gilbert 1827), 21.

10 Strachan, *A Sermon Preached at York ... on the Death of the Late Lord Bishop of Quebec.*

11 *Ibid.*

12 *Ibid.* For an interesting discussion of the idea of a Christian nation in Strachan's thought see Norma MacRae, "The Religious Foundation of John Strachan's Social and Political Thought as Contained in His Sermons, 1803 to 1866" (MA thesis, McMaster Univ. 1978), esp. chap. 5, 79–102.

13 Strachan, *A Sermon Preached at York ... On the Death of the Late Lord Bishop of Quebec.*

14 *Ibid.*

15 Ryerson's response was published in the *Colonial Advocate* in June 1826 and reprinted as "A Review of a Sermon, Preached by the Hon. and Rev. John Strachan, D.D. at York, U.C., 3d of July 1825 on the Death of the Late Lord Bishop of Quebec by a Methodist Preacher" in *Claims of Churchmen and Dissenters of Upper Canada Brought to the Test; In a Controversy Betweeen Several Members of the Church of England and a Methodist Preacher* (Kingston, UC 1828). See also Goldwin French, *Parsons and Politics: The Role of the Wesleyan Methodists in Upper Canada and the Maritimes from 1780 to 1855* (Toronto: Ryerson 1962), 111ff. For Ryerson's own account of these events (written considerably later) see Egerton Ryerson, *The Story of My Life: Being Reminiscences of Sixty Years' Public Service in Canada*, ed. J. George Hodgins (Toronto: William Briggs 1883), 48; and Egerton Ryerson, *Canadian Methodism: Its Epochs and Characteristics* (Toronto: W. Briggs 1882), 165–220.

16 For recent considerations of Ryerson see Neil McDonald and Alf Chaiton, *Egerton Ryerson and His Times* (Toronto: Macmillan 1978), and Albert Fiorino, "The Philosophical Roots of Egerton Ryerson's Idea of Education as Elaborated in his Writings Proceeding and Including the Report of 1846" (Ph.D. thesis, Ontario Institute for Studies in Education 1975).

17 This is a paraphrase of the third part of the Homily against Images originally published in 1547 and reprinted many times. See *Certain Sermons Appointed by the Queen's Majesty to be Declared and Read by all Parsons, Vicars, and Curates ...* (Cambridge, 1850), 260–1.

18 "A Review of a Sermon ... by a Methodist Preacher."

19 *Ibid*.

20 Strachan, *A Sermon Preached at York ... on the Death of the Late Lord Bishop of Quebec*.

21 "A Review of a Sermon ... by a Methodist Preacher."

22 II Timothy 4:2.

23 John 3:3, 5; and Acts 9:17.

24 "A Review of a Sermon ... by a Methodist Preacher."

25 Strachan's critique of revivalism contained themes that he himself had articulated as early as 1808. The same critique could be found as well in the writings of any number of Anglican and Presbyterian clergymen. Forty years later for example, the Rev. Charles Forest made the same argument: "Erroneous tests of godliness have been instituted among them, whereby feelings instead of an enlightened judgment and a life-reforming faith, have been set forth as the criteria of true religion." Society for the Propagation of the Gospel Archives, C/Canada/Quebec, folio 394B, Rev. Charles Forest to the Lord Bishop of Montreal, 1 July 1848; see also C/Canada/Quebec, Rev. B.C. Hill to Sect. of UC Church Society, 13 Jan.

1840. The Bishop of Quebec referred to Methodists as "a set of ignorant enthusiasts, whose preaching is calculated only to perplex the understanding, and corrupt the morals and relax the nerves of industry, and dissolve the bonds of society." Provincial Archives of Quebec, Mountain Papers, Bishop of Quebec to Henry Dundas, Quebec, 15 Sept. 1794, as cited in Richard Preston, *Kingston Before the War of 1812: A Collection of Documents* (Toronto: Champlain Society 1959), 292. See also *The Church,* 16 Jan. 1841, 110; 23 Apr. 1842, 166; and 9 May 1845, 175. For a Presbyterian critique of revivalism see "Seventh Annual Report of the Glasgow Society for Promoting the Religious Interests of Scottish Settlers in British North America, 1833," *The Presbyterian Review* 4 (Nov. 1833), 397–414. Similarly, the division of the colony into three parts is a standard way for Anglicans to represent their place in the religious structure of the colony. For the Rev. John Stuart's appraisal see Synod of Ontario Archives, Stuart Letters, Stuart to Dr. Morice, Kingston, 4 Oct. 1791, and Stuart to Bishop of Nova Scotia, Kingston, 25 June 1793, as cited in Preston, *Kingston Before the War of 1812,* 181, 287.

26 Protestants agreed on the central place of the Bible and saw their devotion to the Bible as the feature that joined all Protestants together and separated them from the Roman Catholics. The Methodists put the matter in these terms: "that wherein they all agree, and which they all subscribe with a greater harmony, as a perfect rule of their faith and actions, that is THE BIBLE; THE BIBLE, I say THE BIBLE ONLY IS THE RELIGION OF PROTESTANTS." *Christian Guardian,* 20 Mar. 1839, 77. The quotation is from Chittingworth's *Religion of Protestants,* chap. 6, sec. 56. Strachan put it this way: "Not all the books on earth would compensate the loss of the Bible to mankind; for it is the Bible, and the Bible alone, that points the way to the mansions where God in Christ forever reigneth." John Strachan, *A Charge Delivered to the Clergy of the Diocese of Toronto at the Visitation on Wednesday, 30 April 1856, by John, Lord Bishop of Toronto* (Toronto: Henry Rowsell 1856), 26.

27 The term "dispensation" was often used to describe the various eras of Christian time. The term was a general one and while related to, should not be confused with, the "dispensationalism" of conservative Protestant theology of a later day. See Ernest R. Sandeen, *The Roots of Fundamentalism: British and American Millenarianism 1800–1903* (Chicago: Univ. of Chicago Press 1970). For a clear contemporary expression of this structure of time see *Jubilee Sermon, Delivered at the Request of and Before the Wesleyan Methodist Conference, Assembled at London, C.W. June 6, 1855 by Rev. William Case* (Toronto: G.R. Sanderson 1855), 5ff.

28 During the nineteenth century people and groups differed about the

interpretation of certain elements of this framework rather than about the framework itself. One of these points – the end of time – forms the subject of chapter 6 in this study. Two of the most important intellectual challenges to this framework were evolution and Biblical criticism. Both, however, were incorporated into this framework, although to do this took considerable effort. See A.B. McKillop, *A Disciplined Intelligence: Critical Inquiry and Canadian Thought in the Victorian Era* (Montreal: McGill - Queen's 1979), and Michael Gauvreau, "History and Faith: A Study of the Evangelical Temper in Canada, 1820–1940" (Ph.D. thesis, Univ. of Toronto, 1984); and Michael Gauvreau, "The Taming of History: Reflections on the Methodist Encounter with Biblical Criticism, 1830–1890," *Papers of the Canadian Methodist Historical Society* 3 (1983).

29 For recent treatments of natural theology see McKillop, *A Disciplined Intelligence;* Carl Berger, *Science, God, and Nature in Victorian Canada* (Toronto: Univ. of Toronto Press 1983); and M.L. Clarke, *Paley: Evidences for the Man* (Toronto: Univ. of Toronto Press 1974). Paley's main works were *Principles of Moral and Political Philosophy*, *A View of the Evidences of Christianity*, and *Natural Theology*. See also Horton Davies, *Worship and Theology in England: From Watts and Wesley to Maurice, 1690–1850* (Princeton: Princeton Univ. Press 1961).

30 For a detailed discussion of early Victorian understandings of perception and psychology see McKillop, *A Disciplined Intelligence*, esp. chaps 2 and 3; and Alison Prentice, *The School Promoters: Education and Social Class in Mid-Nineteenth-Century Upper Canada* (Toronto: McClelland and Stewart 1977), esp. chap. 1.

31 The analogy of nature and God has a long history; the specific analogy of the watchmaker and God provides the introduction to Paley's *Natural Theology*. Clarke, *Paley*, 89–92.

32 AO, Strachan Papers, Manuscript Sermon (31), preached on Psalm 19:2, "Day unto Day uttereth speech, and night unto night sheweth knowledge," first preached 30 Dec. 1821; and Manuscript Sermon (4), preached on the Creed "I believe in God the Father Almighty Maker of Heaven and Earth," first preached 1 July 1804.

33 The Rev. John Strachan, A.M., *The Christian Religion Recommended in a Letter to His Pupils* (Montreal: Nahum Mower 1807), 16. The pamphlet is introduced by the maxim "The Good Alone Can Happiness Enjoy."

34 This passage, Romans 8:28-31, provided the biblical text for a great many sermons in the period. Strachan often used the passage as a text or as a reference; see for example John Strachan, *A Sermon Preached at York, Upper Canada, on the Third of June Being the Day Appointed for General Thanksgiving* (Montreal 1814), and AO, Strachan

Papers, Manuscript Sermon (40), preached on II Corinthians 5:8 "We are confident, I say, and willing rather to be absent from the body, and to be present with the Lord," first preached 30 June 1822.

35 Strachan, *A Sermon Preached at York ... on the Death of the Late Lord Bishop of Quebec*. "To become happy is, therefore, the end of our being; to this all the works of nature and all the powers and faculties of our minds are intended to contribute." John Strachan, *A Sermon on the Death of the Honourable Richard Cartwright, with a Short Account of his Life* (Kingston 1815), 9.

36 Anglican fears of deism led in large part to the founding of the Society for the Propagation of the Gospel in Foreign Parts [hereafter SPG] and the Society for Promoting Christian Knowledge [hereafter SPCK]. These were the two key institutions, especially the SPG, that oversaw and supported the Church in Canada. See C.F. Pascoe, *Two Hundred Years of the S.P.G. An Historical Account of the Society for the Propagation of the Gospel in Foreign Parts, 1701–1900* (London: SPG 1901), I, 3. For an account of the Presbyterian integration of revelation and theology see Gauvreau, "History and Faith", Part I. See also AO, Strachan Papers, Manuscript Sermon (39), preached on Ephesians 4:30 "and grieve not the holy Spirit of God, whereby ye are sealed unto the day of redemption," first preached 26 May 1822.

37 The crucial role that prophecy played in natural theology has not been properly acknowledged. In addition to the function described here, it provided the bridge between natural theology and millennialism, and explains the quite rational practice of calculating the exact moment when prophecies, such as the second advent, will be fulfilled.

38 Strachan, *The Christian Religion Recommended to his Pupils*, 22–3. Strachan often spoke about the limitations of reason unaided by revelation. "We well know that human reason when most improved was in this respect dark and doubtful and could never discover upon which terms the sinner was to be pardoned nor upon what conditions received into divine favour." He would then emphasize that revelation was consistent with reason because they both promoted the same goal – "religion and refined reason join in the recommendation of holiness" – and was able in effect to conclude that "surely the voice of enlightened reason is the voice of God." AO, Strachan Papers, Manuscript Sermon (28), preached on Psalm 73:24, "Thou shalt guide me by thy counsel, and afterwards receive me to Glory," first preached 4 Nov. 1821; (6), preached on St Matthew 20:16, "So the last shall be first and the first last; for

many be called but few chosen," first preached 15 Dec. 1804; and
(12), preached on I Corinthians 10:31, "Whether therefore ye eat or
drink or whatsoever ye do - do all to the glory of God," first
preached (at Cornwall before the Governor) 3 Aug. 1806.

39 Strachan, *The Christian Religion Recommended to his Pupils*, 24.

40 AO, Strachan Papers, Manuscript Sermon (12), preached on I Corinthians 10:31. In the same sermon Strachan explained the importance of morality and the future very clearly. "Having fixed these
truths in the mind Christian morality points always to the other
world and considers everything done here as promoting happiness
or misery there."

41 AO, Strachan Papers, Manuscript Sermon (22), preached on II Corinthians, 3:17 "Now the Lord is that Spirit and where the Spirit of
the Lord is there is liberty," first preached 4 July 1821 [archival notation on microfilm suggests, I believe incorrectly, the date of 4
Feb. 1821].

Scholars have often commented on Strachan's conservatism, and
some have appealed to sermons, such as this one, to sustain their
case. While the argument here acknowledges the conservatism of
many of Strachan's ideas, it differs from other analyses of Strachan's thought by emphasizing his appeal to nature as an anal-
ogue of order and hierarchy, rather than to history *per se*.
Strachan's thought was mechanistic and deductive rather than historical and descriptive. See S.F. Wise, "Sermon Literature and
Canadian Intellectual History," *The Bulletin* (Committee on Archives
of the United Church of Canada) 18 (1965), 3–18; and Robert Lochiel Fraser III, "Like Eden in Her Summer Dress: Gentry, Economy, and Society: Upper Canada, 1812–1840" (Ph.D. thesis, Univ. of
Toronto 1979), esp. chaps 1 and 4.

42 AO, Robinson Papers, charge to the grand jury, Kingston, 20 Sept.
1841 as cited in Fraser, "Like Eden in Her Summer Dress," 213.
For a stimulating interpretation of Robinson's thought see David
Howes, "Property, God and Nature in the Thought of Sir John
Beverley Robinson," *McGill Law Journal* 30 (1985), 365–414. Howes
approaches Robinson through the Loyalist Covenant (see Duffy's
work on Loyalism), and although he is also concerned with culture
and myth, he treats conservative thought in the early nineteenth
century quite differently from this study.

43 McKillop, *A Disciplined Intelligence*, esp. chap. 3.

44 For a general discussion of the changing structure of sermons see
Charles Smyth, *The Art of Preaching: A Practical Survey of Preaching
in the Church of England 747–1939* (London: SPCK, 1940). A more
detailed discussion of the structure of sermons follows in chaps 3
and 4. Strachan's own copy of *An Account of Sir Isaac Newton's Phil-*

osophical Discoveries by Colin Maclaurin (1775) has recently been acquired for the Strachan Collection at Trinity College through the generosity of the Friends of the Trinity Library.

45 The argument in fact indicates the vulnerability of the Anglican position, for if social order (and other social values) could be achieved by other means, then the reasons for the state to support the church suddenly disappeared. For a more detailed discussion of church and state, see the fourth chapter of this study and *A Charge Delivered to the Clergy of the Diocese of Quebec by George J. Mountain, D.D. Lord Bishop of Montreal at his Primary Visitation, Completed in 1838* (Quebec: Thomas Carey 1839).

46 AO, *Strachan Letterbook 1827–1834*, Strachan to Archdeacon George Mountain, 31 Dec. 1827.

47 Strachan, *An Appeal to the Friends of Religion and Literature*, 21.

48 Ryerson's response to Strachan's sermon shows that he was quite familiar with a number of Paley's arguments. The two most influential texts on the question of church and state were William Warburton, *The Alliance Between Church and State, or the Necessity and Equity of an Established Religion, and a Test-law, Demonstrated* (1736); and William Paley, *The Principals of Moral and Political Philosophy*, Bk 6, "Elements of Political Knowledge," chap. 10, "Of Religious Establishments and Toleration."

49 "A Review of a Sermon ... by a Methodist Preacher."

50 *Christian Guardian*, 4 Sept. and 11 Sept. 1830, 330 and 337. See also *Journal of the Rev. John Wesley A.M.*, ed., Nehemia Curnock (London, 1909-16); Fred Dreyer, "Faith and Experience in the Thought of John Wesley," *American Historical Review* 88, 1 (Feb. 1983), 12–30. For a stimulating and informative account of revivalism in Nova Scotia see George Rawlyk, *Ravished By the Spirit: Religious Revivals, Baptists, and Henry Alline* (Kingston and Montreal: McGill-Queen's Univ. Press 1984).

51 *Christian Guardian*, "Experimental Religion," 26 Nov. 1834, 9.

52 For an interesting discussion of the issue of theological training see Gerald O. McCulloh, *Ministerial Education in the American Methodist Movement* (Nashville, Tenn.: United Methodist Board of Higher Education 1980).

53 *Christian Guardian*, "The Great Utility of Camp Meetings in Promoting Revivals of Religion," 31 Oct. 1832, 201.

54 For example, *Christian Guardian*, "Prepare for Camp Meetings," 21 Apr. 1842; John Carroll, *Past and Present, or a Description of Persons and Events Connected with Canadian Methodism for the Last Forty Years by a Spectator of the Scenes* (Toronto: Alfred Dredge 1860), 64; and *Christian Guardian*, 23 Sept. 1835, 182; 25 July 1832, 146.

55 For sketches of some contemporary revivalistic sermons see John

Carroll, *Father Corson: Or the Old Style Canadian Itinerant: Embracing the Life and the Gospel Labours of the Rev. Robert Corson, Fifty-Six Years a Minister in Connection with the Central Methodism of Upper Canada* (Toronto: Samuel Rose 1879), 243–77.

56 Arthur E. Kewley, "Mass Evangelism in Upper Canada Before 1830" (D.Th. thesis, Victoria College 1960). This two volume study is an extremely rich compendium of material on revivalism. Any student of revivalism will always be in Dr Kewley's debt, although his desire to show the contemporary value of many features of revivalism leads him in general to interpret revivalism somewhat more conservatively than the present study.

57 For example, *Christian Guardian*, 23 July 1831, 146; 25 July 1832, 146; and 23 Sept. 1835, 132. "Tears are nothing but the juice of a mind pressed and squeezed by grief." George F. Playter, *The History of Methodism in Canada* (Toronto: Anson Green 1862), 372.

58 See for example United Church Archives [hereafter UCA], "Autobiography of Joseph Gatchell, Personal Papers," and "Journals of Rev. George Ferguson, Personal Papers"; Abel Stevens, *Life and Times of Nathan Bangs* (New York, 1863), 28–55; Marguerite Van Die, "Nathanael Burwash and the Conscientious Search for Truth," *Papers of the Canadian Methodist Historical Society* 3 (1983); and Gerald C. Brauer, "Conversion: From Puritanism to Revivalism," *Journal of Religion* 58 (July 1978), 227–43.

59 AO, Strachan Papers, Manuscript sermon preached on Lamentations 3:40, "Let us search and try our ways and turn again to the Lord," first preached 14 Nov. 1824. This sermon seems to have been lost or misplaced in the recent microfilming of the Strachan sermons.

60 AO, Strachan Papers, Manuscript sermon (85), preached on Matthew 25:39, "Then shall the king say unto them on his right hand, come ye blessed of my Father," first preached 31 Mar. 1830.

61 AO, Strachan Papers, Manuscript sermon (31), preached on Psalm 19:2.

62 For example SPG Archives, C/Canada/Quebec, folio 368. Rev. C.B. Fleming to G.J. Mountain, 21 Mar. 1844: folio 415, Rev. Edward Cusak to Bishop of Montreal n.d. (*c.* 1841); C/Canada/Quebec/Upper Canada, folio 508, Copy of Journal of Rev. F.L. Osler, 6 Jan. to 16 Apr. 1841; also Thomas Conant, *Upper Canada Sketches* (Toronto: William Briggs 1898).

63 "Whosoever is born of God doth not commit sin; for his seed remaineth in him; and he cannot sin, because he is born of God" (I John 3:9). "Does it (the fact that God answers prayer) prove that … believers can by prayer obtain the creation, destruction, disorganization, alteration or perpetuation of anything in the material and the immaterial, the natural and the moral worlds?" *Christian Guardian*, 12 Oct. 1836, 193.

64 See Edward Deming Andrews, *The People Called Shakers: A Search for the Perfect Society* (New York: Dome 1963); and J.F.C. Harrison, *The Second Coming: Popular Millenarianism 1780–1850* (New Brunswick, NJ: Rutgers Univ. Press 1979).

65 See Whitney R. Cross, *The Burned-over District: The Social and Intellectual History of Enthusiastic Religion in Western New York, 1800–1850* (Ithaca, NY: Cornell Univ. Press, 1950), esp. chap. 8.

66 For material on David Willson see Thomas Gerry, "From the Quakers to the Children of Peace: the Development of David Willson's Mystical Religion," *Univ. of Toronto Quarterly* 54 (Winter 1984/85), 200–16. Where the spirit might lead, and the consequent instability of revivals is a recurrent theme in the commentaries on this form of religious practice. See the third chapter of this study and Patrick Sheriff, *A Tour Through North America; Together with a Comprehensive View of the Canadas and United States as Adapted for Agricultural Emigration* (Edinburgh: Oliver and Boyd 1835).

67 Paul Romney, "A Struggle for Authority: Toronto Society and Politics in 1834," in Victor L. Russell, ed., *Forging a Consensus: Historical Essays on Toronto* (Toronto: Univ. of Toronto Press 1984), 9–40.

68 AO, Strachan Letterbook, 1812–34, Letter to the Lord Bishop of Quebec, 1 Oct. 1812.

69 SPG Archives, C/Canada/Quebec/Upper Canada, John Strachan to S. Ramsey, 4 Sept. 1840. One doubts if the clergy of our Church can do either at the present time.

70 For an excellent discussion of the transformation of Methodism see Neil Semple, "The Impact of Urbanization on the Methodist Church in Central Canada 1854–1884" (Ph.D. thesis: Univ. of Toronto 1979), and the third chapter of this study.

71 S. D. Clark, *Church and Sect in Canada* (Toronto: Univ. of Toronto Press 1948).

72 For comments on the churching of women see *The Church*, 14 Dec. 1839, 4. In their desire to use the structure of the physical world to predict events, astrology and almanacs worked within the broad framework of natural theology. In this sense astrology is Paley at a popular level.

73 To follow the migration from church to revival and back to church see SPG Archives, C/Canada/Quebec, folio 367, Rev. John Butler to Rev. C.B. Dalton; folio 388, Rev. Christopher Jackson to Lord Bishop of Montreal, 10 June 1842. "It is hard to convince them that there is any harm in frequenting a Methodist meeting House, or an assembly of Brownists, Baptists, or even Millenarians. If a strange preacher comes into the neighbourhood, everyone must go to hear what he has to say, and on such occasion no weather will keep them at home." *Ibid.*, folio 422, Rev. John Butler to Rev. C.B.

Dalton, 23 Jan. 1843. *The Church* suggested that it would be better for Anglicans to stay at home and read a good book than to attend a Methodist revival.

74 John Strachan, *A Letter ot the Congregation of St. James' Church, York, Upper Canada; Occasioned by the Hon. John Elmsley's Publication on the Bishop of Strasbourg's Observations on the 6th Chapter of St. John's Gospel* (York, UC: Robert Stanton *c.* 1834), 52.

75 Strachan's concern with the spirit is also clear when he attacked deism and those who "consider human reason sufficient for all things." On these occasions he defended the importance of the spirit. See AO, Strachan Papers, Manuscript sermons (39), preached on Ephesians 4:30; and (40), preached on II Corinthians 5:8.

76 *Christian Guardian*, "Christian Experience," 10 Apr. 1839, 93.

CHAPTER THREE

1 See Whitney R. Cross, *The Burned-over District: The Social and Intellectual History of Enthusiastic Religion in Western New York, 1800-1850* (Ithaca: Cornell Univ. Press 1950); for a more general comparison of the religious history of Canada and the United States see Robert T. Handy, *A History of the Churches in the United States and Canada* (New York: Oxford 1977).

2 For an excellent discussion of Blake and popular religious culture see J.F.C. Harrison, *The Second Coming: Popular Millenarianism 1780–1850* (New Brunswick, NJ: Rutgers Univ. Press 1979), 215–17.

3 The vindication of Ryerson began within Methodism shortly after the debate itself and has continued to the present day. The *Christian Guardian* almost from its inception championed Ryerson's "triumph," John Carroll sustained this verdict, Ryerson's biographers reached the same conclusion, and the most recent historian of the Methodism in this period carries on the tradition. See John Carroll, *Case and His Cotemporaries; or the Canadian Itinerants' Memorial*, 5 vols. (Toronto: Samuel Rose 1867–7); G.F. Playter, *History of Methodism in Canada* (Toronto: Wesleyan Printing Establishment 1862); C.B. Sissons, *Egerton Ryerson: His Life and Letters* (Toronto: Clark, Irwin 1947); and Goldwin French, *Parsons and Politics: The Role of Wesleyan Methodists in Upper Canada and the Maritimes from 1780 to 1855* (Toronto: Ryerson 1962).

4 This concept also has a long and interesting history. Ryerson himself alluded to the unsuitability of establishments in Canada and the usefulness and popularity of Methodism. Most Methodist historians have returned to the same theme. It also has an interesting sociological strain. The association of enthusiastic styles of religion with

the Canadian environment runs through the "frontier" school and finds its fullest expression in the work of S.D. Clark. See especially S.D. Clark, *The Developing Canadian Community* (Toronto: Univ. of Toronto Press 1959).

5 Rev. William Morley Punshon, *Canada: Its Religious Prospects: An Address Delivered Before the English Wesleyan Conference at Manchester July 26, 1871* (Toronto: Wesleyan Book Room 1871).

6 Neil Semple, "Ontario's Religious Hegemony: The Creation of the National Methodist Church," *Ontario History* 77, 1 (March 1985), 19–42; and William Magney, "The Methodist Church and the National Gospel, 1884–1914, " *Bulletin* (Committee on Archives of the United Church of Canada), 20 (1968), 3–95.

7 Neil Semple, "The Impact of Urbanization on the Methodist Church in Central Canada, 1854–1884," (Ph.D. thesis, Univ. of Toronto 1979).

8 John Carroll, *Case and His Cotemporaries; or the Canadian Itinerants' Memorial*, 5 vols. (Toronto: Samuel Rose 1867–7); John Carroll, *"Father Corson," or the old style Canadian Itinerant: embracing the Life and Gospel Labours of the Rev. Robert Corson, fifty-six years a minister in connection with the central Methodism of Upper Canada* (Toronto: Samuel Rose 1882); John Carroll, *Past and Present, or a description of persons and events connected with Canadian Methodism for the Last Forty Years by a Spectator of the Scene*, published anonymously (Toronto: Alfred Bridge 1860). For an excellent discussion of Carroll see John Webster Grant, ed., *Salvation! O The Joyful Sound* (Toronto: Oxford 1967).

9 *Christian Guardian*, 11 Feb. 1835; see also *Christian Guardian*, 25 July 1832, 146; and 23 Sept. 1835, 182.

10 For example, *Christian Guardian*, 2 July 1831, 131; 9 July 1831, 138; 31 July 1833, 149; 23 Sept. 1835, 182.

11 "Females are thus prompted to exhibit themselves, and I was credibly assured, that at Hatley two young girls were thus in 'the struggles,' the objects of their intercession being two of the troopers quartered in the village." *A Journal of the Visitation to a Part of the Diocese of Quebec by the Lord Bishop of Montreal in the Spring of 1843* (London: Society for the Propagation of the Gospel [hereafter SPG] 1844) 77.

12 For some examples of conversion experiences see Abel Stevens, *Life and Times of Nathan Bangs* (New York, 1863), 29. John Carroll retells the story of William Lossee's conversion in *Case and his Cotemporaries*, vol. 1, 7; Carroll records his own experience in *My Boy Life* (see Grant, *Salvation! O The Joyful Sound*, 145–147); United Church Archives [hereafter UCA], "Journal of Rev. George Ferguson, Personal Papers" esp. his ordination experience, 65.

13 UCA, "Autobiography of Joseph Gatchell, Personal Papers," 13.

14 *Ibid.*, 13.

15 The Rev. William Case, *Jubilee Sermon, Delivered at the Request of and Before the Wesleyan Canada Conference, Assembled at London, C.W., June 6, 1855* (Toronto: G. R. Sanderson 1855); the sermon was reprinted in the *Christian Guardian*, 13 June 1855, 142, and described in *Case and His Cotemporaries*, vol. 1, 18.

16 Carroll, *Case and His Cotemporaries*, vol. 2, 85–6. Carroll attributes this description to the Rev. Charles Giles, "a member of the Conference." Rev. William Case describes the same sermon in his *Jubilee Sermon ... June 6, 1855* and refers to the same source.

17 Patrick Sherriff, *A Tour Through North America; Together with a Comprehensive View of the Canadas and the United States As Adapted for Agricultural Emigration* (Edinburgh: Oliver and Boyd 1835), 186.

18 *Ibid.*

19 *Ibid.*, 186–8.

20 Carroll, *Case and His Cotemporaries*, vol. 1, 11.

21 *Ibid.*, vol. 1, 7–8.

22 The story is repeated many times. In addition to *Case and His Cotemporaries* it appears in W.H. Withrow, *Barbara Heck: A Tale of Early Methodism* (Toronto: William Briggs 1894). The same story (without Brouse) appears in Nathan Bangs, *A History of the Methodist Episcopal Church* (New York, 1839), vol. 2, 74.

23 "Many bystanders were laughing at the exclamations and postures of the worshippers; others were reading newspapers, or carelessly engaged in conversation." Sherriff, *A Tour Through North America*, 186.

24 Thomas Fisher Rare Book Library, University of Toronto, Dr. Mackenzie's Canadian Diary, 1839–43. I am indebted to Dr Carol Wilton-Siegel for bringing this source to my attention.

25 *Ibid.* The handkerchief also appears in Susanna Moodie, *Life in the Clearings* (1853; rpr. Toronto: Macmillan 1959), 107-126. Her accounts are second-hand, but still confirm the thrust of this analysis.

26 *Ibid.*

27 *Christian Guardian*, 21 Apr. 1841, 102; Carroll, *Past and Present*, 64. In the same passage Carroll describes a large fence of slabs "driven in the ground at an angle of forty-five degrees from the perpendicular ... sharpened at the top, thus constituting a sort of *chevaux de frise* which no intruder, however, bold, might dare to scale." *Christian Guardian*, 17 July 1844, 153.

28 United Church Archives, "Journal of Rev. George Ferguson," 63.

29 Carroll, *Father Corson*, 86ff. See also "Why are there so many Backsliders," *Christian Guardian*, 22 Sept. 1841, 189.

30 "Hints for Helping a Revival," *Christian Guardian*, 24 Jan. 1844, 54.

31 Rev. W.C. Walton, "Thoughts on Revivals," *Christian Guardian*,

12 Feb. 1831. "I told them my pockets would not hold water to quench fire, and that I would rather throw oil on it than water." UCA, "Journal of Rev. George Ferguson," and "How Shall We Obtain a Revival of Religion," *Christian Guardian*, 31 July 1830, 291.

32 For an excellent presentation of the discipline of a class meeting see *Christian Guardian*, 14 May 1834, 105.

33 Bangs, *A History of the Methodist Episcopal Church*, II, 71-2.

34 *Ibid.*, 72.

35 The relationship between religious and sexual experience is complex and fascinating, although only certain aspects of this relationship are touched upon in this study. In relation to this chapter the intensity of a religious experience could lead people to believe that their own salvation was so secure they were no longer bound by the moral law and had achieved perfection. Consequently they could indulge in sexual activities that were forbidden to others. This form of antinomianism proved to be a quick road from religious conversion to sexual freedom. A few other aspects of the relationship may also be mentioned, although this is by no means even a minimal representation of the issue. The sexual appeal of revivalists is well known, and the fact that sexual failings were a recurrent problem among them (indeed among all clergy) simply emphasizes this fact. It is also clear that the language of revivalism is highly sexual in its rhythms and images. Although this might stem from the inability of other words to describe such an experience, certainly the concurrence of religious and sexual language drew the two types of experiences more closely together. Sex, as it were, came to imitate religion. And finally there is the critical way religion could provide the context for reorganizing the relationship between the sexes. Women seemed to have played very important roles in revivalism, and many of the most thorough attempts to institutionalize new sexual patterns in the nineteenth century grew out of the same religious nexus.

36 The relationship between revivalism and millennial groups is discussed in more detail in chapter 6. See also Jerald C. Brauer, "Revivalism and Millenarianism in America," in Joseph D. Ban and Paul R. Dekar, eds, *In the Great Tradition in Honour of Withrop S. Hudson: Essays on Pluralism, Voluntarism, and Revivalism* (Valley Forge, Pa.: Judson 1982), 147–59.

37 Rev. J. Scott, letter to *Christian Guardian*, 4 Mar. 1840, 73.

38 *Christian Guardian*, 28 Sept. 1836, 185.

39 See for example "On Ministerial Dignity," *Christian Guardian*, 11 Feb. 1835, 53; 28 Sept. 1836, 185; "Hints on Preaching," *Christian Guardian*, 18 Jan. 1843, 49.

40 Neil Semple provides the most thorough treatment of these changes.

See Semple, "The Impact of Urbanization on the Methodist Church in Central Canada, 1854-1884," esp. chaps 3 and 4. For contemporary discussions of some of these changes see *Christian Guardian*, 21 Mar. 1832, 74, 16 May 1832, 106, 23 September 1840, 190 (Sunday Schools); *Christian Guardian*, 21 Sept. 1842, 190. 10 Dec. 1851, 33 (Educated Ministry); Carroll, *Past and Present*, 125 (Decline of Exhorters); *Christian Guardian*, 27 Aug. 1851, 181, 10 Sept. 1851, 189, 24 Sept. 1851, 197 (Role of Laity). The figures for Methodist growth appear in chapter 1. An account of the growth of church building appears in chapter 5.

41 The process of Methodist church union is described best in an excellent handout from the United Church Archives entitled simply "The Methodist Church." See also Semple, " Ontario's Religious Hegemony," *Ontario History* 77 (Mar. 1985), 19–42; and T.W. Caldwell, "The Unification of Methodism in Canada, 1865-1884," *Bulletin* (Committee on Archives of the United Church of Canada), 19 (1967), 1–61.

42 The work of S.D. Clark provides the best illustration of this approach. For a detailed examination of his treatment of religion and social change see W.E. de Villiers-Westfall, "The Sacred and the Secular," app. 1, 299–323.

43 For a discussion of respectability see Semple, "The Impact of Urbanization," in relation to education see Alison Prentice, *The School Promoters: Education and Social Class in Mid-nineteenth Century Upper Canada* (Toronto: McClelland and Stewart 1977).

44 "Prepare for Camp Meetings," *Christian Guardian*, 21 Apr. 1841, 102.

45 Another illustration of this process is provided by an article in the *Christian Guardian*, entitled "Good Old Methodist Usages." In appealing to what is "good" and "old" the article in fact defends a number of innovations. See "Good Old Methodist Usages," *Christian Guardian*, 7 Sept. 1842, 182.

46 Arthur E. Kewley, "Mass Evangelism in Upper Canada Before 1830" (D.Th. thesis, Emmanuel College, 1960), 14. See also Semple, "The Impact of Urbanization," esp. chap. 5.

47 In the descriptions of early revivals this is a recurring theme. Ministers did not anticipate that a revival would take place – they in fact tried hard to prevent its occurrence – but "the spirit" was too strong and the people initiated the revival.

48 *Christian Guardian*, 17 July 1844, 153; Carroll, *Past and Present*, 64.

49 Carroll, *Past and Present*, 123–6; Semple, "The Impact of Urbanization," chap. 5; *Christian Guardian*, 29 Jan. 1834, 45.

50 For example, "On Inviting Penitents to the Altar," *Christian Guardian*, 15 Dec. 1841 and *Christian Guardian*, 18 Nov. 1840, 14.

51 Carroll, *Past and Present*, 123–6.

52 "Camp and Field Meetings," *Christian Guardian*, 6 Sept. 1843, 182.

53 "On Ministerial Dignity," *Christian Guardian*, 11 Feb. 1835, 53.

54 "Preaching," *Christian Guardian*, 27 Sept. 1837, 185.

55 *Christian Guardian*, 5 June 1833, 118–19.

56 *Christian Guardian*, 7 Sept. 1842, 182.

57 "The Amen," *Christian Guardian*, 9 Nov. 1842, 10.

58 Semple, "The Impact of Urbanization," chap. 5. See also the discussion that follows.

59 *Christian Guardian*, 14 Jan. 1852.

60 *Christian Guardian*, 7 Jan. 1846, 45.

61 *Ibid.*, 45.

62 For a general guide to this debate, see the letters from YOD in the *Christian Guardian*, 24 Sept. 1845, 193; 1 Oct. 1845, 197; 15 Oct. 1845, 205 (signed DOY); and 26 Nov. 1845, 21. For some of the letters on the other side, see *Christian Guardian*, 13 Aug. 1845, 169; 22 Oct. 1845, 1; and 3 Dec. 1845, 25.

63 *Christian Guardian*, a letter from a local preacher, Prince Edward County, 25 Feb. 1846, 73.

64 "Protracted Religious Meetings," *Christian Guardian*, 31 Dec. 1845, 42.

65 This was the same position put forward in Thomas Webster, *History of the Methodist Episcopal Church in Canada* (Hamilton: Canada Christian Advocate 1870), 104.

66 It is interesting to note that Methodists had to fight on two fronts as they moved towards a more moderate representation of experience. They still had to defend themselves from Anglican attacks, although these were less frequent (see "Attack on Camp Meetings," *Christian Guardian*, 7 Sept. 1842, 182); at the same time they had to try to attack the revivalism of those on their own extreme sectarian wing (see "Enthusiasm – A Conversation," *Christian Guardian*, 10 Mar. 1841, 77).

67 "Superstition and Enthusiasm," Christian Guardian, 21 June 1837, 129.

68 *Ibid.*, 129.

69 *Christian Guardian*, 23 Sept. 1835, 182.

70 "What Shall Ensure the Prosperity of the Church," *Christian Guardian*, 21 Oct. 1840, 206.

71 *Ibid.* Compare this article with earlier discussions of sanctification, for example, *Christian Guardian*, 30 Jan. 1830, 85.

72 "Nor was it possible, that any subsequent change in the circumstances of human nature, could in the least weaken man's moral obligation," "On the proper ground of moral obligation," *Christian Guardian*, 21 June 1837, 129.

73 The exchange is recounted in the *Christian Guardian*, 18 Apr. 1838, 95.

74 *Ibid.*, 95.

75 "Christian Experience – Its Influence," *Christian Guardian*, 3 Dec. 1856, 33.

76 United Church Archives, Burwash Papers, box 30, Autobiography. There was at this time a major controversy within Methodism over the class meeting. Egerton Ryerson argued, in fact, that failure to attend class meetings should *not* be grounds for loss of church membership, maintaining that it was more important to lead a proper life, attend church, and do good works. When his position was attacked, Ryerson resigned from the Conference. His resignation was accepted but he was soon reinstated. See *Christian Guardian*, 18 July 1855.

77 By 1845, one finds a growing number of references to an informal evangelical association of Protestant ministers in Toronto that met to listen to a public lecture and discuss it. A similar group, the Evangelical alliance, was formed in England in August 1846. There was also a good deal of discussion of "Evangelical Union" as early as 1846. See "Evangelical Association," *Christian Guardian*, 9 Apr. 1845, 98; and *Christian Guardian*, "To the Friends of Evangelical Union," 5 Aug. 1846, 166.

78 "Christian Experience – Its Nature, " *Christian Guardian*, 15 Oct. 1856, 5.

79 "Do we not become fixed with a noble ambition when we survey the wonderous scenes which surround us, which rise above us sublimely high, and away off in the deep and distance lay hold upon the hopes and fears, the joys and sorrows of other worlds and times ... we patronize, project, and support missions ... we enter with lovable zeal every open door of usefulness, either at home or abroad." *Ibid.*, 5.

80 *Christian Guardian*, 7 Aug. 1844, 166. Strachan and Ryerson met inadvertently on a coach trip between Kingston and Cobourg in February 1842. Much to Ryerson's surprise they had a pleasant journey, and he commented "Conversation took place on several important topics, on scarcely any of which did I see reason to differ from the Bishop." *Christian Guardian*, 23 Feb. 1842, 70.

81 Case, *Jubilee Sermon*, 60.

82 See, for example "The Church and the World: Worldliness in Relation to the Spirit of Devotion," *Christian Guardian*, 3 Oct. 1855, 207. "Christian men ought to know that [it] is a difficult thing to keep the world in its place, subject to them, and not a lord over them. It is always encroaching on the territory of sacred things ... Take care how you yield up your treasures at its demand. Resist, fight, and overcome it."

83 The term "evangelical" appears in the Methodist vocabulary regularly in the late 1830s, and by the mid-1840s becomes one of the most common adjectives to describe a good Methodist. See, for example, the new column entitled "The Evangelical Essayist," which began in the *Christian Guardian* on 11 Nov. 1840, 9. See also Ralph H. Gabriel, "Evangelical Religion and Popular Romanticism in Early Nineteenth-Century America," *Church History* 19 (Mar. 1950), 34-47.

84 Many of these changes are discussed in chap. 5.

85 "Methodist Pastoral Reminiscences," *Christian Guardian*, 9 Aug. 1843 to 20 Dec. 1843; "Traditionary Recollections," *Christian Guardian*, 21 Mar. 1855; and "Bread Cast on the Waters Found After Many Days," *Christian Guardian*, 18 Apr. 1855.

86 See note 8 above for a discussion of John Carroll from a somewhat different perspective.

CHAPTER FOUR

1 John S. Moir, *Enduring Witness: A History of the Presbyterian Church in Canada* ([Toronto]: Presbyterian Publications [1974]), esp. chaps. 5 and 6.

2 John Strachan, *A Sermon Preached at York, Upper Canada, Third of July 1825, on the Death of the Late Lord Bishop of Quebec* (Kingston: Macfarlane 1826).

3 E.R. Norman, *The Conscience of the State in North America* (Cambridge: Cambridge Univ. 1968), esp. preface and chap. 1.

4 See John S. Moir, *Church and State in Canada West: Three Studies in the Relation of Denominationalism and Nationalism, 1841–1867* (Toronto: Univ. of Toronto Press 1959); Alan Wilson, *The Clergy Reserves of Upper Canada: A Canadian Mortmain* (Toronto: Univ. of Toronto Press 1968); L.F. Gates, *The Land Policies of Upper Canada* (Toronto: Univ. of Toronto Press 1968); G.M. Craig, *Upper Canada: The Formative Years, 1784–1841* (Toronto: McClelland and Stewart 1963); J.M.S. Careless, *The Union of the Canadas: The Growth of Canadian Institutions, 1841–1857* (Toronto: McClelland and Stewart 1967).

5 For some useful material on this aspect see J.L.H. Henderson, *John Strachan 1778–1867* (Toronto: Univ. of Toronto Press 1969); Thomas R. Millman, *Jacob Mountain, First Lord Bishop of Quebec, A Study in Church and State* (Toronto: Univ. of Toronto Press 1947); Thomas R. Millman, *The Life of the Right Reverend, The Honourable Charles James Stewart* (Huron College: London, Ont., 1953); and esp. Curtis Fahey, "A Troubled Zion: The Anglican Experience in Upper Canada, 1791–1854," (Ph.D. thesis, Carleton Univ. 1981).

6 For example, see John Charles Dent, *The Story of the Upper Canadian*

Rebellion: Largely derived from Original Sources and Documents (Toronto: C.B. Robinson 1885), 23; and the treatment that Strachan and the establishment receive in Aileen Dunham, *Political Unrest in Upper Canada, 1815–1836* (London, 1927), 80.

7 For an account of some of these petitions see J.J. Talman, ed., *Loyalist Narratives from Upper Canada* (Toronto: Champlain Society 1946).

8 John Strachan, *A Discourse on the Character of King George the Third; Addressed to the Inhabitants of British America* (Montreal, 1810).

9 A detailed description of the religion of order appears in chap. 2; the question of religion and social order is discussed in chap. 7.

10 See for example John Strachan, *An Appeal to the Friends of Religion and Literature, in Behalf of The University of Upper Canada* (London: R. Gilbert 1827), and John Strachan, *A Sermon Preached at York, Upper Canada, Third of July 1825, on the Death of the Late Lord Bishop of Quebec* (Kingston: Macfarlane 1826).

11 John Strachan, *Observations on the Provision Made for the Maintenance of a Protestant Clergy in the Provinces of Upper Canada and Lower Canada* (London: R. Gilbert 1827).

12 The association of religious establishments and social order is a genuine stable of Anglican discourse. Almost any issue of the Anglican newspaper, *The Church,* employs this defence. It was also the standard fare of the Bishop's correspondence and sermons and appears frequently in the letters of the local missionaries. See for example Lambeth Palace Library, Archbishop John Moore Papers, Bundle Four, Bishops Overseas, Jacob Mountain to Moore, 6 June 1803 and 13 June 1803. The major works of Strachan on this topic are John Strachan, *A Sermon Preached at York Upper Canada, Third of July 1825, on the Death of the Late Lord Bishop of Quebec* (1826); *Observations on the Provision Made for the Maintenance of a Protestant Clergy* ... (1827); *A Letter to the Right Honourable Thomas Frankland Lewis* (York: R. Stanton 1830); *An Appeal to the Friends of Religion and Literature* ... (1827). For the arguments of some of the local clergy see Society for the Propagation of the Gospel Archives [hereafter SPG], C/Canada/Toronto, folio 524, Rev. C.B. Gribble to SPG, 1 Apr. 1842: "Our principles teach men to be good subjects on religious grounds, the government will therefore do right to help forward our principles. And they will therefore do what is expedient for the principles of the church, where followed up by a faithful clergyman, beget humility and submission, order and peace." See as well SPG Archives, C/Canada/Toronto, folio 544, Rev. W.M. Herchmer to SPG, 3 Mar. 1845. For more general references to the arguments see Millman, *Jacob Mountain* and *Life of Charles James Stewart.*

13 For a discussion of the Constitutional Act see G.M. Craig, *Upper Canada: the Formative Years*, 13–19.

14 The basic works are William Warburton, *The Alliance Between Church and State, or the Necessity and Equity of Established Religion, and a Test-law, demonstrated* (1736); Edmund Burke, *Reflections on the Revolution in France* (1790); and William Paley, *The Principles of Moral and Political Philosophy* (1785).

15 Warburton, *The Alliance Between Church and State*, book 1, 37. Strachan used almost exactly the same reasoning in one of his most interesting sermons on the topic of religion and order: Archives of Ontario, Strachan Papers, Manuscript sermon (8), preached on II Corinthians 4:3, "But if our gospel be hid it is hid to them that are lost," first preached 30 Mar. 1806.

16 Warburton, *The Alliance Between Church and State*, book 1, chap 5, "The Nature and End of Religion."

17 Warburton, *The Alliance Between Church and State*, book 2, 88.

18 *Ibid.*, 106.

19 *Ibid.*, 166ff.

20 F.G. Selby, ed., *Burke's Reflections on the Revolution in France* (London: Macmillan 1930), 102–20.

21 Paley's discussion appears in chap. 10, "Of Religious Establishments and Toleration," book 6, "The Elements of Political Knowledge, " *The Principles of Moral and Political Philosophy.*

22 Paley, *Principles of Moral and Political Philosophy*, book 6, chap. 10.

23 *Ibid.*

24 "We will have her to exalt her mitred front in courts and parliaments. We will have her mixed throughout the whole mass of life, and blended with all the classes of society." Selby, ed., *Burke's Reflections on the Revolution in France*, 115. Alan Wilson points out that the rents on the reserves were kept low in order to integrate them into the economic life of the colony: Wilson, *The Clergy Reserves of Upper Canada*, 33. John Strachan made basically the same argument: Strachan, *A Letter to the Right Hon. Thomas Frankland Lewis.*

25 Curtis Fahey points out that the Colonial Church emphasized breadth rather than exclusivity in the early nineteenth century but became more exclusive as her position and the establishment came under attack: Fahey, "A Troubled Zion: The Anglican Experience in Upper Canada, 1791–1854."

26 Strachan's famous "Ecclesiastical Chart" is perhaps the best known example of this practice. It was appended to his *Observations on the Provision Made for the Maintenance of a Protestant Clergy.*

27 "A religious establishment is not part of Christianity; it is only the

means of inculcating it." "The authority therefore of a church establishment is founded in its utility": Paley, *Principles of Moral and Political Philosophy*, book 6, chap. 10.

28 See for example A.H. Young, "A Fallacy in Canadian History," *Canadian Historical Review* 15, 4 (Dec. 1934), 351–60; and J.J. Talman,
"The Position of the Church of England in Upper Canada, 1791–
1840," *Canadian Historical Review* 15, 4 (Dec. 1934), 361–75.

29 The tendency to confuse a religious establishment and religious intolerance provides a good example of this point. In fact, according
to both theory and practice religious freedom and an established
church were quite compatible.

30 For an excellent discussion of the crisis in the Church of England,
see G.F.A. Best, "The Constitutional Revolution, 1828–32, and its
Consequences for the Established Church," *Theology*, 42 (Jan. 1959),
226–234; and G.F.A. Best, *Temporal Pillars: Queen Anne's Bounty, The
Ecclesiastical Commissioners, and the Church of England* (Cambridge:
Cambridge Univ. Press 1964).

31 I am indebted here to an unpublished paper on this topic by Mr.
Alec Dufresne, which shed interesting light on the legal character
of the establishment.

32 For a good account of the marriage issue (along with other questions),
see John S. Moir, ed., *Church and State in Canada, 1627–1867: Basic
Documents* (Toronto: McClelland and Stewart 1967), 140ff.

33 J. J. Talman, "The Position of the Church of England in Upper Canada," 372ff.

34 Moir, *Church and State in Canada, 1627–1867*, 68–71.

35 Article XXI. See Adam Shortt and Arthur G. Doughty, eds, *Documents
Relating to the Constitutional History of Canada, 1759–1791* (Ottawa:
King's Printer 1918), Pt II, 1038.

36 *Ibid.* (Article XXXVIII).

37 *Ibid.* (Article XXXVII).

38 A.H. Young, "A Fallacy in Canadian History, " 358.

39 Professor Talman treats this issue in a thorough and convincing
fashion. J.J.Talman, "The Position of the Church of England in
Upper Canada," 361–4.

40 Talman, "The Position of the Church of England," 363. See also A.H.
Young, "Lord Dorchester and the Church of England," Canadian
Historical Association *Report* (1926), 60–5.

41 The document is reprinted in John M. Norris, "Proposals for Promoting Religion and Literature in Canada, Nova Scotia, and New
Brunswick," *Canadian Historical Review* 36 (Dec. 1955), 335–40.

42 "Our claims still unsettled, and the support of our clergy partial,
meagre and precarious to the infinite detriment of religion and the

manifest perpetuation of those very jealousies and contentions of which the apprehension has dictated this temporizing policy, but of which the existence is to be traced to the want of an avowed and decided maintenance of the Church Establishment as it was originally planned." SPG Archives, C/Canada/Quebec, folio 368, *A Charge Delivered to the Clergy of the Diocese of Quebec by George J. Mountain, D.D. Lord Bishop of Montreal at His Primary Visitation, completed in 1838* (Quebec: Thomas Cary 1839).

The argument that if only we had support and resources then we could fulfill our duty is a reflection of the same discrepancy that the Anglicans saw between intent and practice. See for example *A Sermon Preached Before the Incorporated Society for the Propagation of the Gospel in Foreign Parts ... Together with the Report of the Society for the Year 1830* (London: SPG 1831), 35. Another fascinating document here is one of the first histories of colonial church – *A Brief History of the Church in Upper Canada* by Rev. William Bethridge, the rector of Woodstock. He was sent to England with Benjamin Cronyn to lobby on behalf of the reserves. His history is in effect a catalogue of British promises and an appeal that the promises now be kept: William Bethridge, *A Brief History of the Church in Upper Canada* (London, 1838).

43 See Best, *Temporal Pillars,* 43, 191–2.

44 Best, *Temporal Pillars,* 189–90. Lay patronage was clearly present in Upper Canada. Lord Mountcashel, for example, enjoyed the power of presentment to Amherst Island near Kingston. Strachan clearly accepted the practice but was most concerned that presentment should only occur if it had been earned by a patron who had endowed the church on the most generous and substantial terms. "The patronage of a living," he wrote to Ernest Hawkins, "should be its full endowment." SPG Archives, C/Canada/ Toronto, folio 518, Strachan to Hawkins, 4 Oct. 1844, and Strachan to A.M. Campbell, 30 Nov. 1840. The Act in question is the Church Temporalities Act of 1840 (cap. LXXIV, 3rd Vict., 1840) which received royal assent 3 December 1841; see esp. the provisions for an advowson in clause XVII.

45 Best, *Temporal Pillars,* esp. chaps 2, 4, 5, and 6.

46 This conception of the ministry helps to explain why many Anglicans and Presbyterians were unable to believe that Methodist itinerants were clergymen and helps to explain not only the Anglican critique of "uneducated itinerants" but also why Anglicans simply did not include Methodist preachers when they compiled religious surveys of the province.

47 Talman, "The Position of the Church in Upper Canada," 372ff.

48 When Strachan became Bishop he set out the needs of his new Diocese in a series of letters to the SPG. See esp. SPG Archives, C/Canada/Toronto, folio 518, "Missionaries Required for the Following Stations," (c.1841).

49 See for example the millennial rhetoric that T.B. Fuller, missionary at Thorold, used to describe the role of SPG in Canada: SPG Archives, C/Canada/Toronto, folio 523, Fuller to SPG, 2 Jan. 1843.

50 The problems that seem to recur frequently among Anglican missionaries make a fascinating study of the interaction of ideology and environment. For a brief survey of some of the problems see SPG Archives, C/Canada, folio of the Rev. Fleming (alcoholism); Rev. Lefevre (heresy); Rev. Ansley (alcoholism); Rev. Parkin (insanity); Rev. Burwell (heresy); Rev. Jackson ("insensibility"); Mr. Arnold ("lost" himself in Montreal); Rev. Robinson (mental breakdown); Rev. Wade (improper conduct with servant girl). Peterborough seems to have been especially fertile in this regard.

51 If the church were given resources and a fair trial "it [would] universally gain a pre-eminence ... merely on its foundation and by its own inherent strength." SPG Archives, C/Canada/Quebec/Upper Canada, folio 462, A.N. Bethune to Archdeacon Hamilton, 15 Sept. 1830.

52 It was common practice for the colonial church to send an individual or delegation to England to lobby for the political interests of the church and raise money at the same time. On one of these occasions considerable controversy arose when the expenses of the Rev. William Bethridge rivalled the amount he had collected. See Bethridge, *A Brief History of the Church in Upper Canada*, and Millman, *Life of Charles James Stewart*, 135-6.

53 Strachan, *A Letter to the Right Hon. Thomas Frankland Lewis*. Strachan elaborated on this theme in a letter to the SPG when he criticized the proposal to ask congregations to provide the salary of their clergyman. Even if the amount was small "yet it so far partakes of the voluntary principle that they wish to know something of the clergyman ... and are reluctant to bind themselves till after his arrival." SPG Archives, C/Canada/Toronto, folio 518, Strachan to SPG, "Diocese of Toronto: Missionaries Required for the Following Stations" (c.1841).

54 For an Anglican commentary on Chalmers' critique of religious free trade see *The Church*, 28 July 1838, 22. Strachan and Chalmers discussed this matter in some detail in their personal correspondence. See United Church Archives, Strachan – Chalmers Correspondence, esp. Strachan to Chalmers, 29 Jan. 1827.

55 SPG Archives, C/Canada/Toronto, folio 518, Strachan to Hawkins, 22 Mar. 1847.

56 In this sense the subtitle of Alan Wilson's fine book on the reserves, *A Canadian Mortmain*, can be misleading in that it refers to what the reserves might have become rather than to what they were.

57 C.F. Pascoe, *Two Hundred Years of the SPG: An Historical Account of the Society for the Propagation of the Gospel in Foreign Parts 1701–1900* (London: SPG 1901), and Hans Cnattingius, *Bishops and Societies: A Study of Anglican Colonial and Missionary Expansion, 1698–1850* (London: Society for the Propagation of Christian Knowledge 1952).

58 Cnattingius, *Bishops and Societies.* Another society, the Upper Canada Clergy Society, was founded in 1834 in response to an initiative from Bishop Stewart. It began to function in 1837 and supported a number of missionaries, and then in 1840 merged with the SPG. See Millman, *Life of Charles James Stewart*, 130–5.

59 This material is drawn from the financial records of the Society with the local Bishops. For a general overview see Pascoe, *Two Hundred Years of the SPG*; a fascinating pamphlet, John Strachan, *The Secular State of the Church in the Diocese of Toronto, Canada West* (Toronto: Diocesan Press [1849]); and Millman, *Life of Charles James Stewart*, chap. 12.

60 SPG Archives, Copies of Letters Sent, K.18, American Letters, Campbell to Bishop of Quebec, 2 Jan. 1834.

61 SPG Archives, C/Canada/Quebec, folio 368, Mountain to SPG, 30 Apr. 1838 (marked "private"); "Society for the Propagation of the Gospel in Foreign Parts," *The Church*, 2 Sept. 1837.

62 SPG Archives, Copies of Letters Sent, K.18, American Letters, A.M. Campbell to Bishop of Montreal, 6 Dec. 1837, A.M. Campbell to Bishop of Toronto, 30 Nov. 1839.

63 Strachan, *Secular State of the Church.*

64 "An Act to Provide for the sale of the Clergy Reserves in the Province of Canada, and for the distribution of the proceeds thereof," 3 and 4 Vict. cap. 78.

65 "It is not an easy matter to keep them all quiet particularly in matters where their interests are concerned": SPG Archives, C/Canada/Toronto, Strachan to SPG, 13 Sept. 1848. The pamphlet *The Secular State of the Church*, was written in response to this clerical agitation. For the matter of Strachan's arrears see SPG Archives, C/Canada/Toronto, Strachan to SPG, 22 May 1847 and 9 Aug. 1847.

66 The projected deficit of the SPG in 1846 was about £24,000: SPG Archives, Copies of Letters Sent, Toronto, vol I, Hawkins to Strachan, 18 May 1844.

67 During the crisis occasioned by the withdrawal of the government grant in 1832, the Society had written Mountain and pointed out the need for local support: "And while they are aware of the objec-

tions which may be urged against applying to the people for assistance, they conceive that such objections must be answered by the necessity of the case, and hope that application may be made and may succeed." SPG Archives, Copies of Letters Sent, K.18, American Letters, A.M. Campbell to Bishop of Quebec, 6 Aug. 1833.

68 SPG Archives, Copies of Letters Sent, Toronto, vol. I, Hawkins to Bethune, 10 Jan. 1850.

69 Strachan's original proposals would have reduced the voluntary principle and set up three classifications of clergy based on length of service; as openings occurred in the higher class, everyone would move up. For the discussions about the regulations, see the Strachan – Hawkins correspondence in the C Series (letters received) and Copies of Letters Sent. Some of the most important letters in the latter are Copies of Letters Sent, Toronto, vol. I, Hawkins to Strachan, 31 Dec. 1847, 28 Apr. 1848, 26 May 1848, 15 Dec. 1848, 4 May 1849, and 16 Nov. 1849.

70 John Strachan, *A Charge Delivered to the Clergy of the Diocese of Toronto at the Primary Visitation* (Toronto: Rowsell 1841), repr. in J.L. Henderson, *John Strachan: Documents and Opinions* (Toronto: McClelland and Stewart 1969), 233.

71 Careless, *Union of the Canadas*, chaps 7, 10, 11.

72 The best treatment of these events is found in John S. Moir, *Church and State in Canada West: Three Studies in the Relation of Denominationalism and Nationalism, 1841–1867* (Toronto: Univ. of Toronto Press 1959).

73 For an account of the monies paid by the colonial government to various religious groups and individuals see *Journals of the Legislative Assembly for the Province of Canada*, 1851, app. MM.

74 Sir C.P. Lucas, ed., *Lord Durham's Report on the Affairs of British North America*, vol. 2 (Oxford: Clarendon 1912), 16.

75 *Ibid.*, 31.

76 Those who have praised Durham's "liberalism" have found it very difficult to deal with his "racism." Chester New, for example, argues that "these fallacies" marred "what was in many respects a brilliant analysis of the situation in Lower Canada." Those who have tended to treat the *Report* in more materialist terms find it equally difficult to reconcile the principle of responsible government with the *Report* as a whole. Donald Creighton, for example, argues that the *Report* "fitted imperfectly into any categories of Canadian political thinking." See Chester W. New, *Lord Durham: A Biography of George Lambton, First Earl of Durham* (Oxford: Clarendon 1929), 413, 495, and esp. n. 1; Donald Creighton, *The Empire of the St. Lawrence* (Toronto: Macmillan 1956), 326.

77 J.M.S. Careless, "The Toronto *Globe* and Agrarian Radicalism, 1850–1867," *Canadian Historical Review,* 29 (Mar. 1948), 14–39.

78 Robert L. Fraser argues convincingly that the members of the compact were not opposed to economic development and that indeed they supported it quite strongly. But they were essentially "pre-capitalist" in their economic views, seeing development as a way to exploit the bounties of Providence and preserve a hierarchical social system. Robert Lochiel Fraser III, "Like Eden in Her Summer Dress: Gentry, Economy, and Society: Upper Canada, 1812–1840" (Ph.D. thesis, Univ. of Toronto, 1979) esp. chaps 2 and 5.

79 It was the goal of the state, according to Durham, to promote by every possible means "the increase of population and the accumulation of property": Lucas, ed., *Lord Durham's Report,* vol. 2, 48. Alan Wilson points out clearly how Durham regarded land as a commodity that carried with it few if any social obligations: Wilson, *The Clergy Reserves of Upper Canada,* 141.

80 The section on Upper Canada in Lucas, ed., *Lord Durham's Report,* vol. 2, devotes considerable attention to the issue.

81 Durham introduced his "General Review and Recommendations" with an extended analysis of loyalty, prosperity, and the American example. See Lucas, ed., *Lord Durham's Report,* vol. 2, 259–65.

82 John Moir, "The Settlement of the Clergy Reserves, 1840–1855," *Canadian Historical Review* 37 (Mar. 1956), 46-62. Many of the basic documents are reprinted in Henderson, ed., *John Strachan: Documents and Opinions,* 200–27; and John S. Moir, ed., *Church and State in Canada, 1627–1867* (Toronto: McClelland and Stewart 1967), 212–66.

83 M.R. Kingsford, "Church Societies," *Journal of the Canadian Church Historical Society* 7 (Mar. 1965), 3–34.

84 For good contemporary appraisals of the character and goals of the Church Society of the Diocese of Toronto see *The Church,* 23 Oct. 1841, 62, and esp. 26 Mar. 1842, 150.

85 SPG Archives, C/Canada/Toronto, folio 518, John Beverley Robinson to SPG, 5 Sept. 1850. This letter also appears in the Copies of Letters Received [hereafter CLR], II, 52–6.

86 SPG Archives, C/Canada/Toronto, folio 518, Strachan to SPG, 20 June 1851; also SPG Archives, CLR, II, 67–8.

87 Moir, "The Settlement of the Clergy Reserves, 1840–1855." Bethune referred to this "as a sum in bulk … that … might be preserved to the church in perpetuity." SPG Archives, CLR, II, Bethune to SPG, 24 Nov. 1854, 152–54; see also Strachan to SPG, 6 Jan. 1855, 159–61 and 22 June 1855, 171–3. Ernest Hawkins summarized Strachan's efforts very cogently: "You seem to be doing all that can be done

to extract good out of evil, and no doubt if the amount on which you calculate can be secured for a permanency, the church will be far from destitute, and may, moreover set its independence and self-government against the alienation of its patrimony." See SPG Archives, Copies of Letter Sent, Toronto, I, Hawkins to Strachan, 23 Mar. 1855.

88 SPG Archives, CLR, II, Strachan to SPG, 8 Aug. 1851, 72–7.

89 In a long letter to Lord John Russell, Strachan expressed very clearly the peculiar and distressing position of the church. "To speak of the Church, as in unity with the state in the present state of things is as ridiculous as it is untrue. For since the unequal application of the principle of civil and religious liberty ... she has been left as a Target for all sects and denominations to shoot at, and as helpless as such a Target – Because she is not free to exercise in her own defence the rights and inherent powers, which, in Common Justice ought to be confirmed to her from that same principle." SPG Archives, D series/D14, "A Letter to the Right Honourable Lord John Russell First Lord of the Treasury etc. On the Present State of the Church in Canada by the Bishop of Toronto."

90 John Strachan, *A Letter to the Rev. Thomas Chalmers, D.D., Professor of Divinity in the University of Edinburgh, on the Life and Character of the Right Reverend Dr. Hobart, Bishop of New York, North America* (New York: Swords, Stanford 1832).

91 *The Church*, 22 July 1837, 22 and on many occasions thereafter.

92 The best account of the synodical movement is T. R. Millman, "Beginnings of the Synodical Movement in Colonial Anglican Churches with special reference to Canada," *Journal of the Canadian Church Historical Society*, 21 (1979), 3–19. See also R.V. Harris, *An Historical Introduction to the Study of the Canon Law of the Anglican Church of Canada* (Toronto: General Synod 1965).

93 Millman, "Beginning of the Synodical Movement," 9.

94 SPG Archives, D Series/D14, Strachan to SPG setting out questions concerning synods, 1850.

95 Clause 18 of "An Act to enable the Bishops, Clergy, and Laity of the United Church of England and Ireland in Victoria etc."

96 Great Britain, Parliamentary Papers, 1856 vol. 44, #131, 129ff; and, 1857, Session Z, vol. 28, 95ff.

97 Lambeth Palace Library, Ms. 2218 (Miscellaneous Papers), Archbishop Sumner, "Sketch for Bill for regulating the Church in the Colonies, 1853."

98 Lambeth Palace Library, Ms 2218 (Miscellaneous Papers), Archbishop Sumner to Henry Labouchere, 14 July 1856.

99 Lambeth Palace Library, Archibald Campbell Tait Papers, vol. 159, folios 281ff.

100 The battles over the reserves and the theoretical problems of a dual establishment have obscured the cultural affinity of the two establishment churches. Sensitive Anglicans called for an alliance between the two. As the Rev. A.H. Burwell explained, "As far as the abstract principle of Church and State goes, we agree with them exactly." Burwell to John Macaulay, 1 Sept. 1831 as quoted in Peter A. Russell, "Church of Scotland Clergy in Upper Canada: Culture Shock and Conservatism on the Frontier," *Ontario History* 73 (June 1981), 89.

101 The letters that reveal the true character of these events are to be found in the National Library of Scotland, Lee Papers, M 3437, F14, Letter from Thomas Blackwood, 22 Jan 1828, and F73, extract of letter from Thomas Blackwood to Rev. Dr. Harkness, 15 Oct. 1827 enclosed in letter from J. Grant to Rev. John Lee, 8 May 1828.

102 Moir, *Enduring Witness,* esp. chaps 5 and 6.

103 *Ibid.,* 82–6.

104 Stewart J. Brown, *Thomas Chalmers and the Godly Commonwealth in Scotland* (Oxford: Oxford 1982). Strachan was almost fawning in his admiration for Chalmers. See, for example, his letters to Chalmers in the United Church Archives, Strachan – Chalmers Correspondence, and Strachan, *A Letter to the Rev. Thomas Chalmers, D.D. ...* ; and *The Church,* 14 July 1838; 14, 28 July 1838, 22; 11 Aug. 1838, 30.

105 Peter D. James, "'Righteousness Exalteth the Nation': The Toronto *Banner* and the Nineteenth-Century Evangelical Crusade in Upper Canada" (MA thesis, Carleton Univ. 1981); N.G. Smith, "By Schism Rent Assunder: A Study of the disruption of the Presbyterian Church in Canada in 1844," *Canadian Journal of Theology* (Oct. 1955); Moir, *Enduring Witness,* 102–14; and Ian Rennie, "The Free Church and Relations of Church and State in Canada, 1844-54," (MA thesis, Univ. of Toronto, 1954).

106 *The Church,* 5 Sept. 1845, 34. The editorial quotes Burke directly.

107 *Ibid.*

108 The best treatment of Strachan's doctrine of the church is to be found in Rev. Mark Charles McDermott, "The Theology of Bishop Strachan: A Study in Anglican Identity" (Ph.D. thesis, Toronto School of Theology 1983).

109 "Tracts for the Times," *The Church,* 15 June 1839, 205; see also *The Church,* 15 May 1841, 178.

110 John Strachan, *A Charge Delivered to the Clergy of the Diocese of Toronto, at the Visitation ...* (Toronto: Diocesan Press 1847), as quoted in Henderson, ed., *John Strachan: Documents and Opinions,* 245. "The sooner the Church is rid of such wavering Protestants as Mr.

Newman, the sooner will her peace be restored. There may be others, in holy orders, ready to follow his steps; and though their defection would be a serious blow, and a matter of rejoicing to the enemy, yet, we feel assured, that the cloud would soon pass away, and our Reformed Church soon counterbalance the Loss an hundred fold, by the additions from the ranks of Protestant Dissent." *The Church,* 28 Apr. 1843, 170. See also John S. Moir, "The Correspondence of Bishop Strachan and John Henry Newman," *Canadian Journal of Theology* 3 (1957), 219–25. For a fuller treatment of the impact of the Oxford Movement, especially in relation to worship, see Christopher F. Headon, "Developments in Canadian Anglican Worship in Eastern and Central Canada, 1840–1868," *Journal of the Canadian Church Historical Society* 17 (June 1975), 26–37; and C.F. Headon, "The Influence of the Oxford Movement upon the Church of England in Eastern and Central Canada, 1840–1900" (Ph.D. thesis, McGill Univ. 1974).

111 Examples of the dialogue form can be found in almost every number of *The Church.* It was also a form that was used in many Anglican tracts, especially those published by the SPCK.

112 John Strachan, *Pastoral Letter of the Lord Bishop of Toronto.* (Toronto: Rowsell 1842).

113 The fullest account of the history of the divisions within the church is in Harry Ernest Turner's sizeable MA thesis. Certain parts of his analysis are open to debate; he tends to analyse these divisions from a more traditional perspective and argues that Strachan was a high churchman. Nevertheless, he agrees that the divisions in the church became serious only after the 1850s. Harry Ernest Turner, "The Evangelical Movement in the Church of England in the Diocese of Toronto, 1839–1879" (MA thesis, Univ. of Toronto 1959).

114 John Strachan, *A Charge Delivered to the Clergy of the Diocese of Toronto, at the Primary Visitation* (Toronto: Rowsell 1841).

115 John Strachan, *A Charge; Delivered to the Clergy of the Diocese of Toronto, at the Visitation on Wednesday, April 30, 1856 by John, Lord Bishop of Toronto* (Toronto: Henry Rowsell 1856), 12, 33.

116 *Ibid.,* 33.

117 *Ibid.,* 24.

118 The integration of church and state was praised in these terms by Edmund Burke. See Selby, ed., *Burke's Reflections on the Revolution in France,* 115.

119 See Robert T. Handy, "Dominant Patterns of Christian Life in Canada and the United States: Similarities and Differences," in William Westfall, Louis Rousseau *et al.,* eds, *Religion/Culture: Comparative*

Canadian Studies, Canadian Issues, 7 (Ottawa: Association for Canadian Studies 1985), 344-55.

CHAPTER FIVE

1 Mircea Eliade, *The Sacred and the Profane: the Nature of Religion* (New York: Harcourt, Brace and World 1959). The question of place is discussed in this chapter, the question of time in chapter 6.

2 A discussion of these deliberations appears in the second section of this chapter.

3 In 1890 the Presbyterian Church in Canada sponsored a competition for church designs under the auspices of the *Canadian Architect and Builder.* The committee on Church Architecture of the General Assembly of the Presbyterian Church in Canada published the results in 1893 in a pamphlet entitled *Designs for Village, Town and City Churches.*

4 *Census of the Canadas,* 1851–2 (Quebec, 1853); *Census of the Canadas,* 1860–1 (Quebec, 1863); *Census of Canada,* 1870–1 (Ottawa, 1873); *Census of Canada,* 1880–1 (Ottawa, 1882). The statistics for church building in the census of 1861 are not reliable. For a more detailed digest of these statistics see William E. de Villiers-Westfall, "The Sacred and the Secular: Studies in the Cultural History of Protestant Ontario in the Victorian Period" (Ph.D. thesis, Univ. of Toronto 1976), 2, "Denominational Growth, Church Building, Union and Disruption," 324–35.

5 "The commercial depression which began in 1857 has prostrated the whole country and paralysed all our resources." Society for the Propagation of the Gospel [hereafter SPG] Archives, D series, Strachan to Hawkins, 30 Mar. 1860.

6 For classical vernacular and Neoclassical designs see St George's, Kingston (1825), and St Andrew's, Niagara-on-the Lake (1831). Methodist classicism can be seen in the Hay Bay Meeting House (1791) and the Richmond Street Church, Toronto (1844). See Leslie Maitland, *Neoclassical Architecture in Canada* (Ottawa: Parks Canada 1984). For illustrations of a number of these churches see Marion MacRae and Anthony Adamson, *Hallowed Walls* (Toronto: Clark, Irwin 1975).

7 Ralph Greenhill, Ken MacPherson, and Douglas Richardson, *Ontario Towns* (Ottawa: Oberon Press 1974), unpaginated. See especially the section on meeting houses and churches.

8 Charles E. McFaddin, "A Study of the Buildings of the Children of Peace, Sharon, Ontario" (MA thesis, Univ. of Toronto 1953), esp. 86ff,

9 For Gothic additions see Holy Trinity, Chippawa (1840); Christ

Church, Moulinette (1837); Baptist Church, Haldimand (1824); Trinity Anglican, Port Burwell (1836).

10 Greenhill, Macpherson, and Richardson, *Ontario Towns.*

11 F.H. Armstrong, "The First Great Fire of Toronto, 1849," *Ontario History* 53 (Sept. 1961), 201–21.

12 F.H. Armstrong, "The Rebuilding of Toronto After the Great Fire of 1849," *Ontario History* 53 (Dec. 1961), 233–49.

13 Shirley Grace Morriss, "The Church Architecture of Fredrick William Cumberland," (MA thesis, Univ. of Toronto 1976).

14 *The Ecclesiologist* commented upon the "unfinished" and "less correct" character of the Cathedral. *The Ecclesiologist*, 18 (1857), 359.

15 W. Morrison Kelly, *The History of the Congregations forming St. Andrew's United Church* (n.p., n.d.). The architectural drawings for the new St Andrew's are in the Archives of Ontario [hereafter AO], Horwood Collection (#670). The drawings for the new old St Andrew's are in the Metropolitan Toronto Library, Baldwin Room, Langley Collection.

16 United Church Archives ([hereafter UCA], Ontario Histories, Toronto, Metropolitan United Church.

17 *Christian Guardian*, 10 Apr. 1872, 117. See also Mary Louise Mallory, "Three Henry Langley Churches: Victorian Gothic Architecture and the Diversity of Sects in Ontario," (MA thesis, Univ. of Toronto 1979).

18 The plans for this church are in the Metropolitan Toronto Library, Langley Collection. Additional material can be found in the AO, Horwood Collection (#599). John Ross Robertson claimed that this church introduced "ecclesiastical amphitheatral construction" to Toronto. John Ross Robertson, *Landmarks of Toronto: A Collection of Historical Sketches of the Old Town of York from 1792 until 1837 and of Toronto from 1834 to 1914*, Fourth series (Toronto: J.R. Robertson 1904), 42–3.

19 The plans are in the AO, Horwood Collection (#663).

20 Mr. Hay was instructed "forthwith to prepare plans of a gothic church with a spire – the church to seat 500 people." UCA, Ontario Histories, Toronto, *Historical Sketch of St. James Square Presbyterian Congregation, Toronto, 1853–1903* (Toronto: Brown-Searle n.d.), 13.

21 UCA, Ontario Histories, Toronto, Zion Congregational Church.

22 For example, Northern Congregational Church, St Peter's (Anglican), Church of the Redeemer (Anglican), Charles Street Presbyterian, Parliament Street Primitive Methodist Church, Parliament Street Baptist Church.

23 Compare, for example, St Peter's Anglican with the Northern Congregational Church, or the Church of the Redeemer with Charles Street Presbyterian.

24 Two more examples of this "modern Gothic" variation are the West Presbyterian Church and the Oak Street Presbyterian Church, Toronto.

25 An Anglican Romanesque church still stands on Spadina Avenue in Toronto, just south of Queen Street. It was St Margaret's Church; it is now a factory. A visit to the east end of the building, although fraught with difficulties, is well worth the effort.

26 While it is difficult to generalize with authority, there appears to be a clear break not only between the neo-classical and the Gothic, but also between the Gothic work of older architects, such as John Howard, and the work of the young Goths who flourished in the period after 1850. Examine, for example, Howard's attempts at the Gothic in the Metropolitan Toronto Library, Baldwin Room, Howard Collection.

27 In Toronto Langley built churches for the Anglicans, Methodists, Presbyterians, and Baptists. In Oshawa he built the Anglican Church, the Wesleyan Methodist Church, and the Baptist Church. Many of his drawing survive in the Baldwin Room of the Metropolitan Toronto Library and in the AO, Horwood Collection. See also Greenhill, MacPherson, and Richardson, *Ontario Towns;* and Mallory, "Three Henry Langley Churches."

28 William Hay, "The Late Mr. Pugin and the Revival of Christian Architecture," *Anglo-American Magazine* 2 (1853), 70. Hay is following Pugin's strictures on the neo-classical. Hay's words recall this famous passage in *Contrasts*: "[It is] a bastard imitation of pagan edifices, unworthy and unsuited to so sacred a purpose." Augustus Welby Pugin, *Contrasts: Or a parallel between the Noble edifices of the Middle Ages, and Corresponding Builders of the Present Day: Showing the Present Decay of Taste* (privately printed 1836; 2d London: Charles Dolman 1841).

29 See, for example Geoffrey Scott, *The Architecture of Humanism: A Study in the History of Taste* (London: Constable 1914), esp. chap. 5 "The Ethical Fallacy," 121–64; Kenneth Clark, *The Gothic Revival: An Essay in the History of Taste* (London: Constable 1950), "Epilogue," 294–308; and for a Canadian example, Alan Gowans, *Building Canada: An Architectural History of Canadian Life* (Toronto: Oxford 1966), 85–7.

30 Scott, *The Architecture of Humanism*, 13, 159–64.

31 A. Welby Pugin, *Contrasts: Or, A Parallel Between the Noble Edifices of the Middle Ages, and Corresponding Buildings of the Present Day*, 3. Phoebe Stanton emphasizes the importance of Pugin's "fallacy." "When Pugin enlarged his concept of style to include its 'meaning' and 'spirit', he added a new dimension to the use of history and historical data in architecture." Phoebe Stanton, *Pugin* (London:

Thames and Hudson 1971), 191. For a detailed study of the principle of association see George L. Hersey, *High Victorian Gothic: A Study in Associationism* (Baltimore: John Hopkins Univ. Press 1972).

32 William Durandus, *The Symbolism of Christian Churches and Church Ornaments: A Translation of the First Book of the Rationale Divinorum Officiorum with an Introductory Essay and Notes by the Rev. John Mason Neale, B. A. and the Rev. Benjamin Webb, B. A. of Trinity College, Cambridge,* 3rd ed. (London: Gibbings 1906), xxvi. See also James F. White, *The Cambridge Movement: The Ecclesiologists and the Gothic Revival* (Cambridge: Cambridge Univ. Press 1962).

33 John Ruskin, *The Stones of Venice* (London: 1851–1863), esp. vol. 2, "The Sea Stories," chap. 6, "The Nature of Gothic."

34 "A Hint on Modern Church Architecture," *The Ecclesiologist*, 1 (1842).

35 Stuart C. Parker, *The Book of St. Andrew's: A Short History of St. Andrew's Presbyterian Church Toronto* (Toronto, 1930), 7.

36 Douglas Richardson, "Hyperborean gothic; or, wilderness ecclesiology and the wood Churches of Edward Medley," *Architectura*, 2, 1 (Jan. 1972), 48–74.

37 The drawings for this church are in the AO, Horwood Collection (#57). See also Shirley Morriss, "The Nine-Year Odyssey of a High Victorian Goth: Three Churches by Fred Cumberland," *The Journal of Canadian Art History* (Summer 1975), 42–53.

38 Henry Bower Lane's plans to alter the internal arrangement of Holy Trinity are reproduced in Eric Arthur, *Toronto: No Mean City* (Toronto: Univ. of Toronto Press 1964), 84. The plan for a chancel extension to Little Trinity is in the Langley Collection, Baldwin Room, Metropolitan Toronto Public Library. There is also an interesting set of architectural plans for an extension to Grace Church, Toronto, by W.G. Storm in the AO, Horwood Collection (#690). The Anglican Church in Picton (St Mary's) – it is now a museum – clearly shows the addition of a tower and chancel. Here the additions work well, but in St George's Paris, Ontario, where a Gothic chancel was added to a neo-classical nave, they do not.

39 As quoted in Stanton, *Pugin*, 52.

40 "Ecclesiastical Architecture: Village Churches," *Anglo-American Magazine* 4 (1854), 20.

41 Abacus, "Notes on a Trip to the West, " *Canadian Architect and Builder* 1 (Nov. 1888), 5.

42 For an interesting study of hymns see Margaret A. Filshie, "Sacred Harmonies: The Congregational Voice in Canadian Protestant Worship," in William Westfall, Louis Rousseau, *et al.*, eds, *Religion/Culture: Comparative Canadian Studies*, vol. 7 of *Canadian Issues* (Ottawa: Association for Canadian Studies, 1985), 287–309.

43 Compare, for example, John Ruskin's description of the Gothic with Carl Berger's analysis of the "northern" theme in Canadian national thought. See Ruskin, *The Stones of Venice* and Carl Berger, "The True North Strong and Free," in Peter Russell, ed., *Nationalism in Canada* (Toronto: McGraw-Hill 1966), 3–26.

44 Wilfred Campbell, *Canada: Painted by T. Mower Martin R.C.A., Described by Wilfred Campbell LL.D.* (London: A. and C. Black 1907), 104–5. See also R.H. Hubbard, "Canadian Gothic," *Architectural Review* (Aug. 1954), 102–8.

45 This study concentrates upon the process of cultural transformation and especially the development of romantic forms in English Canadian culture. The way romanticism penetrated various art forms and the persistence of this form in English Canadian art, although introduced in this study, are really the subject of a separate analysis. It would be fascinating for example to integrate the work of the Group of Seven, Margaret Atwood, Donald Creighton, and George Grant in relation to this form: Gothic art, literature, history and philosophy respectively. Two works of criticism which provide a pathway into such a study are Dennis Duffy's excellent study, *Gardens, Covenants, Exiles: Loyalism in the Literature of Upper Canada/Ontario* (Toronto: Univ. of Toronto Press 1982) and Dennis Lee's perceptive analysis *Savage Fields: An Essay in Literature and Cosmology* (Toronto: Anansi 1977). See also Margot Northey, *The Haunted Wilderness: The Gothic and Grotesque in Canadian Fiction* (Toronto: Univ. of Toronto Press 1976).

46 *Christian Guardian*, 18 June 1845, 138.

47 *Ibid.*

48 *Christian Guardian*, "Church Architecture," 19 Mar. 1856, 94.

49 *Ibid.*

50 *Ibid.*

51 See for example "Building and Improvement of Churches," *Christian Guardian*, 18 Nov. 1846, 18; and "Fine Churches and Fashionable Religion," *Christian Guardian*, 27 Feb. 1861, 33.

52 *Christian Guardian*, 10 Apr. 1872, 116. See also Judith St John, *Firm Foundations: A Chronicle of Toronto's Metropolitan United Church and Her Methodist Origins, 1795–1984* (Toronto: Metropolitan United Church 1988).

53 1 John 5:4; UCA, "The Metropolitan Church Service Record"; *Christian Guardian*, 10 Apr. 1872, 116.

54 UCA, "Metropolitan Church Service Record." It should also be pointed out that this was a useful text for helping raise money to pay off the large debt on the church.

55 *Ibid.*

56 Psalm 84:1–2.

57 UCA, Punshon, Rev. William Morley, Biography, Sermons, etc. Frederick W. Macdonald, *The Life of William Morley Punshon* (London: Hodder and Stoughton 1887).

58 Anson Green, *Life and Times of the Rev. Anson Green D.D.* (Toronto: Methodist Bookroom, 1877), 269, 421.

59 Psalm 132:7–8.

60 "God's Presence in God's Rest," *Sermons by the Rev. W. Morley Punshon*, vol. 2 (London: T. Woolmer 1884), 97–117.

61 *Ibid.*, 98.

62 *Ibid.*, 105.

63 *Ibid.*, 101.

64 *Ibid.*, 107.

65 *Ibid.*, 111.

66 Compare, for example, the pictures of these two churches that appear in Eric Arthur, *Toronto: No Mean City*: on page 111 the old Adelaide St Church, on page 229 the new Gothic structure.

67 Robertson's *Landmarks of Toronto* contains a number of descriptions of the internal arrangement of old churches. For St Andrew's Presbyterian see Parker, *The Book of St. Andrew's*, 7; for St James' Cathedral see W.G. Cooke, *The Pilgrim's Guide to the Cathedral Church of St. James* (pamphlet, n.p., n.d.). A ground plan for St George's Church, Toronto, in 1849 may be found in the National Archives of Canada, SPG Collection, D series, D14, p. 158. There is also good illustrative material in MacRae and Adamson, *Hallowed Walls*, 282–5, 290–6.

68 SPG Archives, Copies of Letters Sent, Toronto I, Hawkins to Strachan, 3 Sept. 1844.

69 SPG Archives, C/Canada/Quebec/Upper Canada, folio 523 (Rev. T.B. Fuller), Fuller to Ernest Hawkins, 16 July 1845. A similar piece (signed "T.R." appears as "A Country Church," in *The Church*, 16 Jan. 1841, 112. For other examples of Fuller's romantic style and architectural appreciation, see his description of the death of Anne Davidson. SPG Archives, C/Canada/Quebec /Upper Canada, folio 523 (Fuller), Fuller to Hawkins, 1 July 1849.

70 *Ibid.*, Fuller to Hawkins, 16 July 1845.

71 In the article Fuller wrote for *The Church* he amplified the scenes at the dedication by introducing a nice piece of romantic ritualism: "And the priests of the Most High were not few nor uninterested on such a day. Six holy men of God, robed in the vestment of the sanctuary, and headed by one a Bishop indeed – one who, like the first of Israel's kings, carried everywhere the impress of his high dignity, entered the holy temple, and took possession of it in the

name of the most high God." "A Country Church," *The Church*, 16 Jan. 1841, 112.

72 Luke, 2:21–34.

73 SPG Archives, C/Canada/Quebec/Upper Canada, folio 523 (Fuller), Fuller to Hawkins, 16 July 1845.

74 SPG Archives, C/Canada/Quebec/Upper Canada, folio 518 (Rev. John Strachan) Strachan to Ernest Hawkins, 10 Oct. 1845. The Rev. W.H. Herchmer of Kingston contacted Dr Richards of the Oxford Architectural Society while in England in 1845. See SPG Archives, Copies of Letters Sent, Hawkins to Strachan, 4 Aug. 1845.

75 *Ibid.* A copy of the *Instrumenta Ecclesiastica* signed by Fred Cumberland is in the Rare Book Room of the Trinity College Library. There is also a listing for Markland's book in the card catalogue, but the volume appears to have been missing since at least 1959. Most of the Cumberland library that was left to Trinity is now in the Thomas Fisher Rare Book Library, University of Toronto.

76 "Ecclesiastical Architecture," *The Church*, 2 Apr. 1842, 153. Praise for Markland, The Oxford Architectural Society, and the Cambridge Camden Society appears in *The Church*, 14 Oct. 1842, 57; "Symbolical Language of Primitive Church Architecture," *The Church*, 18 Sept. 1846, 37; and "Church Arrangements Emblematical," *The Church*, 30 July 1847, 9.

77 Rev. Henry Scadding, "Christian Architecture," *The Church*, 3 July 1846, 205.

78 *The Church*, 28 Apr. 1843, 170, sets out the background on the establishment of the committee. "Recommendations by the Church Building Committee of the Church Society in regard to churches and their precincts," *The Church*, 11 Apr. 1850, 145.

79 *Ibid.* The same instructions were also circulated to the clergy of the Diocese of Quebec. See *The Canadian Ecclesiastical Gazette*, 9 Jan. 1851 and 13 Feb. 1851. I am indebted to Father Robert Black for bringing the Quebec reference to my attention.

80 "To the Parishioners of St. James Parish, Toronto," *The Church*, 11 Apr. 1850, 145.

81 "The Rebuilding of St. James's Church, Toronto," *The Church*, 13 Sept. 1849, 26.

82 Shirley Morriss, "The Nine-Year Odyssey of a High Victorian Goth: Three Churches by Fred Cumberland," 47–8.

83 Laying of the Cornerstone of the Cathedral Church of the Diocese," *The Church*, 21 Nov. 1850, 129.

84 Cooke, *The Pilgrim's Guide to the Cathedral Church of St. James.*

85 Two excellent examples of this type of Gothic church are the Anglican churches at Lyn and Almonte in Eastern Ontario.

86 Fred Cumberland, for example, included galleries in both the Church of the Ascension (Hamilton) and St James' Cathedral (Toronto).

87 Some Anglicans also applauded this internal arrangement, although their churches continued to adhere to the older long nave and chancel plan. See, for example Daniel Wilson, "Church Builders," *Evangelical Churchman*, rpr. in *Canadian Architect and Builder* 2 (Apr. 1889), 42–3.

88 The awkwardness of the arced arrangement in a narrow nave can be seen in the Knox Presbyterian (Galt) 1869, Beverley Street Baptist (Toronto) 1886, and especially James Street Baptist (Hamilton) 1879. The last example was built by an Irish Catholic, Joseph Connolly. The change to a squarer sanctuary also helps to explain the growing popularity of the Romanesque style.

89 The Anglican Church in Port Hope provides a good example. See also the plans for a rectory and schoolhouse for the Church of the Redeemer (Toronto) by William Storm. AO, Horwood Collection (#731).

90 Some examples of the basement arrangement are Mount Carmel Methodist Episcopal (Troy), Beamsville First Baptist, and Knox Presbyterian (Elora). Visually this arrangement worked best when the site provided incline to allow both the front door of the church and the back door under the east end to be at grade level. Langley's Baptist Church at Port Hope is a good example: AO, Horwood Collection (#566). Excellent examples of amphitheatrical plans are Central Methodist (Woodstock), Wesleyan Methodist (Port Hope), and First Presbyterian (Brockville).

91 A.J.B. Beresford-Hope, *The English Cathedral of the Nineteenth Century* (London: J. Murray 1861), 235. See also *The Ecclesiologist* 12 (1851), 7. For an excellent study of the Gothic response to place see Douglas Richardson, "Canadian Architecture in the Victorian Era: The Spirit of the Place," *Canadian Collector* 10 (Sept./Oct. 1975), 20–9.

92 For examples of the problems faced by the rural church as it became increasingly lost in an urban environment see St Stephen's in the Fields (Toronto) and St Peter's (Toronto). These were small parish churches that became overwhelmed by their immediate surroundings.

93 For material on classical design and urban growth see Gilbert A. Stelter, "The Classical Ideal: Cultural and Urban Form in Eighteenth-Century Britain and America," *Journal of Urban History* 10 (Aug. 1984), 351–82; Gilbert A. Stelter, "The City Building Process in Canada," and Michael Doucet, "Speculation and the Physical Expansion of Mid-Nineteenth Century Hamilton," in Gilbert A. Stelter and Alan F.J. Artibise, eds, *Shaping the Urban Landscape: Aspects of the*

Canadian City-Building Process (Ottawa: Carleton Univ. Press 1982), 1–29, and 173–199. For an excellent study of one town see Gilbert A. Stelter, "Guelph and the Early Town Planning Tradition," *Ontario History* 77, 2 (June 1985), 83–106.

94 An excellent example of the juxtaposition of the medieval form and the classical plan is the Court House Square, Brockville, where three revival churches face upon a classical square.

95 William Durandus, *The Symbolism of Churches and Church Ornaments*, cxxi–cxxii.

96 The collection of Langley material in the Horwood Collection in the Archives of Ontario contains many good illustrations. Compare, for example, Parkdale Methodist (#532), College St Baptist (#515) and Walmer Road Baptist (#558).

97 AO, Horwood Collection (#599).

98 See Wesleyan Methodist (Port Hope), Central Methodist (Woodstock), and First Baptist (Brockville). Plans to redesign the pulpit platform of Jarvis Street Baptist may be seen in AO, Horwood Collection (#972a).

99 For the growing criticism of old-style pews and the private ownership of church furniture see "Editorial," *The Church*, 27 Mar. 1841, 150; *The Church*, 20 Oct. 1843, 57; and *The Church*, 14 Oct. 1842, 57.

CHAPTER SIX

1 "[The Bible] brings prominently before us the church and the world, which, though consisting of the same beings, exhibit two societies as distinct from each other as if each of the parties composing them were of different natures." John Strachan, *A Charge: Delivered to the Clergy of the Diocese of Toronto, at the Visitation, on Wednesday, April 30, 1856, by John, Lord Bishop of Toronto* (Toronto: Henry Rowsell 1856), 24.

2 G. M. Craig, ed., *Lord Durham's Report* (Toronto: McClelland and Stewart 1963), 19–20.

3 J.M.S. Careless, "The Toronto *Globe* and Agrarian Radicalism, 1850–1867," *Canadian Historical Review* 29 (Mar. 1948), 14–39; and Donald Creighton, "The Commercial Class in Canadian Politics, 1792–1840," *Papers and Proceedings of the Canadian Political Science Association* 5 (1933).

4 Rev. J. M. Neale, "A Catena Symbolica from Writers of the Western Church, AD 540–1736," *The Ecclesiologist* 11 (1850) 217–26, and 12 (1851), 3–11.

5 "I would pray ... that all who enter those courts may enter the courts of God's house in heaven; and that all, who on that glori-

ous day rejoice together, may rejoice forever in the paradise of God." Society for the Propagation of the Gospel [hereafter SPG] Archives, C/Canada/Quebec/Upper Canada, folio 523 (Rev. T. B. Fuller), Fuller to Ernest Hawkins, 16 July 1845. The text, St John 14:2–3, "In my Father's house are many mansions: if it were not so, I would have told you. I go to prepare a place for you," captured this dynamic association. It was often used on such occasions. For a rich source of this type of material see United Church Archives [hereafter UCA], "Ontario Histories."

6 The Anglican Cathedral in Toronto reorganized its interior to accommodate a processional service. W.G. Cooke, *The Pilgrim's Guide to the Cathedral Church of St. James* (n.p., n.d.) provides an excellent account of the historical development of the interior of this church.

7 Unfortunately people did not describe patterns of worship in detail. John Ross Robertson's monumental collection *Landmarks of Toronto: A Collection of Historical Sketches of York from 1792 until 1837 and of Toronto from 1834 to 1914*, Fourth series (Toronto: J.R. Robertson 1904) does offer, however, a number of useful accounts. The extensive collection of architectural drawings in the Horwood Collection in the Archives of Ontario also contains some excellent material on interior renovations.

8 This argument is a brief distillation of the analysis of the means-end schema upon which Talcott Parsons constructs his theory of social action. See Talcott Parsons, *The Structure of Social Action: A Study in Social Theory with Special Reference to a Group of Recent European Writers* (Glencoe, Ill.: Free Press 1949).

9 This is a paraphrase and extension of part of the basic argument of Talcott Parson's other major work, *The Social System*. Time is an integral element of a common value system; since common values sustain the social system, then time is an important part of the mechanisms that sustain social order. Talcott Parsons, *The Social System* (Glencoe, Ill.: Free Press 1951). C. Wright Mills makes the same general point in his critique of Parsons. See *The Sociological Imagination* (New York: Oxford 1959), 31.

10 For a discussion of the theoretical aspects of this relationship see: William E. de Villiers-Westfall, "The Sacred and the Secular: Studies in the Cultural History of Protestant Ontario in the Victorian Period" (Ph.D. thesis, Univ. of Toronto 1976), esp. chap. 3, "The Sacred, the Secular, and the Social System," 73–126.

11 C.C. Berger, *The Sense of Power: Studies in the Ideas of Canadian Imperialism, 1867–1914* (Toronto: Univ. of Toronto Press 1970), 109. See also L.S. Fallis, Jr, "The Idea of Progress in the Province of Canada: A Study in the History of Ideas," in W.L. Morton, ed., *The Shield of*

Achilles: Aspects of Canada in the Victorian Age (Toronto: McClelland and Stewart 1968), 169–84.

12 Rev. George H. Cornish, "Statistical Record of the Progress of Methodism in Canada," *Centennial of Canadian Methodism* (Toronto: William Briggs 1891), 339.

13 This popular hymn is attributed to Edward Perronet, a "passionate, impulsive, and strong-willed" Protestant of French descent. It first appeared in *The Gospel Magazine,* was recast in Dr John Rippon's *Selection of Hymns,* and appeared in slightly altered form in almost all the hymnals of the Victorian period. It is undoubtedly one of the most popular hymns in the English language. See Alexander Macmillan, *Hymns of the Church: A Companion to the Hymns of the United Church of Canada* (Toronto: United Church Publishing House 1935), 146–8, and John Julian, *A Dictionary of Hymnology: Setting Forth the Origin and History of Christian Hymns of all Ages and Nations* (London: John Murray 1908), 41–2. The text used here is from *The Congregational Church Hymnal* (1883). The hymn was sung at the laying of the cornerstone of the Metropolitan Methodist Church on 24 Aug. 1870. UCA, Ontario Histories, Toronto, Metropolitan United Church.

14 Rev. John Roaf, *Lectures on the Millennium* (Toronto, 1844), 1.

15 Whitney R. Cross, *The Burned-Over District: The Social and Intellectual History of Enthusiastic Religion in Western New York, 1800–1850* (New York: Harper and Row 1950), 287.

16 Wesleyan Methodist Church, Great Britain, Foreign Missions: America, the British Dominions in North America, Correspondence 1840–50. John Tompkins to Wesleyan Missionary Society, 18 Apr. 1843.

17 *A Journal of Visitation to a Part of the Diocese of Quebec by the Lord Bishop of Montreal in the Spring of 1843.* (London: Society for the Propagation of the Gospel 1844), 76.

18 *Christian Guardian,* 7 Aug. 1844, 166; Cross, *The Burned-Over District,* 308.

19 Various versions of this disaster–prophetic calendar appear in the Montreal millennial newspaper, *The Voice of Elijah.* See, for example, "The Beasts and the Four Great Kingdoms," 16 Feb. 1844, 4–5. Copies of this newspaper survive in the Library of the American Antiquarian Society, Worcester, Mass.

20 The confusion over terminology in the study of this topic is an expression of the power and extent of millennial thought in the nineteenth century. Millennialist, millenarian, pre-millennialist, post-millennialist, Augustinian, and chiliast are some of the titles that scholars have advanced in an attempt to impose some order on the diverse patterns of millenial experience. The issue is further complicated by the widespread belief among nearly all Protestants

that Revelation pointed toward a future blessed state on earth, although the specific nature of this millennium changed according to a variety of factors. To attempt to describe all the forms of millennial expectancy in Canada would only add to this confusion. Consequently, this study has adopted contemporary usage as much as possible. "Millennium," refers to a future blessed state upon which many might agree. "Millennial sect" and a "millennialist" refer respectively to a group and an individual who place extraordinary emphasis upon questions and doctrines dealing with the "millennium." "Pre-millennial" and "post-millennial" are used when their meanings have become clear during the course of this analysis. In brief, the former describes the belief that Christ will come in a personal form *at the beginning* of the millennium, whereas the latter asserts that the millennium is a moral or spiritual state that *will be concluded by* Christ's appearance. While the two differed in their interpretation of the event, both believed in the future reality of the event itself. For the standard late Victorian definitions see Philip Schaff, ed., *A Religious Encyclopedia or Dictionary of Biblical, Historical, Doctrinal, and Practical Theology*, 3rd ed. (New York: Funk and Wagnalls 1891), vol. 3, 1514–16. I would like to thank Professors Paul Christianson and Klaus Hansen of the Department of History, Queen's University, for their guidance through this terminological jungle.

For material on the Mormons see *A History of the Mormon Church in Canada* (Lethbridge, Alta: Lethbridge Herald 1968). For a sample of contemporary comments on the Mormons see SPG Archives, C/Canada/UC, folio 534, Rev. John Gibson to Rev. W.J.D. Waddilove, 8 Dec. 1840; *The Church*, 1 Feb. 1840, 121, and 15 May 1841, 177; *Christian Guardian*, 29 Nov. 1837, 13, 6 Dec. 1837, 17, and 26 June 1839, 139. Leo Johnson, *History of the County of Ontario 1615–1875* (Whitby: Corporation of the County of Ontario 1973), 167–9, also contains some interesting accounts. See also Janet Virginia Noel, "Dry Millennium: Temperance and a New Social Order in Pre-Confederation Canada and Red River," (Ph.D. thesis, Univ. of Toronto 1987). Dr Noel traces the way the temperance movement began as a revivalist and pre-millennial movement and became a mainstream Protestant movement. See esp. chap. 6.

21 For general material on the Irvingites see: Rev. Alexander Miller, *Plymouthism and the Modern Churches or Life, Light, Law and Learning* (Toronto, 1900). The best overview of this group is in a manuscript in the Lambeth Palace Library, Manuscript 2689, Rev. Reginald Somerset Ward, "The Death of a Church and the Problems Arising Therefrom" (1935). See also UCA, Church Histories, Toronto, Cath-

olic Apostolic Church. For a brief overview of the Catholic Apostolic Church in Toronto see UCA, Susan Miller, "The Catholic Apostolic Church in Canada: The Methodist Perspective" (typescript); and Charles Dougall, "George Ryerson," *Dictionary of Canadian Biography*, vol. 9 (*1881 to 1890*), 795–8.

22 Wesleyan Methodist Church, Great Britain, Foreign Missions: BNA, John Tompkins to Wesleyan Missionary Society, 18 Apr. 1843; SPG Archives, C/Canada/Quebec, folio 368, Rev. C.B. Fleming to G.J. Mountain, 21 Mar. 1844; Francis David Nichol, *The Midnight Cry; a defense of the character and conduct of William Miller and the Millerites, who mistakenly believed that the second coming of Christ would take place in the year 1844* (Takoma Park, Washington, DC: Review and Herald Publishing Association 1945); Sylvester Bliss, *Memoirs of William Miller, generally known as a lecturer on the prophecies, and the second coming of Christ* (Boston: J.V. Himes 1853); Cross, *The Burned-Over District*, 287–321; Louis Billington, "The Millerite Adventists in Great Britain, 1840–1850," *Journal of American Studies* 1 (1967), 191–212.

23 Ernest R. Sandeen, *The Roots of Fundamentalism: British and American Millenarianism 1800–1930* (Chicago: Univ. of Chicago Press 1970).

24 Phyllis D. Airhart, "The Eclipse of Revivalist Spirituality: The Transformation of Canadian Methodist Piety, 1884–1925," (Ph.D. thesis, Univ. of Chicago 1985), chap. 3, "Piety and the Challenge of Innovation," 94–149.

25 *The Second Coming of Our Lord: Being Papers read at a Conference held at Niagara, Ontario July 14th to 17th, 1885* (Toronto: S.R. Briggs [1885–6]).

26 Sandeen, *The Roots of Fundamentalism*; E.R. Sandeen, "Toward a Historical Interpretation of the Origins of Fundamentalism," *Church History* 36 (Mar. 1967), 66–83; and LeRoy Moore, Jr, "Another Look at Fundamentalism: A Response to Ernest R. Sandeen," *Church History* 37 (June 1968), 195–202.

27 Airhart, "The Eclipse of Revivalist Spirituality," chap. 3; and Brian R. Ross, "Ralph Cecil Horner: A Methodist Sectarian Deposed," *The Bulletin*. (Committee on Archives of the United Church of Canada), 26 (1977), 94–103.

28 *Remarkable Visions! Revealed to W. Russell, near Millbrook, Canada West, Regarding the Second Coming of Christ to Take Place Not Later than the Year 1877* (Millbrook, CW: S. Russell 1864), 5.

29 The frustrated adventist who had tried to fly upwards to meet God only to land rather unceremoniously on earth is told by Thomas Conant in *Upper Canada Sketches* (Toronto: William Briggs 1898), 92–6. He also describes Mormons raising the dead. Even though

these were written some fifty years after the supposed event, they are nonetheless repeated without reservation by Leo Johnson in his *History of the County of Ontario 1615–1875*, 167ff and by John Moir in his collection, *The Cross in Canada* (Toronto: Ryerson 1966), 128–30.

30 S.D. Clark, *Church and Sect in Canada* (Toronto: Univ. of Toronto Press 1948), chap. 6 "New Frontiers and New Sects, 1832–1860," 273–328; and S.D. Clark, "Religious Organization and the Rise of the Canadian Nation, 1850–85," Canadian Historical Association *Report* (1944), 86–96. For a more detailed analysis of the work of S.D. Clark see William Edward de Villiers-Westfall, "The Sacred and the Secular," app. 1, "Canadian Society and Religion: Historiography and the Work of S.D. Clark," 299–323.

31 William Edward Biederwolf, *The Millennium Bible: Being a Help to the Study of the Holy Scriptures in their Testimony to the Second Coming of Our Lord and Saviour Jesus Christ* (Chicago: W.D. Blessing 1924).

32 For example, at the Eucharist, in the lessons for Advent, and on such days as All Saints. See also Stephen S. Smalley. "The Delay of the Parousia," *Journal of Biblical Literature* 83 (Mar. 1964), 41–54.

33 William Paley, *A View of the Evidences of Christianity* (London: Faulder 1805). See also the second chapter of this study.

34 *The Church*, 8 July 1837, 15. See also "The Signs of the Times – No 1," *Christian Guardian*, 19 May 1841, 118.

35 Archives of Ontario [hereafter AO], Strachan Papers, Manuscript Sermon (119), preached on Romans 13:11–12, "And that, knowing the time, that now it is high time to awake out of sleep: for now is our salvation nearer than when we believe it. The night is far spent, the day is at hand, let us therefore cast off the works of darkness, and let us put on the armour of light," first preached 15 July 1838. This was preached only once, on the Sunday after the death of the Rev. Peter Robinson.

36 UCA, Rev. Mark Young Stark Papers, Stark to Mrs. Stark (mother), 11 Apr. 1843.

37 See the second and third chapters of this study for an analysis of the assumptions and practice of revivalism.

38 Mark Young Stark, *Sermons by the late Rev. Mark Y. Stark, A.M. Formerly Minister of Knox's Church Dundas, With a Memoir by the Rev. William Reid A.M.* (Toronto: James Campbell 1871), 145.

39 "Revolting as such scenes may appear, yet when mixed up with the awful realities of future judgment, they take on a prodigious effect." *A Journal of Visitation to a Part of the Diocese of Quebec by the Lord Bishop of Montreal in the Spring of 1843*, 78. Jerald C. Brauer, "Revivalism and Millenarianism in America," in Joseph D. Ban and

Paul R. Dekar, eds, *In the Great Tradition: In Honor of Winthrop S. Hudson* (Valley Forge, Penn.: Judson Press 1982), 147–60.

40 UCA, Egerton Ryerson Papers, 1824–1844, George Ryerson to Egerton, 6 Apr. 1832. See also George Ryerson to Egerton, 29 Mar. 1832; and Dougall, "George Ryerson," *Dictionary of Canadian Biography*, vol. 9, 795–8.

41 UCA, Egerton Ryerson Papers, 1824-1844, George Ryerson to Egerton, 6 Apr. 1832.

42 *Ibid.*, "Minutes of the Proceedings at Mr. Irving's Chapel on the Evening of 4th June, 1833." "Mr. Irving is very courteous and pleasing in his manners – his wife is sensible."

43 "Mr. Miller, " *Christian Guardian*, 7 Aug. 1844, 166.

44 Wesleyan Methodist Church, Great Britain, Foreign Missions: BNA, William Harvard to Wesleyan Missionary Society, 19 Apr. 1843.

45 *Ibid.*, Richard Hutchinson to Rev. John Hannah, 11 June 1843; and letter of Hutchinson to a friend [Brownell?], 21 Mar. 1843, which is enclosed in a letter from William Harvard to Wesleyan Missionary Society, 6 Apr. 1843.

46 UCA, Church Records, Metropolitan Church, Stewards and Leaders Meetings (York Station Chapel), Minutes, 1829–34, Mon., 22 Dec. 1834.

47 Thomas R. Millman, *The Life of the Right Reverend, The Honourable Charles James Stewart D.D. Oxon, Second Anglican Bishop of Quebec* (London, Ont.: Huron College 1953), 194, and Carl F. Klinck, "The Poems of Adam Hood Burwell: Pioneer Poet of Upper Canada," *Western Ontario History Nuggets* 30 (May 1963), 1–110.

48 SPG Archives, C/Canada/Quebec, folio 368, G.J. Mountain to SPG, 4 Nov. 1836.

49 In Burwell's major works, *Doctrine of the Holy Spirit* and *A Voice of Warning*, he described himself as a "missionary from the Society for Propagating the Gospel in Foreign Parts." The SPG in London raised the matter of this usage with the leaders of the colonial church. See Rev. Adam Hood Burwell, *Doctrine of the Holy Spirit; In Its Application to the Wants and Interests of Corporate Man Under the Providence and Moral Government of God, Stated and Defended from Holy Writ and the Practice of the Apostles of Our Lord and Saviour Jesus Christ; and in These Days Received in Britain by the Rev. Edward Irving Exhibiting the Sole Means of National Reformation and Preservation* (Toronto: W.J. Cootes 1835); and *A Voice of Warning and Instruction Concerning the Signs of the Times and the Coming of the Son of Man, To Judge the Nations, and Restore All Things* (Kingston: Upper Canada Herald Office 1835).

A.M. Campbell, Secretary of the SPG, felt obliged to ask the Bishop of Quebec why Burwell had not been disciplined after his book on prophecy had appeared. SPG Archives, Copies of Letters Sent, American Letters, 1833 –, Campbell to Quebec, 12 March 1835.

50 "'Claims and Character of Mesmerism Rationally Considered,' by A.H. Burwell, Kingston," *The Church*, 18 Aug. 1845, 2; see also *The Church*, 11 Apr. 1840, 162.

51 AO, Strachan Papers, Strachan Letterbook, 1844–1849, Strachan to A.H. Burwell, 12 July 1844.

52 J.F.C. Harrison, *The Second Coming: Popular Millenarianism 1780–1850* (New Brunswick, NJ: Rutgers Univ. Press 1979), esp. part 3, 161–230.

53 Anson Green, *The Life and Times of Anson Green* (Toronto: Methodist Bookroom 1877), 201.

54 "The End of the World – No. 1" *Christian Guardian*, 19 Apr. 1843, 101.

55 See for example *A Journal of Visitation to a Part of the Diocese of Quebec ... in the Spring of 1843*, 78; Wesleyan Methodist Church, Great Britain, Foreign Missions: BNA, R. Cooney to Wesleyan Missionary Society, 20 Jan. 1843; Anson Green, *Life and Times of Anson Green*. (Toronto: Methodist Bookroom 1877), 370ff.

56 Roaf, *Lectures on the Millennium*, 106. For a similar statement of Anglican expectancy see Bishop Mountain's millennial interpretations of the "signs of the times." *A Charge Delivered to the Clergy of the Diocese of Quebec by George J. Mountain D.D., Lord Bishop of Montreal At His Primary Visitation, Completed in 1838* (Quebec: Thomas Cary 1839), 8.

57 Clark, *Church and Sect in Canada*, 273–328.

58 Burwell saw "two especial signs of the times indicative of a deep and growing apostacy from God." These were the separation of church and state and "the devil's twin engines of moral and physical desolation – the political press and popular elections." Burwell, *Doctrines of the Holy Spirit*, iii–iv.

59 Jerald C. Brauer, "Revivalism and Millenarianism in America."

60 Airhart, "The Eclipse of Revivalist Spirituality," esp. chap. 3; and John S. Moir, *Enduring Witness. A History of the Presbyterian Church in Canada*.

61 David T. Arthur, "Millerism," in Edwin S. Gaustad, ed., *The Rise of Adventism: Religion and Society in Mid-Nineteenth-Century America* (New York: Harper and Row 1974), 154–72.

62 UCA, Church Records, Metropolitan Church, Stewards and Leaders Meetings (York Station Chapel), Minutes, 1829–34, Mon. 22 Dec. 1834. Patrick's religious group also provided a prominent convert

to Mormonism, John Taylor. See *A History of the Mormon Church in Canada*, chap. 1.

63 See UCA, Egerton Ryerson Papers, 1824–44, Egerton Ryerson to S.S. Junkin, 15 July 1835. It is also suggestive that the minutes of this meeting are the last ones entered in the minute book, even though the book was only about half-filled.

64 Susan Miller, "The Catholic Apostolic Church in Canada"; and Dougall, "George Ryerson," *Dictionary of Canadian Biography*, vol. 9, 797–8. See also Anna Jameson's comments on the number of important social and political figures who were Irvingites. Anna Brownell Jameson, *Winter Studies and Summer Rambles in Canada*, ed. James J. Talman and Elsie McLeod Murray (Toronto: Thomas Nelson 1943), 35. I am indebted to Dr Jan Noel for reminding me of this passage.

65 *Christian Guardian*, 19 Apr. 1843, 101.

66 "General Remarks – Cause of Decrease," *Canada Christian Advocate*, 2 Oct. 1845, (unpaginated); see also Rev. John Kay, *Biography of the Rev. William Gundy for Twenty Years a Minister of the Methodist New Connexion Church in Canada* (Toronto: James Campbell 1871), 77–8.

67 UCA, Journal of the Rev. George Ferguson, 111 [typescript copy].

68 "The Miller Delusion," *Christian Guardian*, 6 Mar. 1844, 78; and *Christian Guardian*, 6 Nov. 1844, 9.

69 UCA, Journal of the Rev. George Ferguson, 111.

70 *Christian Guardian*, 26 June 1839, 139; and *The Church*, 1 Feb. 1840, 121, and 15 May 1841, 177.

71 John Borland, *An Examination of and Reply to "A Brief Statement of Facts, for the Consideration of the Methodist People, and the Public in General, particularly of Eastern Canada" by R. Hutchinson M.D. Late Wesleyan Missionary* (Stanstead, Canada East, 1850).

72 *Christian Guardian*, 20 Sept. 1843, 190. Most of the outlandish stories about the seemingly bizarre conduct of millennialists were based upon this line of attack. See, for example, the account of the Rev. John Swazey who was fined £50. 10s for stamping on the chest of (and nearly killing) a Mr Sawyer while under the influence of the spirit during the "struggle." "Millerism," *The Church*, 20 Jan. 1843, 114, or the story of the young boys who terrorized a Millerite meeting in Picton by setting off a charge of gunpowder. "Millerism," *The Church*, 12 May 1843, 178.

73 "In Toronto itself, we are told, men weak enough had their ascension robes ready." "The Miller Delusion," *Christian Guardian*, 6 Mar. 1844, 78.

74 "Millerism, Numbered," *Christian Guardian*, 7 Feb. 1844, 62.

75 The Lord Bishop of Montreal, for example, acknowledged that "unthinking sinners have been brought by the alarm of Millerism, to a care for their souls." *A Journal of Visitation to a Part of the Diocese of Quebec by the Lord Bishop of Montreal*, 78–9.

76 The SPG papers are filled with references to the problems of heresy, drunkenness, moral failure, and insanity that plagued Anglican missionaries in this period.

77 *Christian Guardian*, 9 Oct. 1861, 160.

78 According to the *Guardian* it took the failure of time to break "a spell which had alike defied reason and ridicule." *Christian Guardian*, 7 Feb. 1844, 62.

79 "The Miller Delusion," *Christian Guardian*, 6 Mar. 1844, 78.

80 The *Christian Guardian* described this as the "infidel tendency of Millerism," *Christian Guardian*, 17 Jan. 1844, 50.

81 "Religious Madness," *The Church*, 18 Nov. 1842, 77; and *Christian Guardian*, 17 Jan. 1844, 50. See also David J. Rothman, *The Discovery of Asylum: Social Order and Disorder in the New Republic* (Boston: Little Brown 1971), esp. chap 5, "Insanity and the Social Order," 109–29.

82 Green, *The Life and Times of Anson Green*, 272; see also the remarks of the Rev. John B. Brownell, "if those gentlemen have the correct date in their calculation which I think highly probable, then the world will end as they say." Wesleyan Methodist Church G.B.) Foreign Missions: BNA, William Harvard to W.M.S., 6 Mar. 1843.

83 See the *Guardian's* review of Burwell's book, *The Doctrine of the Holy Spirit* and Burwell's spirited reply. *Christian Guardian*, 25 Feb. 1835, 62, and 7 Jan. 1835, 34..

84 "Second Advent Man," *Christian Guardian*, 20 Sept. 1843, 190. The same critique was made of the Irvingites. "To others who look with the eye of reason instead of imagination, and whose faith is founded on evidence, and not feeling only this illusion is calculated to bring experimental Christianity into discredit, and to subvert the fabric of Revelation." "The Rev. Edward Irving and his Doctrines," *Christian Guardian*, 26 Nov. 1834, 10.

85 "Fundamental Principles in which the Second Advent Cause is Based," *The Voice of Elijah*, 21 July 1843.

86 Roaf, *Lectures on the Millennium*, 8. See also E. Adams, "The True Millennium, *Christian Guardian*, 26 Feb. 1845, 73; and Borland, *An Examination of and Reply to "A Brief Statement of Facts ..."* 11.

87 "The Miller Delusion," *Christian Guardian*, 6 Mar. 1844, 78.

88 Revelations 20:1-4.

89 Roaf, *Lectures on the Millennium*, 23.

90 "The Nature of Christ's Kingdom: His Office as Mediator etc. Calmly Considered," *Christian Guardian*, 12 Nov. 1834, 1.

91 "By the Kingdom of God we are especially to understand the New Testament dispensation, as introduced into the world in 'the fulness of time' by God himself, in the person of his well-beloved son – whose life and death, resurrection and ascension, confirmed and established it for the salvation of all the guilty family of man." "On the Kingdom of God," *Christian Guardian*, 27 Sept. 1837, 185.

92 *Christian Guardian*, 19 Nov. 1834, 6. Irvingism, in the words of the *Guardian*, combined "perfect obsequiousness in one respect, with perfect intolerance in another." It attempted "to bring into perfect contempt everything that has been done and is doing in the religious world." *Christian Guardian*, 19 Nov. 1834, 6.

93 Rev. James S. Douglas, *The Reign of Peace, Commonly Called the Millenium: An exposition of the Nineteenth and Twentieth Chapters of the Book of Revelation* (Toronto: W.C. Chewett 1867), 37.

94 *Ibid.*, 97. "Thus, as the view we take of the Millenium must influence immediately our present action, and the direction of our prayers, it is of the utmost consequence that we hold right views as to its character."

95 Roaf, *Lectures on the Millennium*, 99.

96 The final lecture in Roaf's collection is entitled "The Moral Means by which the Millennium is to be presented."

97 Roaf, *Lectures on the Millennium*, 148–51.

98 John Strachan, *A Charge; Delivered to the Clergy of the Diocese of Toronto, at the Visitation, on Wednesday, April 30, 1856 by John, Lord Bishop of Toronto* (Toronto: Henry Rowsell 1856).

99 Douglas, *The Reign of Peace, Commonly Called the Millenium*, 248.

100 *Ibid.*, 298.

101 Strachan himself made this tie between post-millennialism and missionary endeavour. See AO, Strachan Papers, Manuscript Sermon (213), preached on Isaiah 60:3, "And the Gentiles shall come to thy light, and Kings to the Brightness of thy rising," first preached 6 Jan. 1848 (Epiphany).

102 The nature of popular conceptions of time would make an important and fascinating study. Such a study could include the material in this chapter as an introduction to a large and diverse body of writing. The vision of a lost golden age, the belief that history is unprogressive, and the call for the immediate intervention of an external force join together these sectarian groups, nativist fanatics, English preservationists (*The Tragedy of Quebec*), Quebec separatists,

and the authors of that recent – and least elegant – pre-millennial tract, *The Great Brain Robbery*.

103 Roaf, *Lectures on the Millennium*, 165.
104 Alexander Miller, *Heaven and Hell Here* (Toronto: William Briggs 1908), 179, 181.
105 *Ibid.*, 188.
106 Berger, *The Sense of Power*, 109.

CHAPTER SEVEN

1 See especially Richard Allen, *The Social Passion: Religion and Social Reform in Canada, 1914–1928* (Toronto: Univ. of Toronto Press 1971) and G.R. Cook, *The Regenerators: Social Criticism in Late Victorian English Canada* (Toronto: Univ. of Toronto Press 1985). See also Steward Crysdale, *The Industrial Struggle and Protestant Ethics in Canada* (Toronto: Ryerson 1961).
2 Richard Allen, "The Social Gospel and the Reform Tradition in Canada 1890–1928," *Canadian Historical Review* 49 (Dec. 1968), 381–99.
3 For a general overview of this tradition see Raymond Aron, *Main Currents in Sociological Thought* (London: Weidenfeld and Nicolson 1968). For a more specific and detailed analysis of values, religion, and social order see Talcott Parsons, *The Structure of Social Action: A Study in Social Theory with Special Reference to a Group of Recent European Writers* (Glencoe, Ill.: Free Press 1949). C. Wright Mills summarizes the Parsonian conclusion in the following epigram: "We are asked: How is social order possible? The answer we are given seems to be: commonly accepted values." C. Wright Mills, *The Sociological Imagination* (New York: Oxford 1959).
4 Archives of Ontario [hereafter AO], Strachan Papers, Manuscript Sermon (22), preached on 2 Corinthians 3:17, "Now the Lord is that Spirit: and where the Spirit of the Lord is, there is liberty," first preached 4 July 1821. [The microfilm suggests the date 4 Feb. 1821.]
5 *Ibid.*
6 *Ibid.*
7 AO, Strachan Papers, Manuscript Sermon (8), preached on 2 Corinthians 4:3 "But if our gospel be hid, it is hid to them that are lost," first preached 30 Mar. 1806.
8 *Ibid.*
9 Robinson Papers, Charge to the grand jury Kingston, 20 Sept. 1841, as quoted in Robert Lochiel Fraser III, "Like Eden in Her Summer Dress: Gentry, Economy, and Society: Upper Canada, 1812–1840" (PhD. thesis, Univ. of Toronto 1981), 213.

10 John Strachan, *A Charge; Delivered to the Clergy of the Diocese of Toronto, at the Visitation, on Wednesday, April 30, 1856, by John, Lord Bishop of Toronto* (Toronto: Henry Rowsell 1856), 24.

11 John S. Moir, *The Church in the British Era* (Toronto: McGraw-Hill, Ryerson 1972), 173.

12 Bishop Bethune was addressing the Synod of the Diocese of Toronto in June of 1872. As quoted in Egerton Ryerson, *The Story of My Life: Being the Reminiscences of Sixty Years' Public Service in Canada*, ed., J. George Hodgins (Toronto: W. Briggs 1883), 566.

13 Ryerson, *The Story of My Life*, 428.

14 For a more detailed study of the breakdown of this accommodation in architectural terms, see William Westfall and Malcolm Thurlby, "Church Architecture and Urban Space: Cultural Symbolism and Social Change in Nineteenth Century Ontario," in David R. Keane and Colin Read, eds, *Metropolis and Hinterland: Essays on Old Ontario Presented to J.M.S. Careless* (forthcoming).

15 George Grant, *Technology and Empire* (Toronto: Anansi 1969), 142.

16 Charles G.D. Roberts, *A History of Canada* (London: Lamson, Wolffe 1897), 437.

17 For example, George Grant, *Lament for a Nation: The Defeat of Canadian Nationalism* (Toronto: McClelland and Stewart 1965) and Donald Creighton, *Canada's First Century* (Toronto: Macmillan 1970).

Index